Pioneers of
The New World
France And England In North America
(Volume II)

Francis Parkman

Alpha Editions

This Edition Published in 2021

ISBN: 9789354482120

Design and Setting By
Alpha Editions
www.alphaedis.com
Email – info@alphaedis.com

As per information held with us this book is in Public Domain.
This book is a reproduction of an important historical work. Alpha Editions uses the best technology to reproduce historical work in the same manner it was first published to preserve its original nature. Any marks or number seen are left intentionally to preserve its true form.

FRANCE AND ENGLAND IN
NORTH AMERICA · PART FIRST
BY FRANCIS PARKMAN

IN TWO VOLUMES
VOL. II.

BOSTON
MDCCCXCVII

Copyright, 1865, 1885,
By Francis Parkman.

Copyright, 1897,
By Little, Brown, and Company.

𝕌niversity 𝕡ress:
John Wilson and Son, Cambridge, U.S.A.

CONTENTS.

CHAMPLAIN AND HIS ASSOCIATES.

	PAGE
PREFATORY NOTE	3

CHAPTER I.
1488-1543.
EARLY FRENCH ADVENTURE IN NORTH AMERICA.

Traditions of French Discovery. — Cousin. — Normans, Bretons, Basques. — Legends and Superstitions. — Francis the First. — Verrazzano. — His Voyage to North America. — Jacques Cartier. — His First Voyage. — His Second Voyage. — Anchors at Quebec. — Indian Masquerade. — Visits Hochelaga. — His Reception. — Mont Royal. — Winter at Quebec. — Scurvy. — Wonderful Cures. — Kidnapping. — Return to France. — Roberval. — Spanish Jealousy. — Cartier's Third Voyage. — Cap Rouge. — Roberval sails for New France. — His Meeting with Cartier. — Marguerite and the Isles of Demons. — Roberval at Cap Rouge. — His Severity. — Ruin of the Colony. — His Death 7

CHAPTER II.
1542-1604.
LA ROCHE. — CHAMPLAIN. — DE MONTS.

French Fishermen and Fur-Traders. — La Roche. — His Voyage. — The Convicts of Sable Island. — Pontgravé and Chauvin. — Tadoussac. — Henry the Fourth. — Tranquillity restored in

France. — Samuel de Champlain. — He visits the West Indies and Mexico. — His Character. — De Chastes and Champlain. — Champlain and Pontgravé explore the St. Lawrence. — Death of De Chastes. — De Monts. — His Acadian Schemes. — His Patent 51

CHAPTER III.
1604, 1605.
ACADIA OCCUPIED.

Catholic and Calvinist. — The Lost Priest. — Port Royal. — The Colony of St. Croix. — Winter Miseries. — Explorations of Champlain. — He visits the Coast of Massachusetts. — De Monts at Port Royal 68

CHAPTER IV.
1605-1607.
LESCARBOT AND CHAMPLAIN.

De Monts at Paris. — Marc Lescarbot. — Rochelle. — A New Embarkation. — The Ship aground. — The Outward Voyage. — Arrival at Port Royal. — Disappointment. — Voyage of Champlain. — Skirmish with Indians. — Masquerade of Lescarbot. — Winter Life at Port Royal. — L'Ordre de Bon-Temps. — Excursions. — Spring Employments. — Hopes blighted. — Port Royal abandoned. — Membertou. — Return to France . 81

CHAPTER V.
1610, 1611.
THE JESUITS AND THEIR PATRONESS.

Schemes of Poutrincourt. — The Jesuits and the King. — The Jesuits disappointed. — Sudden Conversions. — Indian Proselytes. — Assassination of the King. — Biencourt at Court. — Madame de Guercheville. — She resists the King's Suit. — Becomes a Devotee. — Her Associates at Court. — She aids the Jesuits. — Biard and Massé. — They sail for America . 99

CONTENTS.

CHAPTER VI.
1611, 1612.
JESUITS IN ACADIA.

The Jesuits arrive. — Collision of Powers Temporal and Spiritual. — Excursion of Biencourt. — Father Masse. — His Experience as a Missionary. — Death of Membertou. — Father Biard's Indian Studies. — Dissension. — Misery at Port Royal. — Grant to Madame de Guercheville. — Gilbert du Thet. — Quarrels. — Anathemas. — Truce 113

CHAPTER VII.
1613.
LA SAUSSAYE. — ARGALL.

Forlorn Condition of Poutrincourt. — Voyage of La Saussaye. — Mount Desert. — St. Sauveur. — The Jesuit Colony. — Captain Samuel Argall. — He attacks the French. — Death of Du Thet. — Knavery of Argall. — St. Sauveur destroyed. — The Prisoners 124

CHAPTER VIII.
1613–1615.
RUIN OF FRENCH ACADIA.

The Jesuits at Jamestown. — Wrath of Sir Thomas Dale. — Second Expedition of Argall. — Port Royal demolished. — Equivocal Posture of the Jesuits. — Jeopardy of Father Biard. — Biencourt and Argall. — Adventures of Biard and Quentin. — Sequel of Argall's History. — Death of Poutrincourt. — The French will not abandon Acadia 136

CHAPTER IX.
1608, 1609.
CHAMPLAIN AT QUEBEC.

A New Enterprise. — The St. Lawrence. — Conflict with Basques. — Tadoussac. — The Saguenay. — Quebec founded. — Conspiracy. — The Montagnais. — Winter at Quebec. — Spring. — Projects of Exploration 149

CONTENTS.

CHAPTER X.
1609.
LAKE CHAMPLAIN.

Champlain joins a War Party. — Preparation. — War-Dance. — Departure. — The River Richelieu. — The Rapids of Chambly. — The Spirits consulted. — Discovery of Lake Champlain. — Battle with the Iroquois. — Fate of Prisoners. — Panic of the Victors 164

CHAPTER XI.
1610–1612.
WAR. — TRADE. — DISCOVERY.

Champlain at Fontainebleau. — Champlain on the St. Lawrence. — Alarm. — Battle. — Victory. — War Parties. — Rival Traders. — Icebergs. — Adventurers. — Champlain at Montreal. — Return to France. — Narrow Escape of Champlain. — The Comte de Soissons. — The Prince de Condé. — Designs of Champlain 179

CHAPTER XII.
1612, 1613.
THE IMPOSTOR VIGNAU.

Illusions. — A Path to the North Sea. — Champlain on the Ottawa. — Forest Travellers. — The Chaudière. — Isles des Allumettes. — Ottawa Towns. — Tessouat. — Indian Cemetery. — Feast. — The Impostor exposed. — Return of Champlain. — False Alarm. — Arrival at Montreal 194

CHAPTER XIII.
1615.
DISCOVERY OF LAKE HURON.

Religious Zeal of Champlain. — Récollet Friars. — St. Francis. — The Franciscans. — The Friars in New France. — Dolbeau. — Le Caron. — Policy of Champlain. — Missions. — Trade. — Exploration. — War. — Le Caron on the Ottawa. — Cham-

plain's Expedition. — He reaches Lake Nipissing. — Embarks
on Lake Huron. — The Huron Villages. — Meeting with Le
Caron. — Mass in the Wilderness 212

CHAPTER XIV.
1615, 1616.
THE GREAT WAR PARTY.

Muster of Warriors. — Departure. — The River Trent. — Deer
Hunt. — Lake Ontario. — The Iroquois Town. — Attack. —
Repulse. — Champlain wounded. — Retreat. — Adventures of
Étienne Brulé. — Winter Hunt. — Champlain lost in the Forest. — Returns to the Huron Villages. — Visits the Tobacco
Nation and the *Cheveux Relevés*. — Becomes Umpire of Indian
Quarrels. — Returns to Quebec 227

CHAPTER XV.
1616-1627.
HOSTILE SECTS. — RIVAL INTERESTS.

Quebec. — Condition of the Colonists. — Dissensions. — Montmorency. — Arrival of Madame de Champlain. — Her History
and Character. — Indian Hostility. — The Monopoly of William and Émery de Caen. — The Duc de Ventadour. — The
Jesuits. — Their Arrival at Quebec. — Catholics and Heretics. — Compromises. — The Rival Colonies. — Despotism in
New France and in New England. — Richelieu. — The Company of the Hundred Associates 245

CHAPTER XVI.
1628, 1629.
THE ENGLISH AT QUEBEC.

Revolt of Rochelle. — War with England. — David Kirke. — The
English on the St. Lawrence. — Alarms at Quebec. — Bold
Attitude of Champlain. — Naval Battle. — The French Squadron destroyed. — Famine at Quebec. — Return of the English.
— Quebec surrendered. — Another Naval Battle. — Michel. —
His Quarrel with Brébeuf. — His Death. — Exploit of Daniel.
— Champlain at London 261

CHAPTER XVII.
1632-1635.
DEATH OF CHAMPLAIN.

New France restored to the French Crown. — Motives for reclaiming it. — Caen takes possession of Quebec. — Return of Jesuits. — Arrival of Champlain. — Daily Life at Quebec. — Policy and Religion. — Death of Champlain. — His Character. — Future of New France 274

INDEX 285

LIST OF ILLUSTRATIONS.

VOLUME TWO.

HENRY IV. AND MADAME DE GUERCHEVILLE . . *Frontispiece*
Goupilgravure facsimile in color of the drawing by F. de Myrbach.

JACQUES CARTIER . . . . *Page* 21
From the original painting by F. Riss, in the Town Hall of St. Malo, France.

JACQUES CARTIER DISCOVERS THE RIVER ST. LAW-
RENCE . . . . " 24
From the original painting by Gudin, in the Versailles Gallery.

SAMUEL DE CHAMPLAIN . . . . " 60
From the Ducornet Portrait.

HENRY IV. AND MADAME DE GUERCHEVILLE . . . " 108
Drawn by F. de Myrbach.

ROUTE OF CHAMPLAIN, 1615–1616 . . . . " 227

HE SOON DISCOVERED THE SMOKE OF THE INDIAN
FIRES . . . . " 240
Drawn by F. de Myrbach.

PIONEERS OF FRANCE IN THE
NEW WORLD.

𝔓art II.
SAMUEL DE CHAMPLAIN.

PREFATORY NOTE

TO

CHAMPLAIN AND HIS ASSOCIATES.

SAMUEL DE CHAMPLAIN has been fitly called the Father of New France. In him were embodied her religious zeal and romantic spirit of adventure. Before the close of his career, purged of heresy, she took the posture which she held to the day of her death, — in one hand the crucifix, in the other the sword. His life, full of significance, is the true beginning of her eventful history.

In respect to Champlain, the most satisfactory authorities are his own writings. These consist of the journal of his voyage to the West Indies and Mexico, of which the original is preserved at Dieppe; the account of his first voyage to the St. Lawrence, published at Paris, in 1604, under the title of *Des Sauvages;* a narrative of subsequent adventures and explorations, published at Paris in 1613, 1615, and 1617, under the title of *Voyage de la Nouvelle France;* a narrative of still later discoveries, published at Paris in 1620 and 1627; and, finally, a compendium of all his previous publications, with much additional matter, published in quarto at Paris in 1632, and illustrated by a very curious and interesting map.

Next in value to the writings of Champlain are those of his associate, Lescarbot, whose *Histoire de la Nouvelle France* is of great interest and authority as far as it relates the author's personal experience. The editions here consulted are those of 1612 and 1618. The *Muses de la Nouvelle France*, and other minor works of Lescarbot, have also been examined.

The *Établissement de la Foy* of Le Clerc is of great value in connection with the present subject, containing documents and extracts from documents not elsewhere to be found. It is of extreme rarity, having been suppressed by the French government soon after its appearance in 1691.

The *Histoire du Canada* of Sagard, the *Première Mission des Jésuites* of Carayon, the curious *Relation* of the Jesuit Biard, and those of the Jesuits Charles Lalemant, Le Jeune, and Brebeuf, together with two narratives — one of them perhaps written by Champlain — in the eighteenth and nineteenth volumes of the *Mercure Français*, may also be mentioned as among the leading authorities of the body of this work. Those of the introductory portion need not be specified at present.

Of manuscripts used, the principal are the *Bref Discours* of Champlain, or the journal of his voyage to the West Indies and Mexico; the *Grand Insulaire et Pilotage d'André Thevet*, an ancient and very curious document, in which the superstitions of Breton and Norman fishermen are recounted by one who shared them; and a variety of official papers, obtained for me through the agency of Mr. B. P. Poore, from the archives of France.

I am indebted to G. B. Faribault, Esq., of Quebec, and to the late Jacques Viger, Esq., of Montreal, for the use of valuable papers and memoranda; to the Rev. John Cordner, of Montreal, for various kind acts of co-operation; to Jared Sparks, LL.D., for the use of a copy of Le Clerc's *Établissement de la Foy;* to Dr. E. B. O'Callaghan, for assistance in examining rare books in the State Library of New York; to John Carter Brown, Esq., and Colonel Thomas Aspinwall, for the use of books from their admirable collections; while to the libraries of Harvard College and of the Boston Athenæum I owe a standing debt of gratitude.

The basis of descriptive passages was supplied through early tastes and habits, which long since made me familiar with most of the localities of the narrative.

PIONEERS OF FRANCE IN THE NEW WORLD.

Part II.
SAMUEL DE CHAMPLAIN.

CHAPTER I.
1488-1543.
EARLY FRENCH ADVENTURE IN NORTH AMERICA.

TRADITIONS OF FRENCH DISCOVERY.— NORMANS, BRETONS, BASQUES. — LEGENDS AND SUPERSTITIONS. — VERRAZZANO. — JACQUES CARTIER. — QUEBEC. — HOCHELAGA. — WINTER MISERIES. — ROBERVAL. — THE ISLES OF DEMONS. — THE COLONISTS OF CAP ROUGE.

WHEN America was first made known to Europe, the part assumed by France on the borders of that new world was peculiar, and is little recognized. While the Spaniard roamed sea and land, burning for achievement, red-hot with bigotry and avarice, and while England, with soberer steps and a less dazzling result, followed in the path of discovery and gold-hunting, it was from France that those barbarous shores first learned to serve the ends of peaceful commercial industry.

A French writer, however, advances a more ambitious claim. In the year 1488, four years before the first voyage of Columbus, America, he maintains, was found by Frenchmen. Cousin, a navigator of Dieppe, being at sea off the African coast, was forced westward, it is said, by winds and currents to within sight of an unknown shore, where he presently descried the mouth of a great river. On board his ship was one Pinzon, whose conduct became so mutinous that, on his return to Dieppe, Cousin made complaint to the magistracy, who thereupon dismissed the offender from the maritime service of the town. Pinzon went to Spain, became known to Columbus, told him the discovery, and joined him on his voyage of 1492.[1]

[1] *Mémoires pour servir à l'Histoire de Dieppe;* Vitet, *Histoire de Dieppe,* 226; Gaffarel, *Brésil Français,* 1. *Compte-rendu du Congrès International des Américanistes,* I. 398–414; Guérin, *Navigateurs Français,* 47; Estancelin, *Navigateurs Normands,* 332. This last writer's research to verify the tradition was vain. The bombardment of 1694 nearly destroyed the archives of Dieppe, and nothing could be learned from the Pinzons of Palos. Yet the story may not be quite void of foundation. In 1500, Cabral was blown within sight of Brazil in a similar manner. Herrera (*Hist. General,* Dec. I. Lib. I. c. 3) gives several parallel instances as having reached the ears of Columbus before his first voyage. Compare the Introduction to Lok's translation of Peter Martyr, and Eden and Willes, *History of Travayles,* fol. 1; also a story in the *Journal de l'Amérique* (Troyes, 1709), and Gomara, *Hist. Gen. des Indes Occidentales,* Lib. I. c. 13. These last, however, are probably inventions.

In the *Description des Costes de la Mer Océane,* a manuscript of the seventeenth century, it is said that a French pilot of St. Jean de Luz first discovered America: "Il fut le premier jeté en la coste de l'Amérique par une violente tempeste, laissa son papier journal, communiqua la route qu'il avoit faite à Coulon, chez qui il mourut." (See Monteil, *Traité de Matériaux Manuscrits,* I. 340.) The story is scarcely worth the mention. Harrisse (*Les Cortereal,* 27) thinks there is reason to believe that the Portuguese reached the American continent as early as 1474, or even ten years earlier.

To leave this cloudland of tradition, and approach the confines of recorded history. The Normans, offspring of an ancestry of conquerors, — the Bretons, that stubborn, hardy, unchanging race, who, among Druid monuments changeless as themselves, still cling with Celtic obstinacy to the thoughts and habits of the past, — the Basques, that primeval people, older than history, — all frequented from a very early date the cod-banks of Newfoundland. There is some reason to believe that this fishery existed before the voyage of Cabot, in 1497;[1] there is strong evidence

[1] "Terra hæc ob lucrosissimam piscationis utilitatem summa litterarum memoria a Gallis adiri solita, & ante mille sexcentos annos frequentari solita est." Postel, cited by Lescarbot, I. 237, and by Hornot, 260.

"De toute mémoire, & dès plusieurs siècles noz Diepois, Maloins, Rochelois, & autres mariniers du Havre de Grace, de Honfleur & autres lieux, font les voyages ordinaires en ces païs-là pour la pêcherie des Moruës." Lescarbot, I. 236.

Compare the following extracts: —

"Les Basques et les Bretons sont depuis plusieurs siècles les seuls qui se soient employés à la pêche de balaines et des molues; et il est fort remarquable que S. Cabot, découvrant la côte de Labrador, y trouva le nom de *Bacallos*, qui signifie des Molues en langue des Basques." — *MS. in the Royal Library of Versailles.*

"Quant au nom de *Bacalos*, il est de l'imposition de nos Basques, lesquels appellent une Moruë, *Bacaillos*, & à leur imitation nos peuples de la Nouvelle France ont appris à nommer aussi la Moruë *Bacaillos*, quoyqu'en leur langage le nom propre de la moruë soit *Apegé.*" Lescarbot, I. 237.

De Laet also says, incidentally (p. 39), that "Bacalaos" is Basque for a codfish. I once asked a Basque gentleman the name for a codfish in his language, and he at once answered *Baccalaos*. The word has been adopted by the Spaniards.

"Sebastian Cabot himself named those lands Baccalaos, because that in the seas thereabout he found so great multitudes of certain bigge fishes, much like unto Tunies (which the inhabitants call Bac-

that it began as early as the year 1504;[1] and it is well established that, in 1517, fifty Castilian, French, and Portuguese vessels were engaged in it at once; while in 1527, on the third of August, eleven sail of Norman, one of Breton, and two of Portuguese fishermen were to be found in the Bay of St. John.[2]

calaos), that they sometimes stayed his shippes." Peter Martyr in Hakluyt, III. 30; Eden and Willes, 125.

If, in the original Basque, *Bacealaos* is the word for a codfish, and if Cabot found it in use among the inhabitants of Newfoundland, it is hard to escape the conclusion that Basques had been there before him.

This name *Baccalaos* is variously used by the old writers. Cabot gave it to the continent, as far as he coasted it. The earliest Spanish writers give it an application almost as comprehensive. On Wytfleit's map (1597) it is confined to Newfoundland and Labrador; on Ramusio's (1556), to the southern parts of Newfoundland; on Lescarbot's (1612), to the island of Cape Breton; on De Laet's (1640), to a small island east of Newfoundland.

[1] *Discorso d' un gran Capitano di Mare Francese*, Ramusio, III. 423. Ramusio does not know the name of the "gran capitano," but Estancelin proves him to have been Jean Parmentier, of Dieppe. From internal evidence, his memoir was written in 1539, and he says that Newfoundland was visited by Bretons and Normans thirty-five years before. "Britones et Normani anno a Christo nato M,CCCCC,-IIII has terras invenére." Wytfleit, *Descriptionis Ptolemaicæ Augmentum*, 185. The translation of Wytfleit (Douay, 1611) bears also the name of Antoine Magin. It is cited by Champlain as "Niflet & Antoine Magin." See also Ogilby, *America*, 128; Forster, *Voyages*, 431; Baumgartens, I. 516; Biard, *Relation*, 2; Bergeron, *Traité de la Navigation*, c. 14.

[2] Herrera, Dec. II. Lib. V. c. 3; Letter of John Rut, dated St. John's, 3 August, 1527, in Purchas, III. 809.

The name of Cape Breton, found on the oldest maps, is a memorial of these early French voyages. Cartier, in 1534, found the capes and bays of Newfoundland already named by his countrymen who had preceded him. In 1565, Charles IX. of France informed the Spanish ambassador that the coast of North America had been discovered by French subjects more than a hundred years before, and is therefore

From this time forth, the Newfoundland fishery was never abandoned. French, English, Spanish, and Portuguese made resort to the Banks, always jealous, often quarrelling, but still drawing up treasure from those exhaustless mines, and bearing home bountiful provision against the season of Lent.

On this dim verge of the known world there were other perils than those of the waves. The rocks and shores of those sequestered seas had, so thought the voyagers, other tenants than the seal, the walrus, and the screaming sea-fowl, the bears which stole away their fish before their eyes,[1] and the wild natives dressed in seal-skins. Griffins — so ran the story — infested the mountains of Labrador.[2] Two islands, north of Newfoundland, were given over to the fiends from whom they derived their name, the Isles of Demons. An old map pictures their occupants at length, — devils rampant, with wings, horns, and tail.[3] The passing voyager heard the din of their infernal orgies, and woe to the sailor or the fisherman who ventured alone into the haunted woods.[4]

called "Terre aux Bretons." *Papiers d'Estat de Forquevaulx,* in Gaffarel, *Floride,* 413.

Navarrete's position, that the fisheries date no farther back than 1540, is wholly untenable.

[1] "The Beares also be as bold, which will not spare at midday to take your fish before your face." — *Letter of Anthonie Parkhurst,* 1578, in Hakluyt, III. 170.

[2] Wytfleit, 190; Gomara, Lib. I. c. 2.

[3] See Ramusio, III. Compare La Popelinière, *Les Trois Mondes,* II. 25.

[4] *Le Grand Insulaire et Pilotage d'André Thevet, Cosmographe du Roy* (1586). I am indebted to G. B. Faribault, Esq., of Quebec, for a

"True it is," writes the old cosmographer Thevet, "and I myself have heard it, not from one, but from a great number of the sailors and pilots with whom I have made many voyages, that, when they passed this way, they heard in the air, on the tops and about the masts, a great clamor of men's voices, confused and inarticulate, such as you may hear from the crowd at a fair or market-place; whereupon they well knew that the Isle of Demons was not far off." And he adds, that he himself, when among the Indians, had seen them so tormented by these infernal persecutors, that they would fall into his arms for relief; on which, repeating a passage of the Gospel of St. John, he had driven the imps of darkness to a speedy exodus. They are comely to look upon, he further tells us; yet, by reason of their malice, that island is of late abandoned, and all who dwelt there have fled for refuge to the main.[1]

While French fishermen plied their trade along these gloomy coasts, the French government spent

copy of this curious manuscript. The islands are perhaps those of Belle Isle and Quirpon. More probably, however, that most held in dread, "pour autant que les Demons y font terrible tintamarre," is a small island near the northeast extremity of Newfoundland, variously called, by Thevet, Isle de Fiche, Isle de Roberval, and Isle des Démons. It is the same with the Isle Fichet of Sanson, and the Fishot Island of some modern maps. A curious legend connected with it will be given hereafter.

[1] Thevet, *Cosmographie* (1575), II. c. 5. A very rare book. I am indebted to Dr. E. B. O'Callaghan for copies of the passages in it relating to subjects within the scope of the present work. Thevet here contradicts himself in regard to the position of the haunted island, which he places at 60° north latitude.

its energies on a different field. The vitality of the kingdom was wasted in Italian wars. Milan and Naples offered a more tempting prize than the wilds of Baccalaos.[1] Eager for glory and for plunder, a swarm of restless nobles followed their knight-errant King, the would-be paladin, who, misshapen in body and fantastic in mind, had yet the power to raise a storm which the lapse of generations could not quell. Under Charles the Eighth and his successor, war and intrigue ruled the day; and in the whirl of Italian politics there was no leisure to think of a new world.

Yet private enterprise was not quite benumbed. In 1506, one Denis of Honfleur explored the Gulf of St. Lawrence;[2] two years later, Aubert of Dieppe followed on his track;[3] and in 1518, the Baron de Léry made an abortive attempt at settlement on Sable Island, where the cattle left by him remained and multiplied.[4]

The crown passed at length to Francis of Angoulême. There were in his nature seeds of nobleness, — seeds destined to bear little fruit. Chivalry and honor were always on his lips; but Francis the First, a forsworn gentleman, a despotic king, vainglorious, selfish, sunk in debaucheries, was but the type of an era which retained the forms of the Middle Age without its soul, and added to a still prevailing barbarism the pestilential vices which hung fog-like

[1] See *ante*, p. 9, note 1.
[2] Parmentier in Ramusio, III. 423; Estancelin, 42-222.
[3] Ibid.
[4] Lescarbot, I. 22; De Laet, *Novus Orbis*, 39; Bergeron, c. 15.

around the dawn of civilization. Yet he esteemed arts and letters, and, still more, coveted the *éclat* which they could give. The light which was beginning to pierce the feudal darkness gathered its rays around his throne. Italy was rewarding the robbers who preyed on her with the treasures of her knowledge and her culture; and Italian genius, of whatever stamp, found ready patronage at the hands of Francis. Among artists, philosophers, and men of letters enrolled in his service stands the humbler name of a Florentine navigator, John Verrazzano.

He was born of an ancient family, which could boast names eminent in Florentine history, and of which the last survivor died in 1819. He has been called a pirate, and he was such in the same sense in which Drake, Hawkins, and other valiant sea-rovers of his own and later times, merited the name; that is to say, he would plunder and kill a Spaniard on the high seas without waiting for a declaration of war.

The wealth of the Indies was pouring into the coffers of Charles the Fifth, and the exploits of Cortés had given new lustre to his crown. Francis the First begrudged his hated rival the glories and profits of the New World. He would fain have his share of the prize; and Verrazzano, with four ships, was despatched to seek out a passage westward to the rich kingdom of Cathay.

Some doubt has of late been cast on the reality of this voyage of Verrazzano, and evidence, mainly negative in kind, has been adduced to prove the story of it a fabrication; but the difficulties of incredulity appear greater than those of belief, and no ordinary degree of scepticism is required to reject the evidence that the narrative is essentially true.[1]

Towards the end of the year 1523, his four ships sailed from Dieppe; but a storm fell upon him, and, with two of the vessels, he ran back in distress to a port of Brittany. What became of the other two does not appear. Neither is it clear why, after a preliminary cruise against the Spaniards, he pursued his voyage with one vessel alone, a caravel called the "Dauphine." With her he made for Madeira, and, on the seventeenth of January, 1524, set sail from a barren islet in its neighborhood, and bore away for the unknown world. In forty-nine days they neared a low shore, not far from the site of Wilmington in North Carolina, "a newe land," exclaims the voyager, "never before seen of any man, either auncient or moderne."[2] Verrazzano steered southward in search of a harbor, and, finding none, turned northward again. Presently he sent a boat ashore. The inhabitants, who had fled at first, soon came down to the strand in wonder and admiration, pointing out a landing-place, and making gestures of friendship. "These people," says Verrazzano, "goe altogether naked, except only certain skinnes of beastes like unto marterns [martens], which they fasten onto a narrowe girdle made of grasse. They are of colour

---

[1] See note, end of chapter.
[2] Hakluyt's translation from Ramusio, in *Divers Voyages* (1582).

russet, and not much unlike the Saracens, their hayre blacke, thicke, and not very long, which they tye togeather in a knot behinde, and weare it like a taile."[1]

He describes the shore as consisting of small low hillocks of fine sand, intersected by creeks and inlets, and beyond these a country "full of Palme [pine?] trees, Bay trees, and high Cypresse trees, and many other sortes of trees, vnknowne in Europe, which yeeld most sweete sauours, farre from the shore." Still advancing northward, Verrazzano sent a boat for a supply of water. The surf ran high, and the crew could not land; but an adventurous young sailor jumped overboard and swam shoreward with a gift of beads and trinkets for the Indians, who stood watching him. His heart failed as he drew near; he flung his gift among them, turned, and struck out for the boat. The surf dashed him back, flinging him with violence on the beach among the recipients of his bounty, who seized him by the arms and legs, and, while he called lustily for aid, answered him with outcries designed to allay his terrors. Next they kindled a great fire, — doubtless to roast and devour him before the eyes of his comrades, gazing in horror from their boat. On the contrary, they carefully warmed him, and were trying to dry his clothes, when, recovering from his bewilderment, he betrayed a strong desire to escape to his friends; whereupon, "with great love, clapping him fast

[1] Hakluyt's translation from Ramusio, in *Divers Voyages* (1582).

about, with many embracings," they led him to the shore, and stood watching till he had reached the boat.

It only remained to requite this kindness, and an opportunity soon occurred; for, coasting the shores of Virginia or Maryland, a party went on shore and found an old woman, a young girl, and several children, hiding with great terror in the grass. Having, by various blandishments, gained their confidence, they carried off one of the children as a curiosity, and, since the girl was comely, would fain have taken her also, but desisted by reason of her continual screaming.

Verrazzano's next resting-place was the Bay of New York. Rowing up in his boat through the Narrows, under the steep heights of Staten Island, he saw the harbor within dotted with canoes of the feathered natives, coming from the shore to welcome him. But what most engaged the eyes of the white men were the fancied signs of mineral wealth in the neighboring hills.

Following the shores of Long Island, they came to an island, which may have been Block Island, and thence to a harbor, which was probably that of Newport. Here they stayed fifteen days, most courteously received by the inhabitants. Among others appeared two chiefs, gorgeously arrayed in painted deer-skins, — kings, as Verrazzano calls them, with attendant gentlemen; while a party of squaws in a canoe, kept by their jealous lords at a safe distance from the caravel, figure in the narrative as the queen and her maids. The Indian wardrobe had been taxed to its utmost to do the strangers honor, — copper bracelets, lynx-skins, raccoon-skins, and faces bedaubed with gaudy colors.

Again they spread their sails, and on the fifth of May bade farewell to the primitive hospitalities of Newport, steered along the rugged coasts of New England, and surveyed, ill pleased, the surf-beaten rocks, the pine-tree and the fir, the shadows and the gloom of mighty forests. Here man and nature alike were savage and repellent. Perhaps some plundering straggler from the fishing-banks, some man-stealer like the Portuguese Cortereal, or some kidnapper of children and ravisher of squaws like themselves, had warned the denizens of the woods to beware of the worshippers of Christ. Their only intercourse was in the way of trade. From the brink of the rocks which overhung the sea the Indians would let down a cord to the boat below, demand fish-hooks, knives, and steel, in barter for their furs, and, their bargain made, salute the voyagers with unseemly gestures of derision and scorn. The French once ventured ashore; but a war-whoop and a shower of arrows sent them back to their boats.

Verrazzano coasted the seaboard of Maine, and sailed northward as far as Newfoundland, whence, provisions failing, he steered for France. He had not found a passage to Cathay, but he had explored the American coast from the thirty-fourth degree to the fiftieth, and at various points had penetrated several leagues into the country. On the eighth of July, he wrote from Dieppe to the King the earliest description known to exist of the shores of the United States.

Great was the joy that hailed his arrival, and great were the hopes of emolument and wealth from the new-found shores.[1] The merchants of Lyons were in a flush of expectation. For himself, he was earnest to return, plant a colony, and bring the heathen tribes within the pale of the Church. But the time was inauspicious. The year of his voyage was to France a year of disasters, — defeat in Italy, the loss of Milan, the death of the heroic Bayard; and, while Verrazzano was writing his narrative at Dieppe, the traitor Bourbon was invading Provence. Preparation, too, was soon on foot for the expedition which, a few months later, ended in the captivity of Francis on the field of Pavia. Without a king, without an army, without money, convulsed within, and threatened from without, France after that humiliation was in no condition to renew her Transatlantic enterprise.

Henceforth few traces remain of the fortunes of Verrazzano. Ramusio affirms, that, on another voyage, he was killed and eaten by savages, in sight of his followers;[2] and a late writer hazards the conjecture that this voyage, if made at all, was made in the

---

[1] *Fernando Carli à suo Padre*, 4 Aug., 1524.
[2] Ramusio, III. 417; Wytfleit, 185. Compare Le Clerc, *Établissement de la Foy*, I. 6.

service of Henry the Eighth of England.[1] But a
Spanish writer affirms that, in 1527, he was hanged
at Puerto del Pico as a pirate,[2] and this assertion is
fully confirmed by authentic documents recently
brought to light.

The fickle-minded King, always ardent at the outset of an enterprise and always flagging before its
close, divided, moreover, between the smiles of his
mistresses and the assaults of his enemies, might
probably have dismissed the New World from his
thoughts. But among the favorites of his youth was
a high-spirited young noble, Philippe de Brion-
Chabot, the partner of his joustings and tennis-playing, his gaming and gallantries.[3] He still stood high
in the royal favor, and, after the treacherous escape
of Francis from captivity, held the office of Admiral
of France. When the kingdom had rallied in some
measure from its calamities, he conceived the purpose
of following up the path which Verrazzano had
opened.

The ancient town of St. Malo — thrust out like a
buttress into the sea, strange and grim of aspect,
breathing war from its walls and battlements of ragged
stone, a stronghold of privateers, the home of a race
whose intractable and defiant independence neither
time nor change has subdued — has been for centuries
a nursery of hardy mariners. Among the earliest

---

[1] Biddle, *Memoir of Cabot*, 275.
[2] Barcia, *Ensayo Cronologico*, 8.
[3] Brantôme, II. 277; *Biographie Universelle*, Art. *Chabot*.

and most eminent on its list stands the name of Jacques Cartier. His portrait hangs in the town-hall of St. Malo, — bold, keen features bespeaking a spirit not apt to quail before the wrath of man or of the elements. In him Chabot found a fit agent of his design, if, indeed, its suggestion is not due to the Breton navigator.[1]

Sailing from St. Malo on the twentieth of April, 1534, Cartier steered for Newfoundland, passed through the Straits of Belle Isle, entered the Gulf of Chaleurs, planted a cross at Gaspé, and, never doubting that he was on the high road to Cathay, advanced up the St. Lawrence till he saw the shores of Anticosti. But autumnal storms were gathering. The voyagers took counsel together, turned their prows eastward, and bore away for France, carrying thither, as a sample of the natural products of the New World, two young Indians, lured into their clutches by an act of villanous treachery. The voyage was a mere reconnoissance.[2]

The spirit of discovery was awakened. A passage to India could be found, and a new France built up beyond the Atlantic. Mingled with such views of interest and ambition was another motive scarcely less

[1] Cartier was at this time forty years of age, having been born in December, 1494. I examined the St. Malo portrait in 1881. It is a recent work (1839), and its likeness is more than doubtful.

[2] Lescarbot, I. 232 (1612); *Relation originale du Voyage de Jacques Cartier en* 1534 (Paris, 1867); Cartier, *Discours du Voyage*, reprinted by the Literary and Historical Society of Quebec. Compare translations in Hakluyt and Ramusio; MS. Map of Cartier's route in *Dépôt des Cartes*, Carton V.

potent.[1] The heresy of Luther was convulsing Germany, and the deeper heresy of Calvin infecting France. Devout Catholics, kindling with redoubled zeal, would fain requite the Church for her losses in the Old World by winning to her fold the infidels of the New. But, in pursuing an end at once so pious and so politic, Francis the First was setting at naught the supreme Pontiff himself, since, by the preposterous bull of Alexander the Sixth, all America had been given to the Spaniards.

In October, 1534, Cartier received from Chabot another commission, and, in spite of secret but bitter opposition from jealous traders of St. Malo, he prepared for a second voyage. Three vessels, the largest not above a hundred and twenty tons, were placed at his disposal, and Claude de Pontbriand, Charles de la Pommeraye, and other gentlemen of birth, enrolled themselves for the adventure. On the sixteenth of May, 1535, officers and sailors assembled in the cathedral of St. Malo, where, after confession and mass, they received the parting blessing of the bishop. Three days later they set sail. The dingy walls of the rude old seaport, and the white rocks that line the neighboring shores of Brittany, faded from their sight, and soon they were tossing in a furious tempest. The scattered ships escaped the danger, and, reuniting at the Straits of Belle Isle, steered westward along the coast of Labrador, till they reached a small bay opposite the island

[1] *Lettre de Cartier au Roy très Chrétien.*

1535.]   SECOND VOYAGE OF CARTIER.   23

of Anticosti. Cartier called it the Bay of St. Lawrence, — a name afterwards extended to the entire gulf, and to the great river above.[1]

To ascend this great river, and tempt the hazards of its intricate navigation with no better pilots than

[1] Cartier calls the St. Lawrence the "River of Hochelaga," or "the great river of Canada." He confines the name of *Canada* to a district extending from the Isle aux Coudres in the St. Lawrence to a point at some distance above the site of Quebec. The country below, he adds, was called by the Indians *Saguenay*, and that above, *Hochelaga*. In the map of Gérard Mercator (1569) the name Canada is given to a town, with an adjacent district, on the river *Stadin* (St. Charles). Lescarbot, a later writer, insists that the country on both sides of the St. Lawrence, from Hochelaga to its mouth, bore the name of *Canada*.

In the second map of Ortelius, published about the year 1572, New France, Nova Francia, is thus divided: *Canada*, a district on the St. Lawrence above the river Saguenay; *Chilaga* (Hochelaga), the angle between the Ottawa and the St. Lawrence; *Saguenai*, a district below the river of that name; *Moscosa*, south of the St. Lawrence and east of the river Richelieu; *Avacal*, west and south of Moscosa; *Norumbega*, Maine and New Brunswick; *Apalachen*, Virginia, Pennsylvania, etc.; *Terra Corterealis*, Labrador; *Florida*, Mississippi, Alabama, Florida.

Mercator confines the name of New France to districts bordering on the St. Lawrence. Others give it a much broader application. The use of this name, or the nearly allied names of Francisca and La Franciscane, dates back, to say the least, as far as 1525, and the Dutch geographers are especially free in their use of it, out of spite to the Spaniards.

The derivation of the name of Canada has been a point of discussion. It is, without doubt, not Spanish, but Indian. In the vocabulary of the language of Hochelaga, appended to the journal of Cartier's second voyage, *Canada* is set down as the word for a town or village. "Ils appellent une ville, Canada." It bears the same meaning in the Mohawk tongue. Both languages are dialects of the Iroquois. Lescarbot affirms that *Canada* is simply an Indian proper name, of which it is vain to seek a meaning. Belleforest also calls it an Indian word, but translates it "Terre," as does also Thevet.

the two young Indians kidnapped the year before, was a venture of no light risk. But skill or fortune prevailed; and, on the first of September, the voyagers reached in safety the gorge of the gloomy Saguenay, with its towering cliffs and sullen depth of waters. Passing the Isle aux Coudres, and the lofty promontory of Cape Tourmente, they came to anchor in a quiet channel between the northern shore and the margin of a richly wooded island, where the trees were so thickly hung with grapes that Cartier named it the Island of Bacchus.[1]

Indians came swarming from the shores, paddled their canoes about the ships, and clambered to the decks to gaze in bewilderment at the novel scene, and listen to the story of their travelled countrymen, marvellous in their ears as a visit to another planet.[2]

---

[1] Now the Island of Orleans.

[2] Doubt has been thrown on this part of Cartier's narrative, on the ground that these two young Indians, who were captured at Gaspé, could not have been so intimately acquainted as the journal represents with the savages at the site of Quebec. From a subsequent part of the journal, however, it appears that they were natives of this place, — "et là est la ville et demeurance du Seigneur Donnacona, et de nos deux hommes qu'avions pris le premier voyage." This is curiously confirmed by Thevet, who personally knew Cartier, and who, in his *Singularités de la France Antarctique* (p. 147), says that the party to which the two Indians captured at Gaspé belonged spoke a language different from that of the other Indians seen in those parts, and that they had come on a war expedition from the river Chelogna (Hochelaga). Compare *New Found Worlde* (London, 1568), 124. This will also account for Lescarbot's remark, that the Indians of Gaspé had changed their language since Cartier's time. The language of Stadaconé, or Quebec, when Cartier visited it, was apparently a dialect of the Iroquois.

Cartier received them kindly, listened to the long harangue of the great chief Donnacona, regaled him with bread and wine; and, when relieved at length of his guests, set forth in a boat to explore the river above.

As he drew near the opening of the channel, the Hochelaga again spread before him the broad expanse of its waters. A mighty promontory, rugged and bare, thrust its scarped front into the surging current. Here, clothed in the majesty of solitude, breathing the stern poetry of the wilderness, rose the cliffs now rich with heroic memories, where the fiery Count Frontenac cast defiance at his foes, where Wolfe, Montcalm, and Montgomery fell. As yet, all was a nameless barbarism, and a cluster of wigwams held the site of the rock-built city of Quebec.[1] Its name was Stadaconé, and it owned the sway of the royal Donnacona.

Cartier set out to visit this greasy potentate; ascended the river St. Charles, by him called the St. Croix,[2] landed, crossed the meadows, climbed the rocks, threaded the forest, and emerged upon a

---

[1] On ground now covered by the suburbs of St. Roque and St. John.

[2] Charlevoix denies that the St. Croix and the St. Charles are the same; but he supports his denial by an argument which proves nothing but his own gross carelessness. Champlain, than whom no one was better qualified to form an opinion, distinctly affirms the identity of the two rivers. See his Map of Quebec, and the accompanying key, in the edition of 1613. La Potherie is of the same opinion; as also, among modern writers, Faribault and Fisher. In truth, the description of localities in Cartier's journal cannot, when closely examined, admit a doubt on the subject. See also Berthelot, *Dissertation sur le Canon de Bronze.*

squalid hamlet of bark cabins. When, having satisfied their curiosity, he and his party were rowing for the ships, a friendly interruption met them at the mouth of the St. Charles. An old chief harangued them from the bank, men, boys, and children screeched welcome from the meadow, and a troop of hilarious squaws danced knee-deep in the water. The gift of a few strings of beads completed their delight and redoubled their agility; and, from the distance of a mile, their shrill songs of jubilation still reached the ears of the receding Frenchmen.

The hamlet of Stadaconé, with its king, Donnacona, and its naked lords and princes, was not the metropolis of this forest state, since a town far greater — so the Indians averred — stood by the brink of the river, many days' journey above. It was called Hochelaga, and the great river itself, with a wide reach of adjacent country, had borrowed its name. Thither, with his two young Indians as guides, Cartier resolved to go; but misgivings seized the guides as the time drew near, while Donnacona and his tribesmen, jealous of the plan, set themselves to thwart it. The Breton captain turned a deaf ear to their dissuasions; on which, failing to touch his reason, they appealed to his fears.

One morning, as the ships still lay at anchor, the French beheld three Indian devils descending in a canoe towards them, dressed in black and white dogskins, with faces black as ink, and horns long as a man's arm. Thus arrayed, they drifted by, while the principal fiend, with fixed eyes, as of one piercing the secrets of futurity, uttered in a loud voice a long harangue. Then they paddled for the shore; and no sooner did they reach it than each fell flat like a dead man in the bottom of the canoe. Aid, however, was at hand; for Donnacona and his tribesmen, rushing pell-mell from the adjacent woods, raised the swooning masqueraders, and, with shrill clamors, bore them in their arms within the sheltering thickets. Here, for a full half-hour, the French could hear them haranguing in solemn conclave. Then the two young Indians whom Cartier had brought back from France came out of the bushes, enacting a pantomime of amazement and terror, clasping their hands, and calling on Christ and the Virgin; whereupon Cartier, shouting from the vessel, asked what was the matter. They replied, that the god Coudouagny had sent to warn the French against all attempts to ascend the great river, since, should they persist, snows, tempests, and drifting ice would requite their rashness with inevitable ruin. The French replied that Coudouagny was a fool; that he could not hurt those who believed in Christ; and that they might tell this to his three messengers. The assembled Indians, with little reverence for their deity, pretended great contentment at this assurance, and danced for joy along the beach.[1]

[1] M. Berthelot, in his *Dissertation sur le Canon de Bronze,* discovers in this Indian pantomime a typical representation of the supposed shipwreck of Verrazzano in the St. Lawrence. This shipwreck, it is needless to say, is a mere imagination of this ingenious writer.

Cartier now made ready to depart. And, first, he caused the two larger vessels to be towed for safe harborage within the mouth of the St. Charles. With the smallest, a galleon of forty tons, and two open boats, carrying in all fifty sailors, besides Pontbriand, La Pommeraye, and other gentlemen, he set out for Hochelaga.

Slowly gliding on their way by walls of verdure brightened in the autumnal sun, they saw forests festooned with grape-vines, and waters alive with wild-fowl; they heard the song of the blackbird, the thrush, and, as they fondly thought, the nightingale. The galleon grounded; they left her, and, advancing with the boats alone, on the second of October neared the goal of their hopes, the mysterious Hochelaga.

Just below where now are seen the quays and storehouses of Montreal, a thousand Indians thronged the shore, wild with delight, dancing, singing, crowding about the strangers, and showering into the boats their gifts of fish and maize; and, as it grew dark, fires lighted up the night, while, far and near, the French could see the excited savages leaping and rejoicing by the blaze.

At dawn of day, marshalled and accoutred, they marched for Hochelaga. An Indian path led them through the forest which covered the site of Montreal. The morning air was chill and sharp, the leaves were changing hue, and beneath the oaks the ground was thickly strewn with acorns. They soon met an Indian chief with a party of tribesmen, or, as the old narrative has it, "one of the principal lords of the said city," attended with a numerous retinue.[1] Greeting them after the concise courtesy of the forest, he led them to a fire kindled by the side of the path for their comfort and refreshment, seated them on the ground, and made them a long harangue, receiving in requital of his eloquence two hatchets, two knives, and a crucifix, the last of which he was invited to kiss. This done, they resumed their march, and presently came upon open fields, covered far and near with the ripened maize, its leaves rustling, and its yellow grains gleaming between the parting husks. Before them, wrapped in forests painted by the early frosts, rose the ridgy back of the Mountain of Montreal, and below, encompassed with its corn-fields, lay the Indian town. Nothing was visible but its encircling palisades. They were of trunks of trees, set in a triple row. The outer and inner ranges inclined till they met and crossed near the summit, while the upright row between them, aided by transverse braces, gave to the whole an abundant strength. Within were galleries for the defenders, rude ladders to mount them, and magazines of stones to throw down on the heads of assailants. It was a mode of fortification practised by all the tribes speaking dialects of the Iroquois.[2]

[1] " . . . l'un des principaulx seigneurs de la dicte ville, accompaigné de plusieurs personnes." Cartier (1545), 23.

[2] That the Indians of Hochelaga belonged to the Huron-Iroquois family of tribes is evident from the affinities of their language (compare Gallatin, *Synopsis of Indian Tribes*), and from the construction

The voyagers entered the narrow portal. Within, they saw some fifty of those large oblong dwellings so familiar in after years to the eyes of the Jesuit apostles in Iroquois and Huron forests. They were

of their houses and defensive works. This was identical with the construction universal, or nearly so, among the Huron-Iroquois tribes. In Ramusio, III. 446, there is a plan of Hochelaga and its defences, marked by errors which seem to show that the maker had not seen the objects represented. Whence the sketch was derived does not appear, as the original edition of Cartier does not contain it. In 1860, a quantity of Indian remains were dug up at Montreal, immediately below Sherbrooke Street, between Mansfield and Metcalfe Streets. (See a paper by Dr. Dawson, in *Canadian Naturalist and Geologist*, V. 430.) They may perhaps indicate the site of Hochelaga. A few, which have a distinctive character, belong not to the Algonquin, but to the Huron-Iroquois type. The short-stemmed pipe of terra-cotta is the exact counterpart of those found in the great Huron deposits of the dead in Canada West, and in Iroquois burial-places of Western New York. So also of the fragments of pottery and the instruments of bone used in ornamenting it.

The assertion of certain Algonquins, who, in 1642, told the missionaries that their ancestors once lived at Montreal, is far from conclusive evidence. It may have referred to an occupancy subsequent to Cartier's visit, or, which is more probable, the Indians, after their favorite practice, may have amused themselves with "hoaxing" their interlocutors.

Cartier calls his vocabulary, *Le Langage des Pays et Royaulmes de Hochelaga et Canada, aultrement appellée par nous la Nouuelle France* (ed. 1545). For this and other reasons it is more than probable that the Indians of Quebec, or Stadaconé, were also of the Huron-Iroquois race, since by *Canada* he means the country about Quebec. Seventy years later, the whole region was occupied by Algonquins, and no trace remained of Hochelaga or Stadaconé.

There was a tradition among the Agniés (Mohawks), one of the five tribes of the Iroquois, that their ancestors were once settled at Quebec. See Lafitau, I. 101. *Canada*, as already mentioned, is a Mohawk word. The tradition recorded by Colden, in his *History of the Five Nations* (Iroquois), that they were formerly settled near Montreal, is of interest here. The tradition declares that they were driven thence by the Adirondacks (Algonquins).

about fifty yards in length, and twelve or fifteen wide, framed of sapling poles closely covered with sheets of bark, and each containing several fires and several families. In the midst of the town was an open area, or public square, a stone's throw in width. Here Cartier and his followers stopped, while the surrounding houses of bark disgorged their inmates, — swarms of children, and young women and old, their infants in their arms. They crowded about the visitors, crying for delight, touching their beards, feeling their faces, and holding up the screeching infants to be touched in turn. The marvellous visitors, strange in hue, strange in attire, with moustached lip and bearded chin, with arquebuse, halberd, helmet, and cuirass, seemed rather demigods than men.

Due time having been allowed for this exuberance of feminine rapture, the warriors interposed, banished the women and children to a distance, and squatted on the ground around the French, row within row of swarthy forms and eager faces, "as if," says Cartier, "we were going to act a play."[1] Then appeared a troop of women, each bringing a mat, with which they carpeted the bare earth for the behoof of their guests. The latter being seated, the chief of the nation was borne before them on a deerskin by a number of his tribesmen, a bedridden old savage, paralyzed and helpless, squalid as the rest in

[1] " . . . comme sy eussions voulu iouer vng mystere." Cartier, 25 (1545).

his attire, and distinguished only by a red fillet, inwrought with the dyed quills of the Canada porcupine, encircling his lank black hair. They placed him on the ground at Cartier's feet and made signs of welcome for him, while he pointed feebly to his powerless limbs, and implored the healing touch from the hand of the French chief. Cartier complied, and received in acknowledgment the red fillet of his grateful patient. Then from surrounding dwellings appeared a woeful throng, the sick, the lame, the blind, the maimed, the decrepit, brought or led forth and placed on the earth before the perplexed commander, "as if," he says, "a god had come down to cure them." His skill in medicine being far behind the emergency, he pronounced over his petitioners a portion of the Gospel of St. John, made the sign of the cross, and uttered a prayer, not for their bodies only, but for their miserable souls. Next he read the passion of the Saviour, to which, though comprehending not a word, his audience listened with grave attention. Then came a distribution of presents. The squaws and children were recalled, and, with the warriors, placed in separate groups. Knives and hatchets were given to the men, and beads to the women, while pewter rings and images of the *Agnes Dei* were flung among the troop of children, whence ensued a vigorous scramble in the square of Hochelaga. Now the French trumpeters pressed their trumpets to their lips, and blew a blast that filled the air with warlike din and the hearts of the hearers with amazement and delight. Bidding their hosts farewell, the visitors formed their ranks and defiled through the gate once more, despite the efforts of a crowd of women, who, with clamorous hospitality, beset them with gifts of fish, beans, corn, and other viands of uninviting aspect, which the Frenchmen courteously declined.

A troop of Indians followed, and guided them to the top of the neighboring mountain. Cartier called it *Mont Royal*, Montreal; and hence the name of the busy city which now holds the site of the vanished Hochelaga. Stadaconé and Hochelaga, Quebec and Montreal, in the sixteenth century as in the nineteenth, were the centres of Canadian population.

From the summit, that noble prospect met his eye which at this day is the delight of tourists, but strangely changed, since, first of white men, the Breton voyager gazed upon it. Tower and dome and spire, congregated roofs, white sail, and gliding steamer, animate its vast expanse with varied life. Cartier saw a different scene. East, west, and south, the mantling forest was over all, and the broad blue ribbon of the great river glistened amid a realm of verdure. Beyond, to the bounds of Mexico, stretched a leafy desert, and the vast hive of industry, the mighty battle-ground of later centuries, lay sunk in savage torpor, wrapped in illimitable woods.

The French re-embarked, bade farewell to Hochelaga, retraced their lonely course down the St. Lawrence, and reached Stadaconé in safety. On the bank of the St. Charles, their companions had built in their absence a fort of palisades, and the ships, hauled up the little stream, lay moored before it.[1] Here the self-exiled company were soon besieged by the rigors of the Canadian winter. The rocks, the shores, the pine-trees, the solid floor of the frozen river, all alike were blanketed in snow beneath the keen cold rays of the dazzling sun. The drifts rose above the sides of their ships; masts, spars, and cordage were thick with glittering incrustations and sparkling rows of icicles; a frosty armor, four inches thick, encased the bulwarks. Yet, in the bitterest weather, the neighboring Indians, "hardy," says the journal, "as so many beasts," came daily to the fort, wading, half naked, waist-deep through the snow. At length, their friendship began to abate; their visits grew less frequent, and during December had wholly ceased, when a calamity fell upon the French.

A malignant scurvy broke out among them. Man after man went down before the hideous disease, till twenty-five were dead, and only three or four were left in health. The sound were too few to attend the sick, and the wretched sufferers lay in helpless despair, dreaming of the sun and the vines of France. The ground, hard as flint, defied their feeble efforts,

[1] In 1608, Champlain found the remains of Cartier's fort. See Champlain (1613), 184-191. Charlevoix is clearly wrong as to the locality. M. Faribault, who has collected the evidence (see *Voyages de Découverte au Canada*, 109-119), thinks the fort was near the junction of the little river Lairet with the St. Charles.

and, unable to bury their dead, they hid them in snow-drifts. Cartier appealed to the saints; but they turned a deaf ear. Then he nailed against a tree an image of the Virgin, and on a Sunday summoned forth his woe-begone followers, who, haggard, reeling, bloated with their maladies, moved in procession to the spot, and, kneeling in the snow, sang litanies and psalms of David. That day died Philippe Rougemont, of Amboise, aged twenty-two years. The Holy Virgin deigned no other response.

There was fear that the Indians, learning their misery, might finish the work that scurvy had begun. None of them, therefore, were allowed to approach the fort; and when a party of savages lingered within hearing, Cartier forced his invalid garrison to beat with sticks and stones against the walls, that their dangerous neighbors, deluded by the clatter, might think them engaged in hard labor. These objects of their fear proved, however, the instruments of their salvation. Cartier, walking one day near the river, met an Indian, who not long before had been prostrate, like many of his fellows, with the scurvy, but who was now, to all appearance, in high health and spirits. What agency had wrought this marvellous recovery? According to the Indian, it was a certain evergreen, called by him *ameda*,[1] a decoction of the leaves of which was sovereign against the disease.

[1] *Ameda*, in the edition of 1545; *annedda*, in Lescarbot, Ternaux-Compans, and Faribault. The wonderful tree seems to have been a spruce, or, more probably, an arbor-vitæ.

The experiment was tried. The sick men drank copiously of the healing draught, — so copiously indeed that in six days they drank a tree as large as a French oak. Thus vigorously assailed, the distemper relaxed its hold, and health and hope began to revisit the hapless company.

When this winter of misery had worn away, and the ships were thawed from their icy fetters, Cartier prepared to return. He had made notable discoveries; but these were as nothing to the tales of wonder that had reached his ear, — of a land of gold and rubies, of a nation white like the French, of men who lived without food, and of others to whom Nature had granted but one leg. Should he stake his credit on these marvels? It were better that they who had recounted them to him should, with their own lips, recount them also to the King, and to this end he resolved that Donnacona and his chiefs should go with him to court. He lured them therefore to the fort, and led them into an ambuscade of sailors, who, seizing the astonished guests, hurried them on board the ships. Having accomplished this treachery, the voyagers proceeded to plant the emblem of Christianity. The cross was raised, the fleur-de-lis planted near it, and, spreading their sails, they steered for home. It was the sixteenth of July, 1536, when Cartier again cast anchor under the walls of St. Malo.[1]

[1] Of the original edition (1545) of the narrative of this voyage only one copy is known, — that in the British Museum. It is styled, *Brief Recit, & succincte narration, de la nauigation faicte es ysles de Canada, Hochelage & Saguenay & autres, auec particulieres mœurs, langaige, &*

A rigorous climate, a savage people, a fatal disease, and a soil barren of gold were the allurements of New France. Nor were the times auspicious for a renewal of the enterprise. Charles the Fifth, flushed with his African triumphs, challenged the Most Christian King to single combat. The war flamed forth with renewed fury, and ten years elapsed before a hollow truce varnished the hate of the royal rivals with a thin pretence of courtesy. Peace returned; but Francis the First was sinking to his ignominious grave, under the scourge of his favorite goddess, and Chabot, patron of the former voyages, was in disgrace.[1]

Meanwhile the ominous adventure of New France had found a champion in the person of Jean François de la Roque, Sieur de Roberval, a nobleman of Picardy. Though a man of high account in his own province, his past honors paled before the splendor of the titles said to have been now conferred on him, — Lord of Norembega, Viceroy and Lieutenant-General in Canada, Hochelaga, Saguenay, Newfoundland, Belle Isle, Carpunt, Labrador, the Great Bay, and Baccalaos.[2] To this windy gift of ink and parch-

---

ceremonies des habitans d'icelles; fort delectable à veoir. As may be gathered from the title, the style and orthography are those of the days of Rabelais. It has been reprinted (1863) with valuable notes by M. d'Avezac.

[1] Brantôme, II. 283; Anquetil, V. 397; Sismondi, XVII. 62.

[2] Labrador — *Laboratoris Terra* — is so called from the circumstance that Cortereal in the year 1500 stole thence a cargo of Indians for slaves. Belle Isle and Carpunt, — the strait and islands between Labrador and Newfoundland. The Great Bay, — the Gulf of St. Law-

ment was added a solid grant from the royal treasury, with which five vessels were procured and equipped; and to Cartier was given the post of Captain-General. "We have resolved," says Francis, "to send him again to the lands of Canada and Hochelaga, which form the extremity of Asia towards the west."[1] His commission declares the objects of the enterprise to be discovery, settlement, and the conversion of the Indians, who are described as "men without knowledge of God or use of reason,"[2] — a pious design, held doubtless in full sincerity by the royal profligate, now, in his decline, a fervent champion of the Faith and a strenuous tormentor of heretics. The machinery of conversion was of a character somewhat questionable, since Cartier and Roberval were empowered to ransack the prisons for thieves, robbers, and other

rence. Norembega, or Norumbega, more properly called Arambec (Hakluyt, III. 167), was, in Ramusio's map, the country embraced within Nova Scotia, southern New Brunswick, and a part of Maine. De Laet confines it to a district about the mouth of the Penobscot. Wytfleit and other early writers say that it had a capital city of the same name; and in several old maps this fabulous metropolis is laid down, with towers and churches, on the river Penobscot. The word is of Indian origin.

Before me is the commission of Roberval, *Lettres Patentes accordées à Jehan Françoys de la Roque Sr de Roberval*, copied from the French archives. Here he is simply styled "notre Lieutenant-General, Chef Ducteur et Cappitaine de la d. entreprinse." The patent is in Lescarbot (1618). In the Archives de la Bibliothèque Publique de Rouen, an edict is preserved authorizing Roberval to raise "une armée de volontaires avec victuailles artillerie, etc. pour aller au pays de Canada." Harrisse has printed curious original documents concerning Roberval in his *Notes sur la Nouvelle France*.

[1] *De par le Roy*, 17 *Oct.*, 1540 (Harrisse).
[2] See the commission in Lescarbot, I. 411; and Hazard, I. 19.

malefactors, to complete their crews and strengthen the colony. "Whereas," says the King, "we have undertaken this voyage for the honor of God our Creator, desiring with all our heart to do that which shall be agreeable to Him, it is our will to perform a compassionate and meritorious work towards criminals and malefactors, to the end that they may acknowledge the Creator, return thanks to Him, and mend their lives. Therefore we have resolved to cause to be delivered to our aforesaid lieutenant (Roberval), such and so many of the aforesaid criminals and malefactors detained in our prisons as may seem to him useful and necessary to be carried to the aforesaid countries."[1] Of the expected profits of the voyage the adventurers were to have one third and the King another, while the remainder was to be reserved towards defraying expenses.

With respect to Donnacona and his tribesmen, basely kidnapped at Stadaconé, their souls had been better cared for than their bodies; for, having been duly baptized, they all died within a year or two, to the great detriment, as it proved, of the expedition.[2]

Meanwhile, from beyond the Pyrenees, the Most Catholic King, with alarmed and jealous eye, watched the preparations of his Most Christian enemy. America, in his eyes, was one vast province of Spain,

[1] *Pouvoir donné par le Roy au Seigneur de Roberval*, 7 *Feb.*, 1540 (Harrisse).
[2] *M. Charles Cunat à M. L. Hovins, Maire de St. Malo.* This is a

to be vigilantly guarded against the intruding foreigner. To what end were men mustered, and ships fitted out in the Breton seaports? Was it for colonization, and if so, where? Was it in Southern Florida, or on the frozen shores of Baccalaos, of which Breton cod-fishers claimed the discovery? Or would the French build forts on the Bahamas, whence they could waylay the gold ships in the Bahama Channel? Or was the expedition destined against the Spanish settlements of the islands or the Main? Reinforcements were despatched in haste, and a spy was sent to France, who, passing from port to port, Quimper, St. Malo, Brest, Morlaix, came back freighted with exaggerated tales of preparation. The Council of the Indies was called. "The French are bound for Baccalaos,"—such was the substance of their report; "your Majesty will do well to send two caravels to watch their movements, and a force to take possession of the said country. And since there is no other money to pay for it, the gold from Peru, now at Panama, might be used to that end." The Cardinal of Seville thought lightly of the danger, and prophesied that the French would reap nothing from their enterprise but disappointment and loss. The King of Portugal, sole acknowledged partner with Spain

report of researches made by M. Cunat in 1844 in the archives of St. Malo.

Extrait Baptistaire des Sauvages amenés en France par Honneste Homme Jacques Cartier.

Thevet says that he knew Donnacona in France, and found him "a good Christian."

in the ownership of the New World, was invited by the Spanish ambassador to take part in an expedition against the encroaching French. "They can do no harm at Baccalaos," was the cold reply; "and so," adds the indignant ambassador, "this King would say if they should come and take him here at Lisbon; such is the softness they show here on the one hand, while, on the other, they wish to give law to the whole world."[1]

The five ships, occasions of this turmoil and alarm, had lain at St. Malo waiting for cannon and munitions from Normandy and Champagne. They waited in vain, and as the King's orders were stringent against delay, it was resolved that Cartier should sail at once, leaving Roberval to follow with additional ships when the expected supplies arrived.

On the twenty-third of May, 1541,[2] the Breton captain again spread his canvas for New France, and, passing in safety the tempestuous Atlantic, the fog-banks of Newfoundland, the island rocks clouded with screaming sea-fowl, and the forests breathing piny odors from the shore, cast anchor again beneath the cliffs of Quebec. Canoes came out from shore filled with feathered savages inquiring for their kidnapped chiefs. "Donnacona," replied Cartier, "is dead;" but he added the politic falsehood, that the others had married in France, and lived in state, like

---

[1] See the documents on this subject in the *Coleccion de Varios Documentos* of Buckingham Smith, I. 107–112.

[2] Hakluyt's date, 1540, is incorrect.

great lords. The Indians pretended to be satisfied; but it was soon apparent that they looked askance on the perfidious strangers.

Cartier pursued his course, sailed three leagues and a half up the St. Lawrence, and anchored off the mouth of the River of Cap Rouge. It was late in August, and the leafy landscape sweltered in the sun. The Frenchmen landed, picked up quartz crystals on the shore and thought them diamonds, climbed the steep promontory, drank at the spring near the top, looked abroad on the wooded slopes beyond the little river, waded through the tall grass of the meadow, found a quarry of slate, and gathered scales of a yellow mineral which glistened like gold, then returned to their boats, crossed to the south shore of the St. Lawrence, and, languid with the heat, rested in the shade of forests laced with an entanglement of grape-vines.

Now their task began, and while some cleared off the woods and sowed turnip-seed, others cut a zigzag road up the height, and others built two forts, one at the summit, and one on the shore below. The forts finished, the Vicomte de Beaupré took command, while Cartier went with two boats to explore the rapids above Hochelaga. When at length he returned, the autumn was far advanced; and with the gloom of a Canadian November came distrust, foreboding, and homesickness. Roberval had not appeared; the Indians kept jealously aloof; the motley colony was sullen as the dull, raw air around it. There was disgust and ire at Charlesbourg-Royal, for so the place was called.[1]

Meanwhile, unexpected delays had detained the impatient Roberval; nor was it until the sixteenth of April, 1542, that, with three ships and two hundred colonists, he set sail from Rochelle. When, on the eighth of June, he entered the harbor of St. John, he found seventeen fishing-vessels lying there at anchor. Soon after, he descried three other sail rounding the entrance of the haven, and, with anger and amazement, recognized the ships of Jacques Cartier. That voyager had broken up his colony and abandoned New France. What motives had prompted a desertion little consonant with the resolute spirit of the man it is impossible to say, — whether sickness within, or Indian enemies without, disgust with an enterprise whose unripened fruits had proved so hard and bitter, or discontent at finding himself reduced to a post of subordination in a country which he had discovered and where he had commanded. The Viceroy ordered him to return; but Cartier escaped with his vessels under cover of night, and made sail for France, carrying with him as trophies a few quartz diamonds from Cap Rouge, and grains of sham gold from the neighboring slate ledges. Thus closed the third Canadian voyage of this notable

[1] The original narrative of this voyage is fragmentary, and exists only in the translation of Hakluyt. Purchas, Belknap, Forster, Chalmers, and the other secondary writers, all draw from this source. The narrative published by the Literary and Historical Society of Quebec is the English version of Hakluyt retranslated into French.

explorer. His discoveries had gained for him a patent of nobility, and he owned the seigniorial mansion of Limoilou,[1] a rude structure of stone still standing. Here, and in the neighboring town of St. Malo, where also he had a house, he seems to have lived for many years.[2]

Roberval once more set sail, steering northward to the Straits of Belle Isle and the dreaded Isles of Demons. And here an incident befell which the all-believing Thevet records in manifest good faith, and which, stripped of the adornments of superstition and a love of the marvellous, has without doubt a nucleus of truth. I give the tale as I find it.

The Viceroy's company was of a mixed complexion. There were nobles, officers, soldiers, sailors, adventurers, with women too, and children. Of the women, some were of birth and station, and among them a damsel called Marguerite, a niece of Roberval himself. In the ship was a young gentleman who

---

[1] This curious relic, which in 1865 was still entire, in the suburbs of St. Malo, was as rude in construction as an ordinary farmhouse. It had only a kitchen and a hall below, and two rooms above. At the side was a small stable, and, opposite, a barn. These buildings, together with two heavy stone walls, enclosed a square court. Adjacent was a garden and an orchard. The whole indicates a rough and simple way of life. See Ramé, *Note sur le Manoir de Jacques Cartier.*

[2] The above account of the departure of Cartier from Canada is from Hakluyt. Since it was written, M. Gosselin, archivist of the Palais de Justice at Rouen, has discovered a paper which shows that Roberval sailed from France, not on the 16th of April, 1542, but on the 22d of August, 1541, thus confusing the narrative of Hakluyt. What remains certain is that Cartier left Canada while Roberval stayed there, and that there were disputes between them. See Ramé, *Documents Inédits* (1865), 22.

had embarked for love of her. His love was too well requited; and the stern Viceroy, scandalized and enraged at a passion which scorned concealment and set shame at defiance, cast anchor by the haunted island, landed his indiscreet relative, gave her four arquebuses for defence, and, with an old Norman nurse named Bastienne, who had pandered to the lovers, left her to her fate. Her gallant threw himself into the surf, and by desperate effort gained the shore, with two more guns and a supply of ammunition.

The ship weighed anchor, receded, vanished, and they were left alone. Yet not so, for the demon lords of the island beset them day and night, raging around their hut with a confused and hungry clamoring, striving to force the frail barrier. The lovers had repented of their sin, though not abandoned it, and Heaven was on their side. The saints vouchsafed their aid, and the offended Virgin, relenting, held before them her protecting shield. In the form of beasts or other shapes abominably and unutterably hideous, the brood of hell, howling in baffled fury, tore at the branches of the sylvan dwelling; but a celestial hand was ever interposed, and there was a viewless barrier which they might not pass. Marguerite became pregnant. Here was a double prize, two souls in one, mother and child. The fiends grew frantic, but all in vain. She stood undaunted amid these horrors; but her lover, dismayed and heartbroken, sickened and died. Her child soon followed;

then the old Norman nurse found her unhallowed rest in that accursed soil, and Marguerite was left alone. Neither her reason nor her courage failed. When the demons assailed her, she shot at them with her gun, but they answered with hellish merriment, and thenceforth she placed her trust in Heaven alone. There were foes around her of the upper, no less than of the nether world. Of these, the bears were the most redoubtable; yet, being vulnerable to mortal weapons, she killed three of them, all, says the story, "as white as an egg."

It was two years and five months from her landing on the island, when, far out at sea, the crew of a small fishing-craft saw a column of smoke curling upward from the haunted shore. Was it a device of the fiends to lure them to their ruin? They thought so, and kept aloof. But misgiving seized them. They warily drew near, and descried a female figure in wild attire waving signals from the strand. Thus at length was Marguerite rescued and restored to her native France, where, a few years later, the cosmographer Thevet met her at Natron in Perigord, and heard the tale of wonder from her own lips.[1]

[1] The story is taken from the curious manuscript of 1586. Compare the *Cosmographie* of Thevet (1575), II. c. 6. Thevet was the personal friend both of Cartier and of Roberval, the latter of whom he calls "mon familier," and the former, "mon grand et singulier amy." He says that he lived five months with Cartier in his house at St. Malo. He was also a friend of Rabelais, who once, in Italy, rescued him from a serious embarrassment. See the *Notice Biographique* prefixed to the edition of Rabelais of Burgaud des Marets and Rathery. The story of

Having left his offending niece to the devils and bears of the Isles of Demons, Roberval held his course up the St. Lawrence, and dropped anchor before the heights of Cap Rouge. His company landed; there were bivouacs along the strand, a hubbub of pick and spade, axe, saw, and hammer; and soon in the wilderness uprose a goodly structure, half barrack, half castle, with two towers, two spacious halls, a kitchen, chambers, store-rooms, workshops, cellars, garrets, a well, an oven, and two water-mills. Roberval named it France-Roy, and it stood on that bold acclivity where Cartier had before intrenched himself, the St. Lawrence in front, and on the right the River of Cap Rouge. Here all the colony housed under the same roof, like one of the experimental communities of recent days, — officers, soldiers, nobles, artisans, laborers, and convicts, with the women and children in whom lay the future hope of New France.

Experience and forecast had both been wanting. There were storehouses, but no stores; mills, but no grist; an ample oven, and a dearth of bread. It was only when two of the ships had sailed for France that they took account of their provision and discovered its lamentable shortcoming. Winter and famine followed. They bought fish from the Indians, and dug

Marguerite is also told in the *Heptameron* of Marguerite de Valois, sister of Francis I. (1559).

In the *Routier* of Jean Alphonse, Roberval's pilot, where the principal points of the voyage are set down, repeated mention is made of "les Isles de la Demoiselle," immediately north of Newfoundland. The inference is obvious that the demoiselle was Marguerite.

roots and boiled them in whale-oil. Disease broke out, and, before spring, killed one third of the colony. The rest would have quarrelled, mutinied, and otherwise aggravated their inevitable woes, but disorder was dangerous under the iron rule of the inexorable Roberval. Michel Gaillon was detected in a petty theft, and hanged. Jean de Nantes, for a more venial offence, was kept in irons. The quarrels of men and the scolding of women were alike requited at the whipping-post, "by which means," quaintly says the narrative, "they lived in peace."

Thevet, while calling himself the intimate friend of the Viceroy, gives a darker coloring to his story. He says that, forced to unceasing labor, and chafed by arbitrary rules, some of the soldiers fell under Roberval's displeasure, and six of them, formerly his favorites, were hanged in one day. Others were banished to an island, and there kept in fetters; while, for various light offences, several, both men and women, were shot. Even the Indians were moved to pity, and wept at the sight of their woes.[1]

And here, midway, our guide deserts us; the ancient narrative is broken, and the latter part is lost, leaving us to divine as we may the future of the ill-starred colony. That it did not long survive is certain. The King, in great need of Roberval, sent Cartier to bring him home, and this voyage seems to have taken place in the summer of 1543.[2] It is said that, in after years, the Viceroy essayed to repossess

[1] Thevet MS. (1586).   [2] Lescarbot (1612), I. 416.

himself of his Transatlantic domain, and lost his life in the attempt.[1] Thevet, on the other hand, with ample means of learning the truth, affirms that Roberval was slain at night, near the Church of the Innocents, in the heart of Paris.

With him closes the prelude of the French-American drama. Tempestuous years and a reign of blood and fire were in store for France. The religious wars begot the hapless colony of Florida, but for more than half a century they left New France a desert. Order rose at length out of the sanguinary chaos; the zeal of discovery and the spirit of commercial enterprise once more awoke, while, closely following, more potent than they, moved the black-robed forces of the Roman Catholic reaction.

[1] Le Clerc, *Établissement de la Foy,* I. 14.

NOTE. — *The Voyage of Verrazzano.* The narrative of the voyage of Verrazzano is contained in a letter from him, dated at Dieppe, 8 July, 1524. The original letter does not exist. An Italian translation was printed by Ramusio in 1556, and there is another translation in the Magliabecchian Library at Florence. This last is accompanied by a letter concerning the voyage from one Fernando Carli, dated at Lyons, 4 August, 1524. Hieronimo da Verrazzano, brother of the navigator, made in 1529 a large map of the world, which is preserved in the College of the Propaganda at Rome. The discoveries of Verrazzano are laid down upon it, and the North American part bears the inscription, "Verazzana sive nova Gallia quale discoprì 5 anni fa Giovanni da Verazzano florentino per ordine e Comandamento del Cristianissimo Re di Francia." A copper globe made by Euphrosynus Ulpius, in 1542, also affirms the discovery of Verrazzano, and gives his name to a part of the continent, while other contemporary maps, notably that of Visconte di Maiollo, 1527, also contain traces of his voyage. Ramusio says that he had conversed with many persons who knew Verrazzano, and he prints a paper called *Discorso d' un gran Capitano di Mare Francese*, in which the voyage of Verrazzano is mentioned by a contemporary navigator of Dieppe.

Various Spanish and Portuguese documents attest the exploits of Verrazzano as a corsair, and a letter of Silveira, Portuguese ambassador to France, shows that in the spring of 1523 he had announced his purpose of a voyage to "Cathay." On the eleventh of May, 1526, he gave a power of attorney to his brother Hieronimo, the maker of the map, and this paper still exists, bearing his autograph. Various other original papers relating to him are extant, one of the most curious being that of the judge of Cadiz, testifying to his capture and his execution at Puerto del Pico. None of the early writers question the reality of the voyage. Among those who affirm it may be mentioned Annibal Caro, 1537; Belleforest, 1570; Herrera, 1601; Wytfleit, 1603; De Laet, 1603; Lescarbot, 1612.

In 1864, Mr. Buckingham Smith questioned the genuineness of the Verrazzano letter in a pamphlet called, *An Inquiry into the Authenticity of Documents concerning a Discovery in North America claimed to have been made by Verrazzano*. Mr. J. Carson Brevoort answered him, in a book entitled *Verrazzano the Navigator*. Mr. Henry C. Murphy followed with another book, *The Voyage of Verrazzano*, in which he endeavored at great length to prove that the evidence concerning the voyage was fabricated. Mr. Henry Harrisse gave a cautious and qualified support to his views in the *Revue Critique*. Mr. Major answered them in the *London Geographical Magazine*, and Mr. De Costa made an elaborate and effective reply in his work called *Verrazzano the Explorer*. An Italian writer, Signor Desimoni, has added some cogent facts in support of the authenticity of the documents. A careful examination of these various writings convinces me that the evidence in favor of the voyage of Verrazzano is far stronger than the evidence against it. Abbé Verreau found a contemporary document in the Bibliothèque Nationale, in which it is mentioned that the "memoirs" of Verrazzano were then in possession of Chatillon (Admiral Coligny). See *Report on Canadian Archives*, 1874, p. 190.

CHAPTER II.

1542–1604.

LA ROCHE. — CHAMPLAIN. — DE MONTS.

FRENCH FISHERMEN AND FUR-TRADERS. — LA ROCHE. — THE CONVICTS OF SABLE ISLAND. — TADOUSSAC. — SAMUEL DE CHAMPLAIN. — VISITS THE WEST INDIES AND MEXICO. — EXPLORES THE ST. LAWRENCE. — DE MONTS. — HIS ACADIAN SCHEMES.

YEARS rolled on. France, long tossed among the surges of civil commotion, plunged at last into a gulf of fratricidal war. Blazing hamlets, sacked cities, fields steaming with slaughter, profaned altars, and ravished maidens, marked the track of the tornado. There was little room for schemes of foreign enterprise. Yet, far aloof from siege and battle, the fishermen of the western ports still plied their craft on the Banks of Newfoundland. Humanity, morality, decency, might be forgotten, but codfish must still be had for the use of the faithful in Lent and on fast days. Still the wandering Esquimaux saw the Norman and Breton sails hovering around some lonely headland, or anchored in fleets in the harbor of St. John; and still, through salt spray and driving mist, the fishermen dragged up the riches of the sea.

In January and February, 1545, about two vessels a day sailed from French ports for Newfoundland.[1] In 1565, Pedro Menendez complains that the French "rule despotically" in those parts. In 1578, there were a hundred and fifty French fishing-vessels there, besides two hundred of other nations, Spanish, Portuguese, and English. Added to these were twenty or thirty Biscayan whalers.[2] In 1607, there was an old French fisherman at Canseau who had voyaged to these seas for forty-two successive years.[3]

But if the wilderness of ocean had its treasures, so too had the wilderness of woods. It needed but a few knives, beads, and trinkets, and the Indians would throng to the shore burdened with the spoils of their winter hunting. Fishermen threw up their old vocation for the more lucrative trade in bear-skins and beaver-skins. They built rude huts along the shores of Anticosti, where, at that day, the bison, it is said, could be seen wallowing in the sands.[4] They outraged the Indians; they quarrelled with each

[1] Gosselin, *Documents Authentiques*.
[2] Hakluyt, III. 132. Comp. Pinkerton, *Voyages*, XII. 174, and Thevet MS. (1586).
[3] Lescarbot, II. 605. Purchas's date is wrong.
[4] Thevet MS. (1586). Thevet says that he had himself seen them. Perhaps he confounds them with the moose.

In 1565, and for some years previous, bison-skins were brought by the Indians down the Potomac, and thence carried along-shore in canoes to the French about the Gulf of St. Lawrence. During two years, six thousand skins were thus obtained. Letters of Pedro Menendez to Philip II., MS.

On the fur-trade, see Hakluyt, III. 187, 193, 233, 292, etc.

other; and this infancy of the Canadian fur-trade showed rich promise of the disorders which marked its riper growth. Others, meanwhile, were ranging the gulf in search of walrus tusks; and, the year after the battle of Ivry, St. Malo sent out a fleet of small craft in quest of this new prize.

In all the western seaports, merchants and adventurers turned their eyes towards America; not, like the Spaniards, seeking treasures of silver and gold, but the more modest gains of codfish and train-oil, beaver-skins and marine ivory. St. Malo was conspicuous above them all. The rugged Bretons loved the perils of the sea, and saw with a jealous eye every attempt to shackle their activity on this its favorite field. When in 1588 Jacques Noel and Estienne Chaton — the former a nephew of Cartier and the latter pretending to be so — gained a monopoly of the American fur-trade for twelve years, such a clamor arose within the walls of St. Malo that the obnoxious grant was promptly revoked.[1]

But soon a power was in the field against which all St. Malo might clamor in vain. A Catholic nobleman of Brittany, the Marquis de la Roche, bargained with the King to colonize New France. On his part, he was to receive a monopoly of the trade, and a profusion of worthless titles and empty privileges. He was declared Lieutenant-General of Canada, Hochelaga, Newfoundland, Labrador, and the coun-

[1] Lescarbot, I. 418. Compare Ramé, *Documents Inédits* (1865). In Hakluyt are two letters of Jacques Noel.

tries adjacent, with sovereign power within his vast and ill-defined domain. He could levy troops, declare war and peace, make laws, punish or pardon at will, build cities, forts, and castles, and grant out lands in fiefs, seigniories, counties, viscounties, and baronies.[1] Thus was effete and cumbrous feudalism to make a lodgement in the New World. It was a scheme of high-sounding promise, but in performance less than contemptible. La Roche ransacked the prisons, and, gathering thence a gang of thieves and desperadoes, embarked them in a small vessel, and set sail to plant Christianity and civilization in the West. Suns rose and set, and the wretched bark, deep freighted with brutality and vice, held on her course. She was so small that the convicts, leaning over her side, could wash their hands in the water.[2] At length, on the gray horizon they descried a long, gray line of ridgy sand. It was Sable Island, off the coast of Nova Scotia. A wreck lay stranded on the beach, and the surf broke ominously over the long, submerged arms of sand, stretched far out into the sea on the right hand and on the left.

Here La Roche landed the convicts, forty in num-

---

[1] *Lettres Patentes pour le Sieur de la Roche*, 12 *Jan.*, 1598; Lescarbot, I. 422; *Édits et Ordonnances* (Quebec, 1804), II. 4. La Roche had received a similar commission in 1577 and 1578, but seems to have made no use of it. Ramé, *Documents Inédits* (1867). There is evidence that, as early as 1564, the King designed an expedition to colonize Canada. See Gosselin, *Documents Inédits pour servir à l'Histoire de la Marine Normande*.

[2] Lescarbot, I. 421.

ber, while, with his more trusty followers, he sailed to explore the neighboring coasts, and choose a site for the capital of his new dominion, to which, in due time, he proposed to remove the prisoners. But suddenly a tempest from the west assailed him. The frail vessel was forced to run before the gale, which, howling on her track, drove her off the coast, and chased her back towards France.

Meanwhile the convicts watched in suspense for the returning sail. Days passed, weeks passed, and still they strained their eyes in vain across the waste of ocean. La Roche had left them to their fate. Rueful and desperate, they wandered among the sand-hills, through the stunted whortleberry bushes, the rank sand-grass, and the tangled cranberry vines which filled the hollows. Not a tree was to be seen; but they built huts of the fragments of the wreck. For food they caught fish in the surrounding sea, and hunted the cattle which ran wild about the island, — sprung, perhaps, from those left here eighty years before by the Baron de Léry.[1] They killed seals, trapped black foxes, and clothed themselves in their skins. Their native instincts clung to them in their exile. As if not content with inevitable miseries, they quarrelled and murdered one another. Season after season dragged on. Five years elapsed, and, of the forty, only twelve were left alive. Sand, sea,

---

[1] Lescarbot, I. 22. Compare De Laet, Lib. II. c. 4. Charlevoix and Champlain say that they escaped from the wreck of a Spanish vessel; Purchas, that they were left by the Portuguese.

and sky, — there was little else around them; though,
to break the dead monotony, the walrus would sometimes
rear his half-human face and glistening sides
on the reefs and sand-bars. At length, on the far
verge of the watery desert, they descried a sail. She
stood on towards the island; a boat's crew landed on
the beach, and the exiles were once more among their
countrymen.

When La Roche returned to France, the fate of
his followers sat heavy on his mind. But the day of
his prosperity was gone. A host of enemies rose
against him and his privileges, and it is said that the
Duc de Mercœur seized him and threw him into
prison. In time, however, he gained a hearing of
the King; and the Norman pilot, Chefdhôtel, was
despatched to bring the outcasts home.

He reached Sable Island in September, 1603, and
brought back to France eleven survivors, whose
names are still preserved.[1] When they arrived,
Henry the Fourth summoned them into his presence.
They stood before him, says an old writer, like river-gods
of yore;[2] for from head to foot they were clothed
in shaggy skins, and beards of prodigious length
hung from their swarthy faces. They had accumulated,
on their island, a quantity of valuable furs.
Of these Chefdhôtel had robbed them; but the pilot
was forced to disgorge his prey, and, with the aid of
a bounty from the King, they were enabled to embark

[1] Gosselin, *Documents Authentiques* (Rouen, 1876).
[2] Charlevoix, I. 110; Guérin, *Navigateurs Français*, 210.

on their own account in the Canadian trade.[1] To their leader, fortune was less kind. Broken by disaster and imprisonment, La Roche died miserably.

In the mean time, on the ruin of his enterprise, a new one had been begun. Pontgravé, a merchant of St. Malo, leagued himself with Chauvin, a captain of the navy, who had influence at court. A patent was granted to them, with the condition that they should colonize the country. But their only thought was to enrich themselves.

At Tadoussac, at the mouth of the Saguenay, under the shadow of savage and inaccessible rocks, feathered with pines, firs, and birch-trees, they built a cluster of wooden huts and store-houses. Here they left sixteen men to gather the expected harvest of furs. Before the winter was over, several of them were dead, and the rest scattered through the woods, living on the charity of the Indians.[2]

But a new era had dawned on France. Exhausted with thirty years of conflict, she had sunk at last to a repose, uneasy and disturbed, yet the harbinger of

---

[1] Purchas, IV. 1807. Before me are several curious papers copied from the archives of the Palais de Justice of Rouen. One of these is entitled *Copie d'un Arrêt rendu contre Chefdhostel*, 27 *Nov.*, 1603. It orders him to deliver to the eleven men whom he had just brought home two thirds of their furs. Another, dated 6 March, 1598, relates to the criminals whom La Roche was empowered to take from the prisons. A third, dated 18 May, 1598, orders that one of these criminals, François de Bauldre, convicted of highway robbery, shall not be allowed to go to Canada, but shall be forthwith beheaded. These papers set at rest the disputed question of the date of La Roche's voyage. I owe them to the kindness of M. Gabriel Gravier, of Rouen.

[2] Champlain (1632), 34; Estancelin, 96.

recovery. The rugged soldier whom, for the weal of France and of mankind, Providence had cast to the troubled surface of affairs, was throned in the Louvre, composing the strife of factions and the quarrels of his mistresses. The bear-hunting prince of the Pyrenees wore the crown of France; and to this day, as one gazes on the time-worn front of the Tuileries, above all other memories rises the small, strong finger, the brow wrinkled with cares of love and war, the bristling moustache, the grizzled beard, the bold, vigorous, and withal somewhat odd features of the mountaineer of Béarn. To few has human liberty owed so deep a gratitude or so deep a grudge. He cared little for creeds or dogmas. Impressible, quick in sympathy, his grim lip lighted often with a smile, and his war-worn cheek was no stranger to a tear. He forgave his enemies and forgot his friends. Many loved him; none but fools trusted him. Mingled of mortal good and ill, frailty and force, of all the kings who for two centuries and more sat on the throne of France Henry the Fourth alone was a man.

Art, industry, and commerce, so long crushed and overborne, were stirring into renewed life, and a crowd of adventurous men, nurtured in war and incapable of repose, must seek employment for their restless energies in fields of peaceful enterprise.

Two small, quaint vessels, not larger than the fishing-craft of Gloucester and Marblehead, — one was of twelve, the other of fifteen tons, — held their way across the Atlantic, passed the tempestuous headlands of Newfoundland and the St. Lawrence, and, with adventurous knight-errantry, glided deep into the heart of the Canadian wilderness. On board of one of them was the Breton merchant, Pontgravé, and with him a man of spirit widely different, a Catholic of good family, — Samuel de Champlain, born in 1567 at the small seaport of Brouage on the Bay of Biscay. His father was a captain in the royal navy, where he himself seems also to have served, though during the war he had fought for the King in Brittany, under the banners of D'Aumont, St. Luc, and Brissac. His purse was small, his merit great; and Henry the Fourth out of his own slender revenues had given him a pension to maintain him near his person. But rest was penance to him. The war in Brittany was over. The rebellious Duc de Mercœur was reduced to obedience, and the royal army disbanded. Champlain, his occupation gone, conceived a design consonant with his adventurous nature. He would visit the West Indies, and bring back to the King a report of those regions of mystery whence Spanish jealousy excluded foreigners, and where every intruding Frenchman was threatened with death. Here much knowledge was to be won and much peril to be met. The joint attraction was resistless.

The Spaniards, allies of the vanquished Leaguers, were about to evacuate Blavet, their last stronghold in Brittany. Thither Champlain repaired; and here he found an uncle, who had charge of the French fleet destined to take on board the Spanish garrison. Champlain embarked with them, and, reaching Cadiz, succeeded, with the aid of his relative, who had just accepted the post of Pilot-General of the Spanish marine, in gaining command of one of the ships about to sail for the West Indies under Don Francisco Colombo.

At Dieppe there is a curious old manuscript, in clear, decisive, and somewhat formal handwriting of the sixteenth century, garnished with sixty-one colored pictures, in a style of art which a child of ten might emulate. Here one may see ports, harbors, islands, and rivers, adorned with portraitures of birds, beasts, and fishes thereto pertaining. Here are Indian feasts and dances; Indians flogged by priests for not going to mass; Indians burned alive for heresy, six in one fire; Indians working the silver mines. Here, too, are descriptions of natural objects, each with its illustrative sketch, some drawn from life and some from memory, — as, for example, a chameleon with two legs; others from hearsay, among which is the portrait of the griffin said to haunt certain districts of Mexico, — a monster with the wings of a bat, the head of an eagle, and the tail of an alligator.

This is Champlain's journal, written and illustrated by his own hand, in that defiance of perspective and absolute independence of the canons of art which mark the earliest efforts of the pencil.

A true hero, after the chivalrous mediæval type, his character was dashed largely with the spirit of romance. Though earnest, sagacious, and penetrating, he leaned to the marvellous; and the faith which was the life of his hard career was somewhat prone to overstep the bounds of reason and invade the domain of fancy. Hence the erratic character of some of his exploits, and hence his simple faith in the Mexican griffin.

His West-Indian adventure occupied him more than two years. He visited the principal ports of the islands, made plans and sketches of them all, after his fashion, and then, landing at Vera Cruz, journeyed inland to the city of Mexico. On his return he made his way to Panama. Here, more than two centuries and a half ago, his bold and active mind conceived the plan of a ship-canal across the isthmus, "by which," he says, "the voyage to the South Sea would be shortened by more than fifteen hundred leagues."[1]

---

[1] ". . . l'on accourciroit par ainsy le chemin de plus de 1500 lieues, et depuis Panama jusques au destroit de Magellan se seroit une isle, et de Panama jusques aux Terres Neufves une autre isle," etc. — Champlain, *Bref Discours*. A Biscayan pilot had before suggested the plan to the Spanish government; but Philip the Second, probably in the interest of certain monopolies, forbade the subject to be again brought forward on pain of death.

The journal is entitled, "Bref Discours des Choses plus Remarquables que Samuel Champlain de Brouage a recognues aux Indes Occidentales." The original manuscript, in Champlain's handwriting, is, or was, in the hands of M. Féret of Dieppe, a collateral descendant of the writer's patron, the Commander de Chastes. It consists of a hun-

On reaching France he repaired to court, and it may have been at this time that a royal patent raised him to the rank of the untitled nobility. He soon wearied of the antechambers of the Louvre. It was here, however, that his destiny awaited him, and the work of his life was unfolded. Aymar de Chastes, Commander of the Order of St. John and Governor of Dieppe, a gray-haired veteran of the civil wars, wished to mark his closing days with some notable achievement for France and the Church. To no man was the King more deeply indebted. In his darkest hour, when the hosts of the League were gathering round him, when friends were falling off, and the Parisians, exulting in his certain ruin, were hiring the windows of the Rue St. Antoine to see him led to the Bastille, De Chastes, without condition or reserve, gave up to him the town and castle of Dieppe. Thus he was enabled to fight beneath its walls the battle of Arques, the first in the series of successes which secured his triumph; and he had been heard to say that to this friend in his adversity he owed his own salvation and that of France.

De Chastes was one of those men who, amid the strife of factions and rage of rival fanaticisms, make reason and patriotism their watchwords, and stand on the firm ground of a strong and resolute modera-

dred and fifteen small quarto pages. I am indebted to M. Jacques Viger for the use of his copy.

A translation of it was published in 1859 by the Hakluyt Society, with notes and a biographical notice by no means remarkable for accuracy.

tion. He had resisted the madness of Leaguer and Huguenot alike; yet, though a foe of the League, the old soldier was a devout Catholic, and it seemed in his eyes a noble consummation of his life to plant the cross and the fleur-de-lis in the wilderness of New France. Chauvin had just died, after wasting the lives of a score or more of men in a second and a third attempt to establish the fur-trade at Tadoussac. De Chastes came to court to beg a patent of Henry the Fourth; "and," says his friend Champlain, "though his head was crowned with gray hairs as with years, he resolved to proceed to New France in person, and dedicate the rest of his days to the service of God and his King."[1]

The patent, costing nothing, was readily granted; and De Chastes, to meet the expenses of the enterprise, and forestall the jealousies which his monopoly would awaken among the keen merchants of the western ports, formed a company with the more prominent of them. Pontgravé, who had some knowledge of the country, was chosen to make a preliminary exploration.

This was the time when Champlain, fresh from the West Indies, appeared at court. De Chastes knew him well. Young, ardent, yet ripe in experience, a skilful seaman and a practised soldier, he above all others was a man for the enterprise. He had many conferences with the veteran, under whom he had served in the royal fleet off the coast of Brittany.

[1] On De Chastes, Vitet, *Histoire de Dieppe*, c. 19, 20, 21.

De Chastes urged him to accept a post in his new company; and Champlain, nothing loath, consented, provided always that permission should be had from the King, "to whom," he says, "I was bound no less by birth than by the pension with which his Majesty honored me." To the King, therefore, De Chastes repaired. The needful consent was gained, and, armed with a letter to Pontgravé, Champlain set out for Honfleur. Here he found his destined companion, and embarking with him, as we have seen, they spread their sails for the west.

Like specks on the broad bosom of the waters, the two pygmy vessels held their course up the lonely St. Lawrence. They passed abandoned Tadoussac, the channel of Orleans, and the gleaming cataract of Montmorenci; the tenantless rock of Quebec, the wide Lake of St. Peter and its crowded archipelago, till now the mountain reared before them its rounded shoulder above the forest-plain of Montreal. All was solitude. Hochelaga had vanished; and of the savage population that Cartier had found here, sixty-eight years before, no trace remained. In its place were a few wandering Algonquins, of different tongue and lineage. In a skiff, with a few Indians, Champlain essayed to pass the rapids of St. Louis. Oars, paddles, and poles alike proved vain against the foaming surges, and he was forced to return. On the deck of his vessel, the Indians drew rude plans of the river above, with its chain of rapids, its lakes and cataracts; and the baffled explorer turned his

SCHEMES OF DE MONTS.

prow homeward, the objects of his mission accomplished, but his own adventurous curiosity unsated. When the voyagers reached Havre de Grace, a grievous blow awaited them. The Commander de Chastes was dead.[1]

His mantle fell upon Pierre du Guast, Sieur de Monts, gentleman in ordinary of the King's chamber, and Governor of Pons. Undaunted by the fate of La Roche, this nobleman petitioned the king for leave to colonize La Cadie, or Acadie,[2] a region defined as extending from the fortieth to the forty-sixth degree of north latitude, or from Philadelphia to beyond Montreal. The King's minister, Sully, as he himself tells us, opposed the plan, on the ground that the colonization of this northern wilderness would never

---

[1] Champlain, *Des Sauvages* (1604). Champlain's Indian informants gave him very confused accounts. They indicated the Falls of Niagara as a mere "rapid." They are laid down, however, in Champlain's great map of 1632 with the following note: "Sault d'eau au bout du Sault [Lac] Sainct Louis fort hault où plusieurs sortes de poissons descendans s'estourdissent."

[2] This name is not found in any earlier public document. It was afterwards restricted to the peninsula of Nova Scotia, but the dispute concerning the limits of Acadia was a proximate cause of the war of 1755.

The word is said to be derived from the Indian *Aquoddiauke*, or *Aquoddie*, supposed to mean the fish called a pollock. The Bay of Passamaquoddy, "Great Pollock Water," if we may accept the same authority, derives its name from the same origin. Potter in *Historical Magazine*, I. 84. This derivation is doubtful. The Micmac word, *Quoddy*, *Kady*, or *Cadie*, means simply a place or region, and is properly used in conjunction with some other noun; as, for example, *Katakady*, the Place of Eels, *Sunakady* (Sunacadie), the Place of Cranberries, *Pestumoquoddy* (Passamaquoddy), the Place of Pollocks. Dawson and Rand, in *Canadian Antiquarian and Numismatic Journal*.

repay the outlay; but De Monts gained his point. He was made Lieutenant-General in Acadia, with viceregal powers; and withered Feudalism, with her antique forms and tinselled follies, was again to seek a new home among the rocks and pine-trees of Nova Scotia. The foundation of the enterprise was a monopoly of the fur-trade, and in its favor all past grants were unceremoniously annulled. St. Malo, Rouen, Dieppe, and Rochelle greeted the announcement with unavailing outcries. Patents granted and revoked, monopolies decreed and extinguished, had involved the unhappy traders in ceaseless embarrassment. De Monts, however, preserved De Chastes's old company, and enlarged it, — thus making the chief malcontents sharers in his exclusive rights, and converting them from enemies into partners.

A clause in his commission empowered him to impress idlers and vagabonds as material for his colony, — an ominous provision of which he largely availed himself. His company was strangely incongruous. The best and the meanest of France were crowded together in his two ships. Here were thieves and ruffians dragged on board by force; and here were many volunteers of condition and character, with Baron de Poutrincourt and the indefatigable Champlain. Here, too, were Catholic priests and Huguenot ministers; for, though De Monts was a Calvinist, the Church, as usual, displayed her banner in the van of the enterprise, and he was forced to promise that he would cause the Indians to be instructed in the dogmas of Rome.[1]

[1] *Articles proposez au Roy par le Sieur de Monts; Commissions du Roy et de Monseigneur l'Admiral au Sieur de Monts; Défenses du Roy Premières et Secondes, à tous ses subjects, autres que le Sieur de Monts, etc. de traffiquer, etc.; Déclaration du Roy; Extraict des Registres de Parlement; Remontrance faict au Roy par le Sieur de Monts;* etc.

CHAPTER III.

1604, 1605.

ACADIA OCCUPIED.

CATHOLIC AND CALVINIST. — THE LOST PRIEST. — ST. CROIX. — WINTER MISERIES. — CHAMPLAIN ON THE COAST OF NEW ENGLAND. — PORT ROYAL.

DE MONTS, with one of his vessels, sailed from Havre de Grace on the seventh of April, 1604. Pontgravé, with stores for the colony, was to follow in a few days.

Scarcely were they at sea, when ministers and priests fell first to discussion, then to quarrelling, then to blows. "I have seen our *curé* and the minister," says Champlain, "fall to with their fists on questions of faith. I cannot say which had the more pluck, or which hit the harder; but I know that the minister sometimes complained to the Sieur de Monts that he had been beaten. This was their way of settling points of controversy. I leave you to judge if it was a pleasant thing to see."[1]

Sagard, the Franciscan friar, relates with horror, that, after their destination was reached, a priest and a minister happening to die at the same time, the

[1] Champlain (1632), 46.

crew buried them both in one grave, to see if they would lie peaceably together.[1]

De Monts, who had been to the St. Lawrence with Chauvin, and learned to dread its rigorous winters, steered for a more southern, and, as he flattered himself, a milder region. The first land seen was Cap la Hêve, on the southern coast of Nova Scotia. Four days later, they entered a small bay, where, to their surprise, they saw a vessel lying at anchor. Here was a piece of good luck. The stranger was a fur-trader, pursuing her traffic in defiance, or more probably in ignorance, of De Monts's monopoly. The latter, as empowered by his patent, made prize of ship and cargo, consoling the commander, one Rossignol, by giving his name to the scene of his misfortune. It is now called Liverpool Harbor.

In an adjacent harbor, called by them Port Mouton, because a sheep here leaped overboard, they waited nearly a month for Pontgravé's store-ship. At length, to their great relief, she appeared, laden with the spoils of four Basque fur-traders, captured at Canseau. The supplies delivered, Pontgravé sailed for Tadoussac to trade with the Indians, while De Monts, followed by his prize, proceeded on his voyage.

He doubled Cape Sable, and entered St. Mary's Bay, where he lay two weeks, sending boats' crews to explore the adjacent coasts. A party one day

[1] Sagard, *Histoire du Canada*, 9.

went on shore to stroll through the forest, and among them was Nicolas Aubry, a priest from Paris, who, tiring of the scholastic haunts of the Rue de la Sorbonne and the Rue d'Enfer, had persisted, despite the remonstrance of his friends, in joining the expedition. Thirsty with a long walk, under the sun of June, through the tangled and rock-encumbered woods, he stopped to drink at a brook, laying his sword beside him on the grass. On rejoining his companions, he found that he had forgotten it; and turning back in search of it, more skilled in the devious windings of the Quartier Latin than in the intricacies of the Acadian forest, he soon lost his way. His comrades, alarmed, waited for a time, and then ranged the woods, shouting his name to the echoing solitudes. Trumpets were sounded, and cannon fired from the ships, but the priest did not appear. All now looked askance on a certain Huguenot, with whom Aubry had often quarrelled on questions of faith, and who was now accused of having killed him. In vain he denied the charge. Aubry was given up for dead, and the ship sailed from St. Mary's Bay; while the wretched priest roamed to and fro, famished and despairing, or, couched on the rocky soil, in the troubled sleep of exhaustion, dreamed, perhaps, as the wind swept moaning through the pines, that he heard once more the organ roll through the columned arches of Sainte Geneviève.

The voyagers proceeded to explore the Bay of Fundy, which De Monts called La Baye Françoise.

Their first notable discovery was that of Annapolis Harbor. A small inlet invited them. They entered, when suddenly the narrow strait dilated into a broad and tranquil basin, compassed by sunny hills, wrapped in woodland verdure, and alive with waterfalls. Poutrincourt was delighted with the scene. The fancy seized him of removing thither from France with his family; and, to this end, he asked a grant of the place from De Monts, who by his patent had nearly half the continent in his gift. The grant was made, and Poutrincourt called his new domain Port Royal.

Thence they sailed round the head of the Bay of Fundy, coasted its northern shore, visited and named the river St. John, and anchored at last in Passamaquoddy Bay.

The untiring Champlain, exploring, surveying, sounding, had made charts of all the principal roads and harbors;[1] and now, pursuing his research, he entered a river which he calls La Rivière des Etechemins, from the name of the tribe of whom the present Passamaquoddy Indians are descendants. Near its mouth he found an islet, fenced round with rocks and shoals, and called it St. Croix, a name now borne by the river itself. With singular infelicity this spot was chosen as the site of the new colony. It commanded the river, and was well fitted for defence: these were its only merits; yet cannon were landed on it, a battery was planted on a detached

---

[1] See Champlain, *Voyages* (1613), where the charts are published.

rock at one end, and a fort begun on a rising ground at the other.[1]

At St. Mary's Bay the voyagers thought they had found traces of iron and silver; and Champdoré, the pilot, was now sent back to pursue the search. As he and his men lay at anchor, fishing, not far from land, one of them heard a strange sound, like a weak human voice; and, looking towards the shore, they saw a small black object in motion, apparently a hat waved on the end of a stick. Rowing in haste to the spot, they found the priest Aubry. For sixteen days he had wandered in the woods, sustaining life on berries and wild fruits; and when, haggard and emaciated, a shadow of his former self, Champdoré carried him back to St. Croix, he was greeted as a man risen from the grave.

In 1783 the river St. Croix, by treaty, was made the boundary between Maine and New Brunswick. But which was the true St. Croix? In 1798, the point was settled. De Monts's island was found; and, painfully searching among the sand, the sedge, and the matted whortleberry bushes, the commissioners could trace the foundations of buildings long crumbled into dust;[2] for the wilderness had resumed its sway, and silence and solitude brooded once more over this ancient resting-place of civilization.

But while the commissioner bends over a moss-grown stone, it is for us to trace back the dim vista

---

[1] Lescarbot, *Hist. de la Nouvelle France* (1612), II. 461.
[2] Holmes, *Annals*, (1829,) I. 122, note 1.

of the centuries to the life, the zeal, the energy, of which this stone is the poor memorial. The rock-fenced islet was covered with cedars, and when the tide was out the shoals around were dark with the swash of sea-weed, where, in their leisure moments, the Frenchmen, we are told, amused themselves with detaching the limpets from the stones, as a savory addition to their fare. But there was little leisure at St. Croix. Soldiers, sailors, and artisans betook themselves to their task. Before the winter closed in, the northern end of the island was covered with buildings, surrounding a square, where a solitary tree had been left standing. On the right was a spacious house, well built, and surmounted by one of those enormous roofs characteristic of the time. This was the lodging of De Monts. Behind it, and near the water, was a long, covered gallery, for labor or amusement in foul weather. Champlain and the Sieur d'Orville, aided by the servants of the latter, built a house for themselves nearly opposite that of De Monts; and the remainder of the square was occupied by storehouses, a magazine, workshops, lodgings for gentlemen and artisans, and a barrack for the Swiss soldiers, the whole enclosed with a palisade. Adjacent there was an attempt at a garden, under the auspices of Champlain; but nothing would grow in the sandy soil. There was a cemetery, too, and a small rustic chapel on a projecting point of rock. Such was the "Habitation de l'Isle Saincte-Croix," as set forth by Champlain in quaint plans and drawings, in that musty little quarto of 1613, sold by Jean Berjon, at the sign of the Flying Horse, Rue St. Jean de Beauvais.

Their labors over, Poutrincourt set sail for France, proposing to return and take possession of his domain of Port Royal. Seventy-nine men remained at St. Croix. Here was De Monts, feudal lord of half a continent in virtue of two potent syllables, "Henri," scrawled on parchment by the rugged hand of the Béarnais. Here were gentlemen of birth and breeding, Champlain, D'Orville, Beaumont, Sourin, La Motte, Boulay, and Fougeray; here also were the pugnacious *curé* and his fellow priests, with the Huguenot ministers, objects of their unceasing ire. The rest were laborers, artisans, and soldiers, all in the pay of the company, and some of them forced into its service.

Poutrincourt's receding sails vanished between the water and the sky. The exiles were left to their solitude. From the Spanish settlements northward to the pole, there was no domestic hearth, no lodgement of civilized men, save one weak band of Frenchmen, clinging, as it were for life, to the fringe of the vast and savage continent. The gray and sullen autumn sank upon the waste, and the bleak wind howled down the St. Croix, and swept the forest bare. Then the whirling snow powdered the vast sweep of desolate woodland, and shrouded in white the gloomy green of pine-clad mountains. Ice in sheets, or broken masses, swept by their island with the ebbing and flowing tide, often debarring all access to the main, and cutting off their supplies of wood and water. A belt of cedars, indeed, hedged the island; but De Monts had ordered them to be spared, that the north wind might spend something of its force with whistling through their shaggy boughs. Cider and wine froze in the casks, and were served out by the pound. As they crowded round their half-fed fires, shivering in the icy currents that pierced their rude tenements, many sank into a desperate apathy.

Soon the scurvy broke out, and raged with a fearful malignity. Of the seventy-nine, thirty-five died before spring, and many more were brought to the verge of death. In vain they sought that marvellous tree which had relieved the followers of Cartier. Their little cemetery was peopled with nearly half their number, and the rest, bloated and disfigured with the relentless malady, thought more of escaping from their woes than of building up a Transatlantic empire. Yet among them there was one, at least, who, amid languor and defection, held to his purpose with indomitable tenacity; and where Champlain was present, there was no room for despair.

Spring came at last, and, with the breaking up of the ice, the melting of the snow, and the clamors of the returning wild-fowl, the spirits and the health of the woe-begone company began to revive. But to misery succeeded anxiety and suspense. Where was the succor from France? Were they abandoned to their fate like the wretched exiles of La Roche? In a happy hour, they saw an approaching sail. Pontgravé, with forty men, cast anchor before their island on the sixteenth of June; and they hailed him as the condemned hails the messenger of his pardon.

Weary of St. Croix, De Monts resolved to seek out a more auspicious site, on which to rear the capital of his wilderness dominion. During the preceding September, Champlain had ranged the westward coast in a pinnace, visited and named the island of Mount Desert, and entered the mouth of the river Penobscot, called by him the Pemetigoet, or Pentegoet, and previously known to fur-traders and fishermen as the Norembega, a name which it shared with all the adjacent region.[1] Now, embarking a second time, in a bark of fifteen tons, with De Monts, several gentlemen, twenty sailors, and an Indian with his squaw, he set forth on the eighteenth of June on a second voyage of discovery. They coasted the strangely indented shores of Maine, with its reefs and surf-washed islands, rocky headlands, and deep embosomed bays, passed Mount Desert and the Penobscot, explored the mouths of the Kennebec, crossed Casco Bay, and descried the distant peaks of the White Mountains. The ninth of July brought

[1] The earliest maps and narratives indicate a city, also called Norembega, on the banks of the Penobscot. The pilot, Jean Alphonse, of Saintonge, says that this fabulous city is fifteen or twenty leagues from the sea, and that its inhabitants are of small stature and dark complexion. As late as 1607 the fable was repeated in the *Histoire Universelle des Indes Occidentales.*

them to Saco Bay. They were now within the limits
of a group of tribes who were called by the French
the Armouchiquois, and who included those whom
the English afterwards called the Massachusetts.
They differed in habits as well as in language from
the Etechemins and Micmacs of Acadia, for they
were tillers of the soil, and around their wigwams
were fields of maize, beans, pumpkins, squashes,
tobacco, and the so-called Jerusalem artichoke. Near
Prout's Neck, more than eighty of them ran down to
the shore to meet the strangers, dancing and yelping
to show their joy. They had a fort of palisades on a
rising ground by the Saco, for they were at deadly
war with their neighbors towards the east.

On the twelfth, the French resumed their voyage,
and, like some adventurous party of pleasure, held
their course by the beaches of York and Wells,
Portsmouth Harbor, the Isles of Shoals, Rye Beach,
and Hampton Beach, till, on the fifteenth, they
descried the dim outline of Cape Ann. Champlain
called it Cap aux Isles, from the three adjacent
islands, and in a subsequent voyage he gave the
name of Beauport to the neighboring harbor of
Gloucester. Thence steering southward and westward, they entered Massachusetts Bay, gave the
name of Rivière du Guast to a river flowing into it,
probably the Charles; passed the islands of Boston
Harbor, which Champlain describes as covered with
trees, and were met on the way by great numbers of
canoes filled with astonished Indians. On Sunday,

the seventeenth, they passed Point Allerton and Nantasket Beach, coasted the shores of Cohasset, Scituate, and Marshfield, and anchored for the night near Brant Point. On the morning of the eighteenth, a head wind forced them to take shelter in Port St. Louis, for so they called the harbor of Plymouth, where the Pilgrims made their memorable landing fifteen years later. Indian wigwams and garden patches lined the shore. A troop of the inhabitants came down to the beach and danced; while others, who had been fishing, approached in their canoes, came on board the vessel, and showed Champlain their fish-hooks, consisting of a barbed bone lashed at an acute angle to a slip of wood.

From Plymouth the party circled round the bay, doubled Cape Cod, called by Champlain Cap Blanc, from its glistening white sands, and steered southward to Nausett Harbor, which, by reason of its shoals and sand-bars, they named Port Mallebarre. Here their prosperity deserted them. A party of sailors went behind the sand-banks to find fresh water at a spring, when an Indian snatched a kettle from one of them, and its owner, pursuing, fell, pierced with arrows by the robber's comrades. The French in the vessel opened fire. Champlain's arquebuse burst, and was near killing him, while the Indians, swift as deer, quickly gained the woods. Several of the tribe chanced to be on board the vessel, but flung themselves with such alacrity into the water that only one was caught. They bound him hand

and foot, but soon after humanely set him at liberty.

Champlain, who we are told "delighted marvellously in these enterprises," had busied himself throughout the voyage with taking observations, making charts, and studying the wonders of land and sea. The "horse-foot crab" seems to have awakened his special curiosity, and he describes it with amusing exactness. Of the human tenants of the New England coast he has also left the first precise and trustworthy account. They were clearly more numerous than when the Puritans landed at Plymouth, since in the interval a pestilence made great havoc among them. But Champlain's most conspicuous merit lies in the light that he threw into the dark places of American geography, and the order that he brought out of the chaos of American cartography; for it was a result of this and the rest of his voyages that precision and clearness began at last to supplant the vagueness, confusion, and contradiction of the earlier map-makers.[1]

At Nausett Harbor provisions began to fail, and

[1] President Eliot of Harvard University, and his son, Mr. Charles Eliot, during many yacht voyages along the New England coast, made a study of the points visited by Champlain. I am indebted to them for useful information, as also to Mr. Henry Mitchell of the Coast Survey, who has made careful comparisons of the maps of Champlain with the present features of the places they represent. I am also indebted to the excellent notes of Rev. Edmund F. Slafter in Mr. Otis's translation of Champlain, and to those of Abbé Laverdière in the Quebec edition of the *Voyages*, 1870. In the new light from these sources, I have revised former conclusions touching several localities mentioned in the original narrative.

steering for St. Croix the voyagers reached that ill-starred island on the third of August. De Monts had found no spot to his liking. He now bethought him of that inland harbor of Port Royal which he had granted to Poutrincourt, and thither he resolved to remove. Stores, utensils, even portions of the buildings, were placed on board the vessels, carried across the Bay of Fundy, and landed at the chosen spot. It was on the north side of the basin opposite Goat Island, and a little below the mouth of the river Annapolis, called by the French the Équille, and, afterwards, the Dauphin. The axe-men began their task; the dense forest was cleared away, and the buildings of the infant colony soon rose in its place.

But while De Monts and his company were struggling against despair at St. Croix, the enemies of his monopoly were busy at Paris; and, by a ship from France, he was warned that prompt measures were needed to thwart their machinations. Therefore he set sail, leaving Pontgravé to command at Port Royal; while Champlain, Champdoré, and others, undaunted by the past, volunteered for a second winter in the wilderness.

CHAPTER IV.

1605-1607.

LESCARBOT AND CHAMPLAIN.

DE MONTS AT PARIS. — MARC LESCARBOT. — DISASTER. — EMBARKATION. — ARRIVAL. — DISAPPOINTMENT. — WINTER LIFE AT PORT ROYAL. — L'ORDRE DE BON-TEMPS. — HOPES BLIGHTED.

EVIL reports of a churlish wilderness, a pitiless climate, disease, misery, and death, had heralded the arrival of De Monts. The outlay had been great, the returns small; and when he reached Paris, he found his friends cold, his enemies active and keen. Poutrincourt, however, was still full of zeal; and, though his private affairs urgently called for his presence in France, he resolved, at no small sacrifice, to go in person to Acadia. He had, moreover, a friend who proved an invaluable ally. This was Marc Lescarbot, "avocat en Parlement," who had been roughly handled by fortune, and was in the mood for such a venture, being desirous, as he tells us, "to fly from a corrupt world," in which he had just lost a lawsuit. Unlike De Monts, Poutrincourt, and others of his associates, he was not within the pale of the *noblesse*, belonging to the class of "gens de robe," which stood at the head of the *bourgeoisie*, and which, in its higher grades, formed within itself a virtual nobility. Lescarbot was no common man, — not that his abundant gift of verse-making was likely to avail much in the woods of New France, nor yet his classic lore, dashed with a little harmless pedantry, born not of the man, but of the times; but his zeal, his good sense, the vigor of his understanding, and the breadth of his views, were as conspicuous as his quick wit and his lively fancy. One of the best, as well as earliest, records of the early settlement of North America is due to his pen; and it has been said, with a certain degree of truth, that he was no less able to build up a colony than to write its history. He professed himself a Catholic, but his Catholicity sat lightly on him; and he might have passed for one of those amphibious religionists who in the civil wars were called "Les Politiques."

De Monts and Poutrincourt bestirred themselves to find a priest, since the foes of the enterprise had been loud in lamentation that the spiritual welfare of the Indians had been slighted. But it was Holy Week. All the priests were, or professed to be, busy with exercises and confessions, and not one could be found to undertake the mission of Acadia. They were more successful in engaging mechanics and laborers for the voyage. These were paid a portion of their wages in advance, and were sent in a body to Rochelle, consigned to two merchants of that port, members of the company. De Monts and Poutrincourt went thither by post. Lescarbot soon followed, and no sooner reached Rochelle than he penned and printed his *Adieu à la France*, a poem which gained for him some credit.

More serious matters awaited him, however, than this dalliance with the Muse. Rochelle was the centre and citadel of Calvinism, — a town of austere and grim aspect, divided, like Cisatlantic communities of later growth, betwixt trade and religion, and, in the interest of both, exacting a deportment of discreet and well-ordered sobriety. "One must walk a strait path here," says Lescarbot, "unless he would hear from the mayor or the ministers." But the mechanics sent from Paris, flush of money, and lodged together in the quarter of St. Nicolas, made day and night hideous with riot, and their employers found not a few of them in the hands of the police. Their ship, bearing the inauspicious name of the "Jonas," lay anchored in the stream, her cargo on board, when a sudden gale blew her adrift. She struck on a pier, then grounded on the flats, bilged, careened, and settled in the mud. Her captain, who was ashore, with Poutrincourt, Lescarbot, and others, hastened aboard, and the pumps were set in motion; while all Rochelle, we are told, came to gaze from the ramparts, with faces of condolence, but at heart well pleased with the disaster. The ship and her cargo were saved, but she must be emptied, repaired, and reladen. Thus a month was lost; at length, on the thirteenth of May, 1606, the disorderly crew were all brought on board, and the "Jonas" put to sea.

Poutrincourt and Lescarbot had charge of the expedition, De Monts remaining in France.

Lescarbot describes his emotions at finding himself on an element so deficient in solidity, with only a two-inch plank between him and death. Off the Azores, they spoke a supposed pirate. For the rest, they beguiled the voyage by harpooning porpoises, dancing on deck in calm weather, and fishing for cod on the Grand Bank. They were two months on their way; and when, fevered with eagerness to reach land, they listened hourly for the welcome cry, they were involved in impenetrable fogs. Suddenly the mists parted, the sun shone forth, and streamed fair and bright over the fresh hills and forests of the New World, in near view before them. But the black rocks lay between, lashed by the snow-white breakers. "Thus," writes Lescarbot, "doth a man sometimes seek the land as one doth his beloved, who sometimes repulseth her sweetheart very rudely. Finally, upon Saturday, the fifteenth of July, about two o'clock in the afternoon, the sky began to salute us as it were with cannon-shots, shedding tears, as being sorry to have kept us so long in pain; . . . but, whilst we followed on our course, there came from the land odors incomparable for sweetness, brought with a warm wind so abundantly that all the Orient parts could not produce greater abundance. We did stretch out our hands as it were to take them, so palpable were they, which I have admired a thousand times since."[1]

[1] The translation is that of Purchas, *Nova Francia*, c. 12.

It was noon on the twenty-seventh when the "Jonas" passed the rocky gateway of Port Royal Basin, and Lescarbot gazed with delight and wonder on the calm expanse of sunny waters, with its amphitheatre of woody hills, wherein he saw the future asylum of distressed merit and impoverished industry. Slowly, before a favoring breeze, they held their course towards the head of the harbor, which narrowed as they advanced; but all was solitude, — no moving sail, no sign of human presence. At length, on their left, nestling in deep forests, they saw the wooden walls and roofs of the infant colony. Then appeared a birch canoe, cautiously coming towards them, guided by an old Indian. Then a Frenchman, arquebuse in hand, came down to the shore; and then, from the wooden bastion, sprang the smoke of a saluting shot. The ship replied; the trumpets lent their voices to the din, and the forests and the hills gave back unwonted echoes. The voyagers landed, and found the colony of Port Royal dwindled to two solitary Frenchmen.

These soon told their story. The preceding winter had been one of much suffering, though by no means the counterpart of the woful experience of St. Croix. But when the spring had passed, the summer far advanced, and still no tidings of De Monts had come, Pontgravé grew deeply anxious. To maintain themselves without supplies and succor was impossible. He caused two small vessels to be built, and set out in search of some of the French vessels on the fishing-stations. This was but twelve days before the arrival of the ship "Jonas." Two men had bravely offered themselves to stay behind and guard the buildings, guns, and munitions; and an old Indian chief, named Membertou, a fast friend of the French, and still a redoubted warrior, we are told, though reputed to number more than a hundred years, proved a stanch ally. When the ship approached, the two guardians were at dinner in their room at the fort. Membertou, always on the watch, saw the advancing sail, and, shouting from the gate, roused them from their repast. In doubt who the new-comers might be, one ran to the shore with his gun, while the other repaired to the platform where four cannon were mounted, in the valorous resolve to show fight should the strangers prove to be enemies. Happily this redundancy of mettle proved needless. He saw the white flag fluttering at the masthead, and joyfully fired his pieces as a salute.

The voyagers landed, and eagerly surveyed their new home. Some wandered through the buildings; some visited the cluster of Indian wigwams hard by; some roamed in the forest and over the meadows that bordered the neighboring river. The deserted fort now swarmed with life; and, the better to celebrate their prosperous arrival, Poutrincourt placed a hogshead of wine in the courtyard at the discretion of his followers, whose hilarity, in consequence, became exuberant. Nor was it diminished when Pontgravé's vessels were seen entering the harbor. A boat sent by Poutrincourt, more than a week before, to explore the coasts, had met them near Cape Sable, and they joyfully returned to Port Royal.

Pontgravé, however, soon sailed for France in the "Jonas," hoping on his way to seize certain contraband fur-traders, reported to be at Canseau and Cape Breton. Poutrincourt and Champlain, bent on finding a better site for their settlement in a more southern latitude, set out on a voyage of discovery, in an ill-built vessel of eighteen tons, while Lescarbot remained in charge of Port Royal. They had little for their pains but danger, hardship, and mishap. The autumn gales cut short their exploration; and, after visiting Gloucester Harbor, doubling Monomoy Point, and advancing as far as the neighborhood of Hyannis, on the southeast coast of Massachusetts, they turned back, somewhat disgusted with their errand. Along the eastern verge of Cape Cod they found the shore thickly studded with the wigwams of a race who were less hunters than tillers of the soil. At Chatham Harbor — called by them Port Fortuné — five of the company, who, contrary to orders, had remained on shore all night, were assailed, as they slept around their fire, by a shower of arrows from four hundred Indians. Two were killed outright, while the survivors fled for their boat, bristling like porcupines with the feathered missiles, — a scene oddly portrayed by the untutored pencil of Champlain. He and Poutrincourt, with eight men, hearing the war-whoops and the cries for aid, sprang up from sleep, snatched their weapons, pulled ashore in their shirts, and charged the yelling multitude, who fled before their spectral assailants, and vanished in the woods. "Thus," observes Lescarbot, "did thirty-five thousand Midianites fly before Gideon and his three hundred." The French buried their dead comrades; but, as they chanted their funeral hymn, the Indians, at a safe distance on a neighboring hill, were dancing in glee and triumph, and mocking them with unseemly gestures; and no sooner had the party re-embarked, than they dug up the dead bodies, burnt them, and arrayed themselves in their shirts. Little pleased with the country or its inhabitants, the voyagers turned their prow towards Port Royal, though not until, by a treacherous device, they had lured some of their late assailants within their reach, killed them, and cut off their heads as trophies. Near Mount Desert, on a stormy night, their rudder broke, and they had a hair-breadth escape from destruction. The chief object of their voyage, that of discovering a site for their colony under a more southern sky, had failed. Pontgravé's son had his hand blown off by the bursting of his gun; several of their number had been killed; others were sick or wounded; and thus, on the fourteenth of November, with somewhat downcast visages, they guided their helpless vessel with a pair of oars to the landing at Port Royal.

"I will not," says Lescarbot, "compare their perils to those of Ulysses, nor yet of Æneas, lest thereby I should sully our holy enterprise with things impure."

1606.] ANOTHER VOYAGE TO NEW ENGLAND. 89

He and his followers had been expecting them with great anxiety. His alert and buoyant spirit had conceived a plan for enlivening the courage of the company, a little dashed of late by misgivings and forebodings. Accordingly, as Poutrincourt, Champlain, and their weather-beaten crew approached the wooden gateway of Port Royal, Neptune issued forth, followed by his tritons, who greeted the voyagers in good French verse, written in all haste for the occasion by Lescarbot. And, as they entered, they beheld, blazoned over the arch, the arms of France, circled with laurels, and flanked by the scutcheons of De Monts and Poutrincourt.[1]

The ingenious author of these devices had busied himself, during the absence of his associates, in more serious labors for the welfare of the colony. He explored the low borders of the river Équille, or Annapolis. Here, in the solitude, he saw great meadows, where the moose, with their young, were grazing, and where at times the rank grass was beaten to a pulp by the trampling of their hoofs. He burned the grass, and sowed crops of wheat, rye, and barley in its stead. His appearance gave so little promise of personal vigor, that some of the party assured him that he would never see France again, and warned him to husband his strength; but he knew himself better, and set at naught these comforting monitions. He was the most diligent of workers. He made

---

[1] Lescarbot, *Muses de la Nouvelle France*, where the programme is given, and the speeches of Neptune and the tritons in full.

gardens near the fort, where, in his zeal, he plied the hoe with his own hands late into the moonlight evenings. The priests, of whom at the outset there had been no lack, had all succumbed to the scurvy at St. Croix; and Lescarbot, so far as a layman might, essayed to supply their place, reading on Sundays from the Scriptures, and adding expositions of his own after a fashion not remarkable for rigorous Catholicity. Of an evening, when not engrossed with his garden, he was reading or writing in his room, perhaps preparing the material of that *History of New France* in which, despite the versatility of his busy brain, his good sense and capacity are clearly made manifest.

Now, however, when the whole company were reassembled, Lescarbot found associates more congenial than the rude soldiers, mechanics, and laborers who gathered at night around the blazing logs in their rude hall. Port Royal was a quadrangle of wooden buildings, enclosing a spacious court. At the southeast corner was the arched gateway, whence a path, a few paces in length, led to the water. It was flanked by a sort of bastion of palisades, while at the southwest corner was another bastion, on which four cannon were mounted. On the east side of the quadrangle was a range of magazines and storehouses; on the west were quarters for the men; on the north, a dining-hall and lodgings for the principal persons of the company; while on the south, or water side, were the kitchen, the forge, and the oven. Except the garden-patches and the cemetery, the adjacent ground was thickly studded with the stumps of the newly felled trees.

Most bountiful provision had been made for the temporal wants of the colonists, and Lescarbot is profuse in praise of the liberality of De Monts and two merchants of Rochelle, who had freighted the ship "Jonas." Of wine, in particular, the supply was so generous, that every man in Port Royal was served with three pints daily.

The principal persons of the colony sat, fifteen in number, at Poutrincourt's table, which, by an ingenious device of Champlain, was always well furnished. He formed the fifteen into a new order, christened "L'Ordre de Bon-Temps." Each was Grand Master in turn, holding office for one day. It was his function to cater for the company; and, as it became a point of honor to fill the post with credit, the prospective Grand Master was usually busy, for several days before coming to his dignity, in hunting, fishing, or bartering provisions with the Indians. Thus did Poutrincourt's table groan beneath all the luxuries of the winter forest, — flesh of moose, caribou, and deer, beaver, otter, and hare, bears and wild-cats; with ducks, geese, grouse, and plover; sturgeon, too, and trout, and fish innumerable, speared through the ice of the Équille, or drawn from the depths of the neighboring bay. "And," says Lescarbot, in closing his bill of fare, "whatever our gourmands at home may think, we found as good cheer at Port Royal as they at their Rue aux Ours [1] in Paris, and that, too, at a cheaper rate." For the preparation of this manifold provision, the Grand Master was also answerable; since, during his day of office, he was autocrat of the kitchen.

Nor did this bounteous repast lack a solemn and befitting ceremonial. When the hour had struck, — after the manner of our fathers they dined at noon, — the Grand Master entered the hall, a napkin on his shoulder, his staff of office in his hand, and the collar of the Order — valued by Lescarbot at four crowns — about his neck. The brotherhood followed, each bearing a dish. The invited guests were Indian chiefs, of whom old Membertou was daily present, seated at table with the French, who took pleasure in this red-skin companionship. Those of humbler degree, warriors, squaws, and children, sat on the floor, or crouched together in the corners of the hall, eagerly waiting their portion of biscuit or of bread, a novel and much coveted luxury. Being always treated with kindness, they became fond of the French, who often followed them on their moose-hunts, and shared their winter bivouac.

At the evening meal there was less of form and circumstance; and when the winter night closed in, when the flame crackled and the sparks streamed up the wide-throated chimney, and the founders of New France with their tawny allies were gathered around

[1] A short street between Rue St. Martin and Rue St. Denis, once renowned for its restaurants.

the blaze, then did the Grand Master resign the collar and the staff to the successor of his honors, and, with jovial courtesy, pledge him in a cup of wine.[1] Thus these ingenious Frenchmen beguiled the winter of their exile.

It was an unusually mild winter. Until January, they wore no warmer garment than their doublets. They made hunting and fishing parties, in which the Indians, whose lodges were always to be seen under the friendly shelter of the buildings, failed not to bear part. "I remember," says Lescarbot, "that on the fourteenth of January, of a Sunday afternoon, we amused ourselves with singing and music on the river Équille; and that in the same month we went to see the wheat-fields two leagues from the fort, and dined merrily in the sunshine."

Good spirits and good cheer saved them in great measure from the scurvy; and though towards the end of winter severe cold set in, yet only four men died. The snow thawed at last, and as patches of the black and oozy soil began to appear, they saw the grain of their last autumn's sowing already piercing the mould. The forced inaction of the winter was over. The carpenters built a water-mill on the stream now called Allen's River; others enclosed fields and laid out gardens; others, again, with scoop-nets and baskets, caught the herrings and alewives as they ran up the innumerable rivulets. The leaders of the colony set a contagious example of activity.

[1] Lescarbot (1612), II. 581.

Poutrincourt forgot the prejudices of his noble birth, and went himself into the woods to gather turpentine from the pines, which he converted into tar by a process of his own invention; while Lescarbot, eager to test the qualities of the soil, was again, hoe in hand, at work all day in his garden.

All seemed full of promise; but alas for the bright hope that kindled the manly heart of Champlain and the earnest spirit of the vivacious advocate! A sudden blight fell on them, and their rising prosperity withered to the ground. On a morning, late in spring, as the French were at breakfast, the ever watchful Membertou came in with news of an approaching sail. They hastened to the shore; but the vision of the centenarian sagamore put them all to shame. They could see nothing. At length their doubts were resolved. A small vessel stood on towards them, and anchored before the fort. She was commanded by one Chevalier, a young man from St. Malo, and was freighted with disastrous tidings. De Monts's monopoly was rescinded. The life of the enterprise was stopped, and the establishment at Port Royal could no longer be supported; for its expense was great, the body of the colony being laborers in the pay of the company. Nor was the annulling of the patent the full extent of the disaster; for, during the last summer, the Dutch had found their way to the St. Lawrence, and carried away a rich harvest of furs, while other interloping traders had plied a busy traffic along the coasts, and, in the excess of their avidity, dug up the bodies of buried Indians to rob them of their funeral robes.

It was to the merchants and fishermen of the Norman, Breton, and Biscayan ports, exasperated at their exclusion from a lucrative trade, and at the confiscations which had sometimes followed their attempts to engage in it, that this sudden blow was due. Money had been used freely at court, and the monopoly, unjustly granted, had been more unjustly withdrawn. De Monts and his company, who had spent a hundred thousand livres, were allowed six thousand in requital, to be collected, if possible, from the fur-traders in the form of a tax.

Chevalier, captain of the ill-omened bark, was entertained with a hospitality little deserved, since, having been intrusted with sundry hams, fruits, spices, sweetmeats, jellies, and other dainties, sent by the generous De Monts to his friends of New France, he with his crew had devoured them on the voyage, alleging that, in their belief, the inmates of Port Royal would all be dead before their arrival.

Choice there was none, and Port Royal must be abandoned. Built on a false basis, sustained only by the fleeting favor of a government, the generous enterprise had come to naught. Yet Poutrincourt, who in virtue of his grant from De Monts owned the place, bravely resolved that, come what might, he would see the adventure to an end, even should it involve emigration with his family to the wilderness. Meanwhile, he began the dreary task of abandonment, sending boat-loads of men and stores to Canseau, where lay the ship "Jonas," eking out her diminished profits by fishing for cod.

Membertou was full of grief at the departure of his friends. He had built a palisaded village not far from Port Royal, and here were mustered some four hundred of his warriors for a foray into the country of the Armouchiquois, dwellers along the coasts of Massachusetts, New Hampshire, and Western Maine. One of his tribesmen had been killed by a chief from the Saco, and he was bent on revenge. He proved himself a sturdy beggar, pursuing Poutrincourt with daily petitions, — now for a bushel of beans, now for a basket of bread, and now for a barrel of wine to regale his greasy crew. Membertou's long life had not been one of repose. In deeds of blood and treachery he had no rival in the Acadian forest; and, as his old age was beset with enemies, his alliance with the French had a foundation of policy no less than of affection. In right of his rank of Sagamore, he claimed perfect equality both with Poutrincourt and with the King, laying his shrivelled forefingers together in token of friendship between peers. Calumny did not spare him; and a rival chief intimated to the French, that, under cover of a war with the Armouchiquois, the crafty veteran meant to seize and plunder Port Royal. Precautions, therefore, were taken; but they were seemingly needless; for, their feasts and dances over, the warriors launched their birchen flotilla and set out. After an absence of six weeks they reappeared with howls of victory, and their exploits were commemorated in French verse by the muse of the indefatigable Lescarbot.[1]

With a heavy heart the advocate bade farewell to the dwellings, the cornfields, the gardens, and all the dawning prosperity of Port Royal, and sailed for Canseau in a small vessel on the thirtieth of July. Poutrincourt and Champlain remained behind, for the former was resolved to learn before his departure the results of his agricultural labors. Reaching a harbor on the southern coast of Nova Scotia, six leagues west of Canseau, Lescarbot found a fishing-vessel commanded and owned by an old Basque, named Savalet, who for forty-two successive years had carried to France his annual cargo of codfish. He was in great glee at the success of his present venture, reckoning his profits at ten thousand francs. The Indians, however, annoyed him beyond measure, boarding him from their canoes as his fishing-boats came alongside, and helping themselves at will to his halibut and cod. At Canseau — a harbor near the strait now bearing the name — the ship "Jonas" still lay, her hold well stored with fish; and here, on the twenty-seventh of August, Lescarbot was rejoined by Poutrincourt and Champlain, who had come from Port Royal in an open boat. For a few days, they amused themselves with gathering raspberries on the islands; then they spread their sails for France, and early in October, 1607, anchored in the harbor of St. Malo.

[1] See *Muses de la Nouvelle France.*

First of Europeans, they had essayed to found an agricultural colony in the New World. The leaders of the enterprise had acted less as merchants than as citizens; and the fur-trading monopoly, odious in itself, had been used as the instrument of a large and generous design. There was a radical defect, however, in their scheme of settlement. Excepting a few of the leaders, those engaged in it had not chosen a home in the wilderness of New France, but were mere hirelings, without wives or families, and careless of the welfare of the colony. The life which should have pervaded all the members was confined to the heads alone. In one respect, however, the enterprise of De Monts was truer in principle than the Roman Catholic colonization of Canada, on the one hand, or the Puritan colonization of Massachusetts, on the other, for it did not attempt to enforce religious exclusion.

Towards the fickle and bloodthirsty race who claimed the lordship of the forests, these colonists, excepting only in the treacherous slaughter at Port Fortuné, bore themselves in a spirit of kindness contrasting brightly with the rapacious cruelty of the Spaniards and the harshness of the English settlers. When the last boat-load left Port Royal, the shore resounded with lamentation; and nothing could console the afflicted savages but reiterated promises of a speedy return.

CHAPTER V.

1610, 1611.

THE JESUITS AND THEIR PATRONESS.

POUTRINCOURT AND THE JESUITS. — HE SAILS FOR ACADIA. — SUDDEN CONVERSIONS. — BIENCOURT. — DEATH OF THE KING. — MADAME DE GUERCHEVILLE. — BIARD AND MASSE. — THE JESUITS TRIUMPHANT.

POUTRINCOURT, we have seen, owned Port Royal in virtue of a grant from De Monts. The ardent and adventurous baron was in evil case, involved in litigation and low in purse; but nothing could damp his zeal. Acadia must become a new France, and he, Poutrincourt, must be its father. He gained from the King a confirmation of his grant, and, to supply the lack of his own weakened resources, associated with himself one Robin, a man of family and wealth. This did not save him from a host of delays and vexations; and it was not until the spring of 1610 that he found himself in a condition to embark on his new and doubtful venture.

Meanwhile an influence, of sinister omen as he thought, had begun to act upon his schemes. The Jesuits were strong at court. One of their number, the famous Father Coton, was confessor to Henry the Fourth, and, on matters of this world as of the next, was ever whispering at the facile ear of the renegade King. New France offered a fresh field of action to the indefatigable Society of Jesus, and Coton urged upon the royal convert, that, for the saving of souls, some of its members should be attached to the proposed enterprise. The King, profoundly indifferent in matters of religion, saw no evil in a proposal which at least promised to place the Atlantic betwixt him and some of those busy friends whom at heart he deeply mistrusted.[1] Other influences, too, seconded the confessor. Devout ladies of the court, and the Queen herself, supplying the lack of virtue with an overflowing piety, burned, we are assured, with a holy zeal for snatching the tribes of the West from the bondage of Satan. Therefore it was insisted that the projected colony should combine the spiritual with the temporal character, — or, in other words, that Poutrincourt should take Jesuits with him. Pierre Biard, Professor of Theology at Lyons, was named for the mission, and repaired in haste to Bordeaux, the port of embarkation, where he found no vessel, and no sign of preparation; and here, in wrath and discomfiture, he remained for a whole year.

That Poutrincourt was a good Catholic appears from a letter to the Pope, written for him in Latin by Lescarbot, asking a blessing on his enterprise, and

[1] The missionary Biard makes the characteristic assertion, that the King initiated the Jesuit project, and that Father Coton merely obeyed his orders. Biard, *Relation*, c. 11.

assuring his Holiness that one of his grand objects was the saving of souls.[1] But, like other good citizens, he belonged to the national party in the Church, — those liberal Catholics, who, side by side with the Huguenots, had made head against the League, with its Spanish allies, and placed Henry the Fourth upon the throne. The Jesuits, an order Spanish in origin and policy, determined champions of ultramontane principles, the sword and shield of the Papacy in its broadest pretensions to spiritual and temporal sway, were to him, as to others of his party, objects of deep dislike and distrust. He feared them in his colony, evaded what he dared not refuse, left Biard waiting in solitude at Bordeaux, and sought to postpone the evil day by assuring Father Coton that, though Port Royal was at present in no state to receive the missionaries, preparation should be made to entertain them the next year after a befitting fashion.

Poutrincourt owned the barony of St. Just in Champagne, inherited a few years before from his mother. Hence, early in February, 1610, he set out in a boat loaded to the gunwales with provisions, furniture, goods, and munitions for Port Royal, descended the rivers Aube and Seine, and reached Dieppe safely with his charge.[2] Here his ship was awaiting him; and on the twenty-sixth of February he set sail, giving the slip to the indignant Jesuit at Bordeaux.

[1] See Lescarbot (1618), 605.

[2] Lescarbot, *Relation Dernière*, 6. This is a pamphlet of thirty-nine pages, containing matters not included in the larger work.

The tedium of a long passage was unpleasantly broken by a mutiny among the crew. It was suppressed, however, and Poutrincourt entered at length the familiar basin of Port Royal. The buildings were still standing, whole and sound save a partial falling in of the roofs. Even furniture was found untouched in the deserted chambers. The centenarian Membertou was still alive, his leathern, wrinkled visage beaming with welcome.

Poutrincourt set himself without delay to the task of Christianizing New France, in an access of zeal which his desire of proving that Jesuit aid was superfluous may be supposed largely to have reinforced. He had a priest with him, one La Flèche, whom he urged to the pious work. No time was lost. Membertou first was catechised, confessed his sins, and renounced the Devil, whom we are told he had faithfully served during a hundred and ten years. His squaws, his children, his grandchildren, and his entire clan were next won over. It was in June, the day of St. John the Baptist, when the naked proselytes, twenty-one in number, were gathered on the shore at Port Royal. Here was the priest in the vestments of his office; here were gentlemen in gay attire, soldiers, laborers, lackeys, all the infant colony. The converts kneeled; the sacred rite was finished, *Te Deum* was sung, and the roar of cannon proclaimed this triumph over the powers of darkness.[1] Membertou was named Henri, after the King; his principal

[1] Lescarbot, *Relation Dernière*, 11.

squaw, Marie, after the Queen. One of his sons received the name of the Pope, another that of the Dauphin; his daughter was called Marguerite, after the divorced Marguerite de Valois, and, in like manner, the rest of the squalid company exchanged their barbaric appellatives for the names of princes, nobles, and ladies of rank.[1]

The fame of this *chef-d'œuvre* of Christian piety, as Lescarbot gravely calls it, spread far and wide through the forest, whose denizens, — partly out of a notion that the rite would bring good luck, partly to please the French, and partly to share in the good cheer with which the apostolic efforts of Father La Flèche had been sagaciously seconded — came flocking to enroll themselves under the banners of the Faith. Their zeal ran high. They would take no refusal. Membertou was for war on all who would not turn Christian. A living skeleton was seen crawling from hut to hut in search of the priest and his saving waters; while another neophyte, at the point of death, asked anxiously whether, in the realms of bliss to which he was bound, pies were to be had comparable to those with which the French regaled him.

A formal register of baptisms was drawn up to be carried to France in the returning ship, of which Poutrincourt's son, Biencourt, a spirited youth of eighteen, was to take charge. He sailed in July, his father keeping him company as far as Port la Hêve, whence, bidding the young man farewell, he attempted

[1] *Regître de Baptême de l'Église du Port Royal en la Nouvelle France.*

to return in an open boat to Port Royal. A north wind blew him out to sea; and for six days he was out of sight of land, subsisting on rain-water wrung from the boat's sail, and on a few wild-fowl which he had shot on an island. Five weeks passed before he could rejoin his colonists, who, despairing of his safety, were about to choose a new chief.

Meanwhile, young Biencourt, speeding on his way, heard dire news from a fisherman on the Grand Bank. The knife of Ravaillac had done its work. Henry the Fourth was dead.

There is an ancient street in Paris, where a great thoroughfare contracts to a narrow pass, the Rue de la Ferronnerie. Tall buildings overshadow it, packed from pavement to tiles with human life, and from the dingy front of one of them the sculptured head of a man looks down on the throng that ceaselessly defiles beneath. On the fourteenth of May, 1610, a ponderous coach, studded with fleurs-de-lis and rich with gilding, rolled along this street. In it was a small man, well advanced in life, whose profile once seen could not be forgotten, — a hooked nose, a protruding chin, a brow full of wrinkles, grizzled hair, a short, grizzled beard, and stiff, gray moustaches, bristling like a cat's. One would have thought him some whiskered satyr, grim from the rack of tumultuous years; but his alert, upright port bespoke unshaken vigor, and his clear eye was full of buoyant life. Following on the footway strode a tall, strong, and somewhat corpulent man, with sinister, deep-set eyes and a red beard, his arm and shoulder covered with his cloak. In the throat of the thoroughfare, where the sculptured image of Henry the Fourth still guards the spot, a collision of two carts stopped the coach. Ravaillac quickened his pace. In an instant he was at the door. With his cloak dropped from his shoulders, and a long knife in his hand, he set his foot upon a guardstone, thrust his head and shoulders into the coach, and with frantic force stabbed thrice at the King's heart. A broken exclamation, a gasping convulsion, — and then the grim visage drooped on the bleeding breast. Henry breathed his last, and the hope of Europe died with him.

The omens were sinister for Old France and for New. Marie de Medicis, "cette grosse banquière," coarse scion of a bad stock, false wife and faithless queen, paramour of an intriguing foreigner, tool of the Jesuits and of Spain, was Regent in the minority of her imbecile son. The Huguenots drooped, the national party collapsed, the vigorous hand of Sully was felt no more, and the treasure gathered for a vast and beneficent enterprise became the instrument of despotism and the prey of corruption. Under such dark auspices, young Biencourt entered the thronged chambers of the Louvre.

He gained audience of the Queen, and displayed his list of baptisms; while the ever present Jesuits failed not to seize him by the button,[1] assuring him,

[1] Lescarbot, (1618,) 662: ". . . ne manquèrent de l'empoigner par les cheveux."

not only that the late King had deeply at heart the establishment of their Society in Acadia, but that to this end he had made them a grant of two thousand livres a year. The Jesuits had found an ally and the intended mission a friend at court, whose story and whose character are too striking to pass unnoticed.

This was a lady of honor to the Queen, Antoinette de Pons, Marquise de Guercheville, once renowned for grace and beauty, and not less conspicuous for qualities rare in the unbridled court of Henry's predecessor, where her youth had been passed. When the civil war was at its height, the royal heart, leaping with insatiable restlessness from battle to battle, from mistress to mistress, had found a brief repose in the affections of his Corisande, famed in tradition and romance; but Corisande was suddenly abandoned, and the young widow, Madame de Guercheville, became the load-star of his erratic fancy. It was an evil hour for the Béarnais. Henry sheathed in rusty steel, battling for his crown and his life, and Henry robed in royalty and throned triumphant in the Louvre, alike urged their suit in vain. Unused to defeat, the King's passion rose higher for the obstacle that barred it. On one occasion he was met with an answer not unworthy of record: —

"Sire, my rank, perhaps, is not high enough to permit me to be your wife, but my heart is too high to permit me to be your mistress." [1]

[1] A similar reply is attributed to Catherine de Rohan, Duchesse de Deux-Ponts: "Je suis trop pauvre pour être votre femme, et de trop

She left the court and retired to her château of La Roche-Guyon, on the Seine, ten leagues below Paris, where, fond of magnificence, she is said to have lived in much expense and splendor. The indefatigable King, haunted by her memory, made a hunting-party in the neighboring forests; and, as evening drew near, separating himself from his courtiers, he sent a gentleman of his train to ask of Madame de Guercheville the shelter of her roof. The reply conveyed a dutiful acknowledgment of the honor, and an offer of the best entertainment within her power. It was night when Henry, with his little band of horsemen, approached the château, where lights were burning in every window, after a fashion of the day on occasions of welcome to an honored guest. Pages stood in the gateway, each with a blazing torch; and here, too, were gentlemen of the neighborhood, gathered to greet their sovereign. Madame de Guercheville came forth, followed by the women of her household; and when the King, unprepared for so benign a welcome, giddy with love and hope, saw her radiant in pearls and more radiant yet in a beauty enhanced by the wavy torchlight and the surrounding shadows, he scarcely dared trust his senses: —

"Que vois-je, madame; est-ce bien vous, et suis-je ce roi méprisé?"

He gave her his hand, and she led him within the château, where, at the door of the apartment destined

bonne maison pour être votre maîtresse." Her suitor also was Henry the Fourth. *Dictionnaire de Bayle*, III. 2182.

for him, she left him, with a graceful reverence. The King, nowise disconcerted, did not doubt that she had gone to give orders for his entertainment, when an attendant came to tell him that she had descended to the courtyard and called for her coach. Thither he hastened in alarm: —

"What! am I driving you from your house?"

"Sire," replied Madame de Guercheville, "where a king is, he should be the sole master; but, for my part, I like to preserve some little authority wherever I may be."

With another deep reverence, she entered her coach and disappeared, seeking shelter under the roof of a friend, some two leagues off, and leaving the baffled King to such consolation as he might find in a magnificent repast, bereft of the presence of the hostess.[1]

---

[1] *Mémoires de l'Abbé de Choisy*, Liv. XII. The elaborate notices of Madame de Guercheville in the *Biographie Générale* and the *Biographie Universelle* are from this source. She figures under the name of Scilinde in *Les Amours du Grand Alcandre* (Henry IV.). See *Collection Petitot*, LXIII. 515, note, where the passage is extracted.

The Abbé de Choisy says that when the King was enamoured of her she was married to M. de Liancourt. This, it seems, is a mistake, this second marriage not taking place till 1594. Madame de Guercheville refused to take the name of Liancourt, because it had once been borne by the Duchesse de Beaufort, who had done it no honor, — a scruple very reasonably characterized by her biographer as "trop affecté."

The following is De Choisy's account: —

"Enfin ce prince s'avisa un jour, pour dernière ressource, de faire une partie de chasse du côté de La Roche-Guyon ; et, sur la fin de la journée, s'étant séparé de la plupart de ses courtisans, il envoya un gentilhomme à La Roche-Guyon demander le couvert pour une nuit. Madame de Guercheville, sans s'embarrasser, répondit au gentilhomme,

Henry could admire the virtue which he could not vanquish; and, long after, on his marriage, he acknowledged his sense of her worth by begging her to accept an honorable post near the person of the Queen.

"Madame," he said, presenting her to Marie de Medicis, "I give you a lady of honor who is a lady of honor indeed."

Some twenty years had passed since the adventure of La Roche-Guyon. Madame de Guercheville had outlived the charms which had attracted her royal

que le Roi lui feroit beaucoup d'honneur, et qu'elle le recevroit de son mieux. En effet, elle donna ordre à un magnifique souper; on éclaira toutes les fenêtres du château avec des torches (c'étoit la mode en ce temps-là); elle se para de ses plus beaux habits, se couvrit de perles (c'étoit aussi la mode); et lorsque le Roi arriva à l'entrée de la nuit, elle alla le recevoir à la porte de sa maison, accompagnée de toutes ses femmes, et de quelques gentilshommes du voisinage. Des pages portoient les torches devant elle. Le Roi, transporté de joie, la trouva plus belle que jamais : les ombres de la nuit, la lumière des flambeaux, les diamans, la surprise d'un accueil si favorable et si peu accoutumé, tout contribuait à renouveler ses anciennes blessures. 'Que vois-je, madame?' lui dit ce monarque tremblant; 'est-ce bien vous, et suis-je ce roi méprisé?' Madame de Guercheville l'interrompit, en le priant de monter dans son appartement pour se reposer. Il lui donna la main. Elle le conduisit jusqu'à la porte de sa chambre, lui fit une grande révérence, et se retira. Le Roi ne s'en étonna pas; il crut qu'elle vouloit aller donner ordre à la fête qu'elle lui préparoit. Mais il fut bien surpris quand on lui vint dire qu'elle étoit descendue dans sa cour, et qu'elle avoit crié tout haut: *Qu'on attelle* mon coche! comme pour aller coucher hors de chez elle. Il descendit aussitôt, et tout éperdu lui dit : 'Quoi! madame, je vous chasserai de votre maison?' 'Sire,' lui répondit-elle d'un ton ferme, 'un roi doit être le maître partout où il est; et pour moi, je suis bien aise d'avoir quelque pouvoir dans les lieux où je me trouve.' Et, sans vouloir l'écouter davantage, elle monta dans son coche, et alla coucher à deux lieues de là chez une de ses amies."

suitor, but the virtue which repelled him was reinforced by a devotion no less uncompromising. A rosary in her hand and a Jesuit at her side, she realized the utmost wishes of the subtle fathers who had moulded and who guided her. She readily took fire when they told her of the benighted souls of New France, and the wrongs of Father Biard kindled her utmost indignation. She declared herself the protectress of the American missions; and the only difficulty, as a Jesuit writer tells us, was to restrain her zeal within reasonable bounds.[1]

She had two illustrious coadjutors. The first was the jealous Queen, whose unbridled rage and vulgar clamor had made the Louvre a hell. The second was Henriette d'Entragues, Marquise de Verneuil, the crafty and capricious siren who had awakened these conjugal tempests. To this singular coalition were joined many other ladies of the court; for the pious flame, fanned by the Jesuits, spread through hall and boudoir, and fair votaries of the Loves and Graces found it a more grateful task to win heaven for the heathen than to merit it for themselves.

Young Biencourt saw it vain to resist. Biard must go with him in the returning ship, and also another Jesuit, Enemond Masse. The two fathers repaired to Dieppe, wafted on the wind of court favor, which they never doubted would bear them to their journey's end. Not so, however. Poutrincourt and his associates, in the dearth of their own resources, had bar-

[1] Charlevoix, I. 122.

gained with two Huguenot merchants of Dieppe, Du Jardin and Du Quesne, to equip and load the vessel, in consideration of their becoming partners in the expected profits. Their indignation was extreme when they saw the intended passengers. They declared that they would not aid in building up a colony for the profit of the King of Spain, nor risk their money in a venture where Jesuits were allowed to intermeddle; and they closed with a flat refusal to receive them on board, unless, they added with patriotic sarcasm, the Queen would direct them to transport the whole order beyond sea.[1] Biard and Masse insisted, on which the merchants demanded reimbursement for their outlay, as they would have no further concern in the business.

Biard communicated with Father Coton, Father Coton with Madame de Guercheville. No more was needed. The zealous lady of honor, "indignant," says Biard, "to see the efforts of hell prevail," and resolved "that Satan should not remain master of the field," set on foot a subscription, and raised an ample fund within the precincts of the court. Biard, in the name of the "Province of France of the Order of Jesus," bought out the interest of the two merchants for thirty-eight hundred livres, thus constituting the Jesuits equal partners in business with their enemies. Nor was this all; for, out of the ample proceeds of the subscription, he lent to the needy associates a further sum of seven hundred and thirty-seven livres,

[1] Lescarbot (1618), 664.

and advanced twelve hundred and twenty-five more to complete the outfit of the ship. Well pleased, the triumphant priests now embarked, and friend and foe set sail together on the twenty-sixth of January, 1611.[1]

[1] *Contract d'Association des Jésuites au Trafique du Canada*, 20 *Jan.*, 1611; a certified copy of the original parchment. It is noteworthy that the first contract of the French Jesuits in America relates to a partnership to carry on the fur-trade. Compare Lescarbot (1618), 665; Biard, *Relation*, c. 12; Champlain (1632), 100; Charlevoix, I. 123; De Laet, Lib. II. c. 21; *Lettre du P. Pierre Biard au T. R. P. Claude Aquaviva, Général de la Compagnie de Jésus à Rome, Dieppe*, 21 *Jan.*, 1611; *Lettre du P. Biard au R. P. Christophe Balthazar, Provincial de France à Paris, Port Royal*, 10 *Juin*, 1611; *Lettre du P. Baird au T. R. P. Claude Aquaviva, Port Royal*, 31 *Jan.* 1612. These letters form part of an interesting collection recently published by R. P. Auguste Carayon, S. J., under the title *Première Mission des Jésuites au Canada* (Paris, 1864). They are taken from the Jesuit archives at Rome.

CHAPTER VI.

1611, 1612.

JESUITS IN ACADIA.

THE JESUITS ARRIVE. — COLLISION OF POWERS TEMPORAL AND SPIRITUAL. — EXCURSION OF BIENCOURT. — BIARD'S INDIAN STUDIES. — MISERY AT PORT ROYAL. — GRANT TO MADAME DE GUERCHEVILLE. — GILBERT DU THET. — QUARRELS. — ANATHEMAS. — TRUCE.

THE voyage was one of inordinate length, — beset, too, with icebergs, larger and taller, according to the Jesuit voyagers, than the Church of Notre Dame; but on the day of Pentecost their ship, "The Grace of God," anchored before Port Royal. Then first were seen in the wilderness of New France the close black cap, the close black robe, of the Jesuit father, and the features seamed with study and thought and discipline. Then first did this mighty Proteus, this many-colored Society of Jesus, enter upon that rude field of toil and woe, where, in after years, the devoted zeal of its apostles was to lend dignity to their order and do honor to humanity.

Few were the regions of the known world to which the potent brotherhood had not stretched the vast network of its influence. Jesuits had disputed in theology with the bonzes of Japan, and taught astronomy to the mandarins of China; had wrought prodigies of sudden conversion among the followers of Brahma, preached the papal supremacy to Abyssinian schismatics, carried the cross among the savages of Caffraria, wrought reputed miracles in Brazil, and gathered the tribes of Paraguay beneath their paternal sway. And now, with the aid of the Virgin and her votary at court, they would build another empire among the tribes of New France. The omens were sinister and the outset was unpropitious. The Society was destined to reap few laurels from the brief apostleship of Biard and Masse.

When the voyagers landed, they found at Port Royal a band of half-famished men, eagerly expecting their succor. The voyage of four months had, however, nearly exhausted their own very moderate stock of provisions, and the mutual congratulations of the old colonists and the new were damped by a vision of starvation. A friction, too, speedily declared itself between the spiritual and the temporal powers. Pontgravé's son, then trading on the coast, had exasperated the Indians by an outrage on one of their women, and, dreading the wrath of Poutrincourt, had fled to the woods. Biard saw fit to take his part, remonstrated for him with vehemence, gained his pardon, received his confession, and absolved him. The Jesuit says that he was treated with great consideration by Poutrincourt, and that he should be forever beholden to him. The latter, however, chafed at Biard's interference.

"Father," he said, "I know my duty, and I beg you will leave me to do it. I, with my sword, have hopes of paradise, as well as you with your breviary. Show me my path to heaven. I will show you yours on earth."[1]

He soon set sail for France, leaving his son Biencourt in charge. This hardy young sailor, of ability and character beyond his years, had, on his visit to court, received the post of Vice-Admiral in the seas of New France, and in this capacity had a certain authority over the trading-vessels of St. Malo and Rochelle, several of which were upon the coast. To compel the recognition of this authority, and also to purchase provisions, he set out along with Biard in a boat filled with armed followers. His first collision was with young Pontgravé, who with a few men had built a trading-hut on the St. John, where he proposed to winter. Meeting with resistance, Biencourt took the whole party prisoners, in spite of the remonstrances of Biard. Next, proceeding along the coast, he levied tribute on four or five traders wintering at St. Croix, and, continuing his course to the Kennebec, found the Indians of that region greatly enraged at the conduct of certain English adventurers, who three or four years before had, as they said, set dogs upon them and otherwise maltreated them. These were the colonists under Popham and Gilbert, who in 1607 and 1608 made an abortive attempt to settle

[1] Lescarbot, (1618,) 669. Compare Biard, *Relation*, c. 14; and Biard, *Lettre au R. P. Christophe Balthazar*, in Carayon, 9.

near the mouth of the river. Nothing now was left of them but their deserted fort. The neighboring Indians were Abenakis, one of the tribes included by the French under the general name of Armouchiquois. Their disposition was doubtful, and it needed all the coolness of young Biencourt to avoid a fatal collision. On one occasion a curious incident took place. The French met six canoes full of warriors descending the Kennebec, and, as neither party trusted the other, the two encamped on opposite banks of the river. In the evening the Indians began to sing and dance. Biard suspected these proceedings to be an invocation of the Devil, and "in order," he says, "to thwart this accursed tyrant, I made our people sing a few church hymns, such as the *Salve*, the *Ave Maris Stella*, and others. But being once in train, and getting to the end of their spiritual songs, they fell to singing such others as they knew, and when these gave out they took to mimicking the dancing and singing of the Armouchiquois on the other side of the water; and as Frenchmen are naturally good mimics, they did it so well that the Armouchiquois stopped to listen; at which our people stopped too; and then the Indians began again. You would have laughed to hear them, for they were like two choirs answering each other in concert, and you would hardly have known the real Armouchiquois from the sham ones."

Before the capture of young Pontgravé, Biard made him a visit at his camp, six leagues up the St. John. Pontgravé's men were sailors from St. Malo, between whom and the other Frenchmen there was much ill blood. Biard had hardly entered the river when he saw the evening sky crimsoned with the dancing fires of a superb aurora borealis, and he and his attendants marvelled what evil thing the prodigy might portend. Their Indian companions said that it was a sign of war. In fact, the night after they had joined Pontgravé a furious quarrel broke out in the camp, with abundant shouting, gesticulating, and swearing; and, says the father, "I do not doubt that an accursed band of furious and sanguinary spirits were hovering about us all night, expecting every moment to see a horrible massacre of the few Christians in those parts; but the goodness of God bridled their malice. No blood was shed, and on the next day the squall ended in a fine calm."

He did not like the Indians, whom he describes as "lazy, gluttonous, irreligious, treacherous, cruel, and licentious." He makes an exception in favor of Membertou, whom he calls "the greatest, most renowned, and most redoubted savage that ever lived in the memory of man," and especially commends him for contenting himself with but one wife, hardly a superlative merit in a centenarian. Biard taught him to say the Lord's Prayer, though at the petition, "Give us this day our daily bread," the chief remonstrated, saying, "If I ask for nothing but bread, I shall get no fish or moose-meat." His protracted career was now drawing to a close, and, being brought to the settlement in a dying state, he was placed in

Biard's bed and attended by the two Jesuits. He was as remarkable in person as in character, for he was bearded like a Frenchman. Though, alone among La Flèche's converts, the Faith seemed to have left some impression upon him, he insisted on being buried with his heathen forefathers, but was persuaded to forego a wish fatal to his salvation, and slept at last in consecrated ground.

Another of the scanty fruits of the mission was a little girl on the point of death, whom Biard had asked her parents to give him for baptism. "Take her and keep her, if you like," was the reply, "for she is no better than a dead dog." "We accepted the offer," says Biard, "in order to show them the difference between Christianity and their impiety; and after giving her what care we could, together with some instruction, we baptized her. We named her after Madame the Marquise de Guercheville, in gratitude for the benefits we have received from that lady, who can now rejoice that her name is already in heaven; for, a few days after baptism, the chosen soul flew to that place of glory."

Biard's greatest difficulty was with the Micmac language. Young Biencourt was his best interpreter, and on common occasions served him well; but the moment that religion was in question he was, as it were, stricken dumb, — the reason being that the language was totally without abstract terms. Biard resolutely set himself to the study of it, — a hard and thorny path, on which he made small progress, and often went astray. Seated, pencil in hand, before some Indian squatting on the floor, whom with the bribe of a mouldy biscuit he had lured into the hut, he plied him with questions which he often neither would nor could answer. What was the Indian word for *Faith, Hope, Charity, Sacrament, Baptism, Eucharist, Trinity, Incarnation?* The perplexed savage, willing to amuse himself, and impelled, as Biard thinks, by the Devil, gave him scurrilous and unseemly phrases as the equivalent of things holy, which, studiously incorporated into the father's Indian catechism, produced on his pupils an effect the reverse of that intended. Biard's colleague, Masse, was equally zealous, and still less fortunate. He tried a forest life among the Indians with signal ill success. Hard fare, smoke, filth, the scolding of squaws, and the cries of children reduced him to a forlorn condition of body and mind, wore him to a skeleton, and sent him back to Port Royal without a single convert.

The dark months wore slowly on. A band of half-famished men gathered about the huge fires of their barn-like hall, moody, sullen, and quarrelsome. Discord was here in the black robe of the Jesuit and the brown capote of the rival trader. The position of the wretched little colony may well provoke reflection. Here lay the shaggy continent, from Florida to the Pole, outstretched in savage slumber along the sea, the stern domain of Nature, — or, to adopt the ready solution of the Jesuits, a realm of the powers

of night, blasted beneath the sceptre of hell. On the
banks of James River was a nest of woe-begone Englishmen, a handful of Dutch fur-traders at the mouth
of the Hudson,[1] and a few shivering Frenchmen
among the snow-drifts of Acadia; while deep within
the wild monotony of desolation, on the icy verge of
the great northern river, the hand of Champlain
upheld the fleur-de-lis on the rock of Quebec. These
were the advance guard, the forlorn hope of civilization, messengers of promise to a desert continent.
Yet, unconscious of their high function, not content
with inevitable woes, they were rent by petty jealousies and miserable feuds; while each of these
detached fragments of rival nationalities, scarcely
able to maintain its own wretched existence on a few
square miles, begrudged to the others the smallest
share in a domain which all the nations of Europe
could hardly have sufficed to fill.

One evening, as the forlorn tenants of Port Royal
sat together disconsolate, Biard was seized with a
spirit of prophecy. He called upon Biencourt to
serve out the little of wine that remained, — a proposal which met with high favor from the company
present, though apparently with none from the youthful Vice-Admiral. The wine was ordered, however,
and, as an unwonted cheer ran round the circle, the
Jesuit announced that an inward voice told him how,

---

[1] It is not certain that the Dutch had any permanent trading-post
here before 1613, when they had four houses at Manhattan. O'Callaghan, *Hist. New Netherland*, I. 69.

within a month, they should see a ship from France. In truth, they saw one within a week. On the twenty-third of January, 1612, arrived a small vessel laden with a moderate store of provisions and abundant seeds of future strife.

This was the expected succor sent by Poutrincourt. A series of ruinous voyages had exhausted his resources; but he had staked all on the success of the colony, had even brought his family to Acadia, and he would not leave them and his companions to perish.[1] His credit was gone; his hopes were dashed; yet assistance was proffered, and, in his extremity, he was forced to accept it. It came from Madame de Guercheville and her Jesuit advisers. She offered to buy the interest of a thousand crowns in the enterprise. The ill-omened succor could not be refused; but this was not all. The zealous protectress of the missions obtained from De Monts, whose fortunes, like those of Poutrincourt, had ebbed low, a transfer of all his claims to the lands of Acadia; while the young King, Louis the Thirteenth, was persuaded to give her, in addition, a new grant of all the territory of North America, from the St. Lawrence to Florida. Thus did Madame de Guercheville, or in other words, the Jesuits who used her name as a cover, become proprietors of the greater part of the future United States and British Provinces. The English colony of Virginia and the Dutch trading-houses of New

---

[1] Biard, *Epistola ex Portu-regali in Acadia*, 1612. Biard says there was no other family in the colony.

York were included within the limits of this destined Northern Paraguay; while Port Royal, the seigniory of the unfortunate Poutrincourt, was encompassed, like a petty island, by the vast domain of the Society of Jesus. They could not deprive him of it, since his title had been confirmed by the late King, but they flattered themselves, to borrow their own language, that he would be "confined as in a prison."[1] His grant, however, had been vaguely worded, and, while they held him restricted to an insignificant patch of ground, he claimed lordship over a wide and indefinite territory. Here was argument for endless strife. Other interests, too, were adverse. Poutrincourt, in his discouragement, had abandoned his plan of liberal colonization, and now thought of nothing but beaver-skins. He wished to make a trading-post; the Jesuits wished to make a mission.

When the vessel anchored before Port Royal, Biencourt, with disgust and anger, saw another Jesuit landed at the pier. This was Gilbert du Thet, a lay brother, versed in affairs of this world, who had come out as representative and administrator of Madame de Guercheville. Poutrincourt, also, had his agent on board; and, without the loss of a day, the two began to quarrel. A truce ensued; then a smothered feud, pervading the whole colony, and ending in a notable explosion. The Jesuits, chafing under the sway of Biencourt, had withdrawn without ceremony, and betaken themselves to the

[1] Biard, *Relation*, c. 19.

vessel, intending to sail for France. Biencourt, exasperated at such a breach of discipline, and fearing their representations at court, ordered them to return, adding that, since the Queen had commended them to his especial care, he could not, in conscience, lose sight of them. The indignant fathers excommunicated him. On this, the sagamore Louis, son of the grisly convert Membertou, begged leave to kill them; but Biencourt would not countenance this summary mode of relieving his embarrassment. He again, in the King's name, ordered the clerical mutineers to return to the fort. Biard declared that he would not, threatened to excommunicate any who should lay hand on him, and called the Vice-Admiral a robber. His wrath, however, soon cooled; he yielded to necessity, and came quietly ashore, where, for the next three months, neither he nor his colleagues would say mass, or perform any office of religion.[1] At length a change came over him; he made advances of peace, prayed that the past might be forgotten, said mass again, and closed with a petition that Brother du Thet might be allowed to go to France in a trading vessel then on the coast. His petition being granted, he wrote to Poutrincourt a letter overflowing with praises of his son; and, charged with this missive, Du Thet set sail.

[1] Lescarbot (1618), 676. Biard passes over the affair in silence. In his letters (see Carayon) prior to this time, he speaks favorably both of Biencourt and Poutrincourt.

CHAPTER VII.

1613.

LA SAUSSAYE.—ARGALL.

VOYAGE OF LA SAUSSAYE. — MOUNT DESERT. — ARGALL ATTACKS THE FRENCH. — DEATH OF DU THET. — ST. SAUVEUR DESTROYED.

PENDING these squabbles, the Jesuits at home were far from idle. Bent on ridding themselves of Poutrincourt, they seized, in satisfaction of debts due them, all the cargo of his returning vessel, and involved him in a network of litigation. If we accept his own statements in a letter to his friend Lescarbot, he was outrageously misused, and indeed defrauded, by his clerical copartners, who at length had him thrown into prison.[1] Here, exasperated, weary, sick of Acadia, and anxious for the wretched exiles who looked to him for succor, the unfortunate man fell ill. Regaining his liberty, he again addressed himself with what strength remained to the forlorn task of sending relief to his son and his comrades.

Scarcely had Brother Gilbert du Thet arrived in France, when Madame de Guercheville and her Jesuits, strong in court favor and in the charity of

[1] See the letter in Lescarbot (1618), 678.

wealthy penitents, prepared to take possession of their empire beyond sea. Contributions were asked, and not in vain; for the sagacious fathers, mindful of every spring of influence, had deeply studied the mazes of feminine psychology, and then, as now, were favorite confessors of the fair. It was on the twelfth of March, 1613, that the "Mayflower" of the Jesuits sailed from Honfleur for the shores of New England. She was the "Jonas," formerly in the service of De Monts, a small craft bearing forty-eight sailors and colonists, including two Jesuits, Father Quentin and Brother Du Thet. She carried horses, too, and goats, and was abundantly stored with all things needful by the pious munificence of her patrons. A courtier named La Saussaye was chief of the colony, Captain Charles Fleury commanded the ship,[1] and, as she winged her way across the Atlantic, benedictions hovered over her from lordly halls and perfumed chambers.

On the sixteenth of May, La Saussaye touched at La Hève, where he heard mass, planted a cross, and displayed the scutcheon of Madame de Guercheville. Thence, passing on to Port Royal, he found Baird, Masse, their servant-boy, an apothecary, and one man beside. Biencourt and his followers were scattered about the woods and shores, digging the tuberous roots called ground-nuts, catching alewives in the

---

[1] *Rapport fait à l'Amirauté de Rouen par Charles Fleury, Capitaine du Jonas, le 27 Aoust,* 1614. I am indebted to M. Gabriel Gravier, of Rouen, for a copy of this document.

brooks, and by similar expedients sustaining their miserable existence. Taking the two Jesuits on board, the voyagers steered for the Penobscot. A fog rose upon the sea. They sailed to and fro, groping their way in blindness, straining their eyes through the mist, and trembling each instant lest they should descry the black outline of some deadly reef and the ghostly death-dance of the breakers. But Heaven heard their prayers. At night they could see the stars.[1] The sun rose resplendent on a laughing sea, and his morning beams streamed fair and full on the wild heights of the island of Mount Desert. They entered a bay that stretched inland between iron-bound shores, and gave it the name of St. Sauveur. It is now called Frenchman's Bay. They saw a coast-line of weather-beaten crags set thick with spruce and fir, the surf-washed cliffs of Great Head and Schooner Head, the rocky front of Newport Mountain, patched with ragged woods, the arid domes of Dry Mountain and Green Mountain, the round bristly backs of the Porcupine Islands, and the waving outline of the Gouldsborough Hills.

La Saussaye cast anchor not far from Schooner Head, and here he lay till evening. The jet-black shade betwixt crags and sea, the pines along the

---

[1] "Suruint en mer vne si espaisse brume, que nous n'y voyons pas plus de iour que de nuict. Nous apprehendions grandement ce danger, parce qu'en cét endroict, il y a beaucoup de brisans et rochers. . . . De sa bonté, Dieu nous exauça, car le soir mesme nous commençasmes à voir les estoiles, et le matin les brouées se dissiperent; nous nous reconnusmes estre au deuant des Monts deserts." Biard, *Relation*, c. 23.

cliff, pencilled against the fiery sunset, the dreamy slumber of distant mountains bathed in shadowy purple, — such is the scene that in this our day greets the wandering artist, the roving collegian bivouacked on the shore, or the pilgrim from stifled cities renewing his jaded strength in the mighty life of Nature. Perhaps they then greeted the adventurous Frenchmen. There was peace on the wilderness and peace on the sea; but none in this missionary bark, pioneer of Christianity and civilization. A rabble of angry sailors clamored on her deck, ready to mutiny over the terms of their engagement. Should the time of their stay be reckoned from their landing at La Hêve, or from their anchoring at Mount Desert? Fleury, the naval commander, took their part. Sailor, courtier, and priest gave tongue together in vociferous debate. Poutrincourt was far away, a ruined man, and the intractable Vice-Admiral had ceased from troubling; yet not the less were the omens of the pious enterprise sinister and dark. The company, however, went ashore, raised a cross, and heard mass.

At a distance in the woods they saw the signal smoke of Indians, whom Biard lost no time in visiting. Some of them were from a village on the shore, three leagues westward. They urged the French to go with them to their wigwams. The astute savages had learned already how to deal with a Jesuit.

"Our great chief, Asticou, is there. He wishes for baptism. He is very sick. He will die unbaptized. He will burn in hell, and it will be all your fault."

This was enough. Biard embarked in a canoe, and they paddled him to the spot, where he found the great chief, Asticou, in his wigwam, with a heavy cold in the head. Disappointed of his charitable purpose, the priest consoled himself with observing the beauties of the neighboring shore, which seemed to him better fitted than St. Sauveur for the intended settlement. It was a gentle slope, descending to the water, covered with tall grass, and backed by rocky hills. It looked southeast upon a harbor where a fleet might ride at anchor, sheltered from the gales by a cluster of islands.[1]

The ship was brought to the spot, and the colonists disembarked. First they planted a cross; then they began their labors, and with their labors their quar-

---

[1] Biard says that the place was only three leagues from St. Sauveur, and that he could go and return in an afternoon. He adds that it was "séparé de la grande Isle des Monts Déserts." He was evidently mistaken in this. St. Sauveur being on the east side of Mount Desert, there is no place separated from it, and answering to his description, which he could have reached within the time mentioned. He no doubt crossed Mount Desert Sound, which, with Soames's Sound, nearly severs the island. The settlement must have been on the western side of Soames's Sound. Here, about a mile from the open sea, on the farm of Mr. Fernald, is a spot perfectly answering to the minute description of Biard: "Le terroir noir, gras, et fertile, ... la jolie colline esleuée doucement sur la mer, et baignée à ses costez de deux fontaines; . . . . les petites islettes qui rompent les flots et les vents." The situation is highly picturesque. On the opposite or eastern shore of the sound are found heaps of clam-shells and other indications of an Indian village, probably that of Asticou. I am indebted to E. L. Hamlin, Esq., of Bangor, for pointing out this locality.

rels. La Saussaye, zealous for agriculture, wished to break ground and raise crops immediately; the rest opposed him, wishing first to be housed and fortified. Fleury demanded that the ship should be unladen, and La Saussaye would not consent.[1] Debate ran high, when suddenly all was harmony, and the disputants were friends once more in the pacification of a common danger.

Far out at sea, beyond the islands that sheltered their harbor, they saw an approaching sail; and as she drew near, straining their anxious eyes, they could descry the red flags that streamed from her masthead and her stern; then the black muzzles of her cannon, — they counted seven on a side; then the throng of men upon her decks. The wind was brisk and fair; all her sails were set; she came on, writes a spectator, more swiftly than an arrow.[2]

Six years before, in 1607, the ships of Captain Newport had conveyed to the banks of James River the first vital germ of English colonization on the continent. Noble and wealthy speculators, with Hispaniola, Mexico, and Peru for their inspiration, had combined to gather the fancied golden harvest of Virginia, received a charter from the Crown, and taken possession of their El Dorado. From tavern, gaming-house, and brothel was drawn the staple of

[1] *Rapport de Fleury à l'Amirauté de Rouen.*
[2] "Le nauire Anglois venoit plus viste qu'un dard, ayant le vent à souhait, tout panis de rogue, les pauillons d'Angleterre flottans, et trois trompettes et deux tambours faisans rage de sonner." Biard, *Relation*, c. 25.

the colony, — ruined gentlemen, prodigal sons, disreputable retainers, debauched tradesmen. Yet it would be foul slander to affirm that the founders of Virginia were all of this stamp; for among the riotous crew were men of worth, and, above them all, a hero disguised by the homeliest of names. Again and again, in direst woe and jeopardy, the infant settlement owed its life to the heart and hand of John Smith.

Several years had elapsed since Newport's voyage; and the colony, depleted by famine, disease, and an Indian war, had been recruited by fresh emigration, when one Samuel Argall arrived at Jamestown, captain of an illicit trading-vessel. He was a man of ability and force, — one of those compounds of craft and daring in which the age was fruitful; for the rest, unscrupulous and grasping. In the spring of 1613 he achieved a characteristic exploit, — the abduction of Pocahontas, that most interesting of young squaws, or, to borrow the style of the day, of Indian princesses. Sailing up the Potomac he lured her on board his ship, and then carried off the benefactress of the colony a prisoner to Jamestown. Here a young man of family, Rolfe, became enamoured of her, married her with more than ordinary ceremony, and thus secured a firm alliance between her tribesmen and the English.

Meanwhile Argall had set forth on another enterprise. With a ship of one hundred and thirty tons, carrying fourteen guns and sixty men, he sailed in

May for islands off the coast of Maine to fish, as he says, for cod.[1] He had a more important errand; for Sir Thomas Dale, Governor of Virginia, had commissioned him to expel the French from any settlement they might have made within the limits of King James's patents.[2] Thick fogs involved him; and when the weather cleared he found himself not far from the Bay of Penobscot. Canoes came out from shore; the Indians climbed the ship's side, and, as they gained the deck, greeted the astonished English with an odd pantomime of bows and flourishes, which, in the belief of the latter, could have been learned from none but Frenchmen.[3] By signs, too, and by often repeating the word *Norman*, — by which they always designated the French, — they betrayed the presence of the latter. Argall questioned them as well as his total ignorance of their language would permit, and learned, by signs, the position and numbers of the colonists. Clearly they were no match for him. Assuring the Indians that the Normans were his friends, and that he longed to see them, he retained one of the visitors as a guide, dismissed the rest with presents, and shaped his course for Mount Desert.[4]

[1] Letter of Argall to Nicholas Hawes, June, 1613, in Purchas, IV. 1764.

[2] *Collections Mass. Hist. Soc.*, Fourth Series, IX. 41, 489.

[3] ". . . et aux cérémonies que les sauvages faisoient pour leur complaire, ils recognoissoient que c'étoient cérémonies de courtoisie et ciuilitez françoises." Biard, *Relation*, c. 25.

[4] Holmes, *American Annals*, by a misapprehension of Champlain's narrative, represents Argall as having a squadron of eleven ships. He certainly had but one.

Now the wild heights rose in view; now the English could see the masts of a small ship anchored in the sound; and now, as they rounded the islands, four white tents were visible on the grassy slope between the water and the woods. They were a gift from the Queen to Madame de Guercheville and her missionaries. Argall's men prepared for fight, while their Indian guide, amazed, broke into a howl of lamentation.

On shore all was confusion. Bailleul, the pilot, went to reconnoitre, and ended by hiding among the islands. La Saussaye lost presence of mind, and did nothing for defence. La Motte, his lieutenant, with Captain Fleury, an ensign, a sergeant, the Jesuit Du Thet, and a few of the bravest men, hastened on board the vessel, but had no time to cast loose her cables. Argall bore down on them, with a furious din of drums and trumpets, showed his broadside, and replied to their hail with a volley of cannon and musket shot. "Fire! Fire!" screamed Fleury. But there was no gunner to obey, till Du Thet seized and applied the match. "The cannon made as much noise as the enemy's," writes Biard; but, as the inexperienced artillerist forgot to aim the piece, no other result ensued. Another storm of musketry, and Brother Gilbert du Thet rolled helpless on the deck.

The French ship was mute. The English plied her for a time with shot, then lowered a boat and boarded. Under the awnings which covered her, dead and wounded men lay strewn about her deck, and among them the brave lay brother, smothering in his blood. He had his wish; for, on leaving France, he had prayed with uplifted hands that he might not return, but perish in that holy enterprise. Like the Order of which he was a humble member, he was a compound of qualities in appearance contradictory. La Motte, sword in hand, showed fight to the last, and won the esteem of his captors.[1]

The English landed without meeting any show of resistance, and ranged at will among the tents, the piles of baggage and stores, and the buildings and defences newly begun. Argall asked for the commander, but La Saussaye had fled to the woods. The crafty Englishman seized his chests, caused the locks to be picked, searched till he found the royal letters and commissions, withdrew them, replaced everything else as he had found it, and again closed the lids. In the morning, La Saussaye, between the English and starvation, preferred the former, and issued from his hiding-place. Argall received him with studious courtesy. That country, he said, belonged to his master, King James. Doubtless they had authority from their own sovereign for thus encroaching upon it; and, for his part, he was prepared to yield all respect to the commissions of the

[1] Fleury, who was wounded, greatly blames the flight of La Saussaye: "Si luy et ses dicts compagnons eussent donné combat et se fussent defendus, le dict navire n'eust esté prins." In a reply to complaints of the French ambassador, it was said that the French fired the first shot. See *Coll. Mass. Hist. Soc.*, Fourth Series, IX. 489.

King of France, that the peace between the two nations might not be disturbed. Therefore he prayed that the commissions might be shown to him. La Saussaye opened his chests. The royal signature was nowhere to be found. At this, Argall's courtesy was changed to wrath. He denounced the Frenchmen as robbers and pirates who deserved the gallows, removed their property on board his ship, and spent the afternoon in dividing it among his followers. The disconsolate French remained on the scene of their woes, where the greedy sailors as they came ashore would snatch from them, now a cloak, now a hat, and now a doublet, till the unfortunate colonists were left half naked. In other respects the English treated their captives well, — except two of them, whom they flogged; and Argall, whom Biard, after recounting his knavery, calls "a gentleman of noble courage," having gained his point, returned to his former courtesy.

But how to dispose of the prisoners? Fifteen of them, including La Saussaye and the Jesuit Masse, were turned adrift in an open boat, at the mercy of the wilderness and the sea. Nearly all were landsmen; but while their unpractised hands were struggling with the oars, they were joined among the islands by the fugitive pilot and his boat's crew. Worn and half starved, the united bands made their perilous way eastward, stopping from time to time to hear mass, make a procession, or catch codfish. Thus sustained in the spirit and in the flesh, cheered too by the Indians, who proved fast friends in need, they crossed the Bay of Fundy, doubled Cape Sable, and followed the southern coast of Nova Scotia, till they happily fell in with two French trading-vessels, which bore them in safety to St. Malo.

CHAPTER VIII.

1613-1615.

RUIN OF FRENCH ACADIA.

THE JESUITS AT JAMESTOWN. — WRATH OF SIR THOMAS DALE. — A NEW EXPEDITION. — PORT ROYAL DEMOLISHED. — EQUIVOCAL POSTURE OF THE JESUITS. — THEIR ADVENTURES. — THE FRENCH WILL NOT ABANDON ACADIA.

"PRAISED be God, behold two thirds of our company safe in France, telling their strange adventures to their relatives and friends. And now you will wish to know what befell the rest of us."[1] Thus writes Father Biard, who with his companions in misfortune, fourteen in all, prisoners on board Argall's ship and the prize, were borne captive to Virginia. Old Point Comfort was reached at length, the site of Fortress Monroe; Hampton Roads, renowned in our day for the sea-fight of the Titans; Sewell's Point; the Rip Raps; Newport News, — all household words in the ears of this generation. Now, far on their right, buried in the damp shade of immemorial verdure, lay, untrodden and voiceless, the fields where stretched the leaguering lines of

[1] "Dieu soit beny. Voyla ja les deux tiers de nostre troupe reconduicts en France sains et sauues parmy leurs parents et amis, qui les oyent conter leurs grandes aventures. Ores consequemment vous desirez scauoir ce qui deuiendra l'autre tiers." Biard, *Relation*, c. 28.

Washington, where the lilies of France floated beside the banners of the new-born republic, and where in later years embattled treason confronted the manhood of an outraged nation.[1] And now before them they could descry the masts of small craft at anchor, a cluster of rude dwellings fresh from the axe, scattered tenements, and fields green with tobacco.

Throughout the voyage the prisoners had been soothed with flattering tales of the benignity of the Governor of Virginia, Sir Thomas Dale; of his love of the French, and his respect for the memory of Henry the Fourth, to whom, they were told, he was much beholden for countenance and favor. On their landing at Jamestown, this consoling picture was reversed. The Governor fumed and blustered, talked of halter and gallows, and declared that he would hang them all. In vain Argall remonstrated, urging that he had pledged his word for their lives. Dale, outraged by their invasion of British territory, was deaf to all appeals; till Argall, driven to extremity, displayed the stolen commissions, and proclaimed his stratagem, of which the French themselves had to that moment been ignorant. As they were accredited by their government, their lives at least were safe. Yet the wrath of Sir Thomas Dale still burned high. He summoned his council, and they resolved promptly to wipe off all stain of French intrusion from shores which King James claimed as his own.

Their action was utterly unauthorized. The two

[1] Written immediately after the War of Secession.

kingdoms were at peace. James the First, by the patents of 1606, had granted all North America, from the thirty-fourth to the forty-fifth degree of latitude, to the two companies of London and Plymouth, — Virginia being assigned to the former, while to the latter were given Maine and Acadia, with adjacent regions. Over these, though as yet the claimants had not taken possession of them, the authorities of Virginia had no color of jurisdiction. England claimed all North America, in virtue of the discovery of Cabot; and Sir Thomas Dale became the self-constituted champion of British rights, not the less zealous that his championship promised a harvest of booty.

Argall's ship, the captured ship of La Saussaye, and another smaller vessel, were at once equipped and despatched on their errand of havoc. Argall commanded; and Biard, with Quentin and several others of the prisoners, were embarked with him.[1] They shaped their course first for Mount Desert. Here they landed, levelled La Saussaye's unfinished defences, cut down the French cross, and planted one of their own in its place. Next they sought out the island of St. Croix, seized a quantity of salt, and razed to the ground all that remained of the dilapidated buildings of De Monts. They crossed the Bay

[1] In his *Relation*, Biard does not explain the reason of his accompanying the expedition. In his letter to the General of the Jesuits, dated Amiens, 26 May, 1614 (Carayon), he says that it was "dans le dessein de profiter de la première occasion qui se rencontrerait, pour nous renvoyer dans notre patrie."

of Fundy to Port Royal, guided, says Biard, by an Indian chief, — an improbable assertion, since the natives of these coasts hated the English as much as they loved the French, and now well knew the designs of the former. The unfortunate settlement was tenantless. Biencourt, with some of his men, was on a visit to neighboring bands of Indians, while the rest were reaping in the fields on the river, two leagues above the fort. Succor from Poutrincourt had arrived during the summer. The magazines were by no means empty, and there were cattle, horses, and hogs in adjacent fields and enclosures. Exulting at their good fortune, Argall's men butchered or carried off the animals, ransacked the buildings, plundered them even to the locks and bolts of the doors, and then laid the whole in ashes; "and may it please the Lord," adds the pious Biard, "that the sins therein committed may likewise have been consumed in that burning."

Having demolished Port Royal, the marauders went in boats up the river to the fields where the reapers were at work. These fled, and took refuge behind the ridge of a hill, whence they gazed helplessly on the destruction of their harvest. Biard approached them, and, according to the declaration of Poutrincourt made and attested before the Admiralty of Guienne, tried to persuade them to desert his son, Biencourt, and take service with Argall. The reply of one of the men gave little encouragement for further parley: —

"Begone, or I will split your head with this hatchet."

There is flat contradiction here between the narrative of the Jesuit and the accounts of Poutrincourt and contemporary English writers, who agree in affirming that Biard, "out of indigestible malice that he had conceived against Biencourt,"[1] encouraged the attack on the settlements of St. Croix and Port Royal, and guided the English thither. The priest himself admits that both French and English regarded him as a traitor, and that his life was in danger. While Argall's ship was at anchor, a Frenchman shouted to the English from a distance that they would do well to kill him. The master of the ship, a Puritan, in his abomination of priests, and above all of Jesuits, was at the same time urging his commander to set Biard ashore and leave him to the mercy of his countrymen. In this pass he was saved, to adopt his own account, by what he calls his simplicity; for he tells us, that, while — instigated, like the rest of his enemies, by the Devil — the robber and the robbed were joining hands to ruin him, he was on his knees before Argall, begging him to take pity on the French, and leave them a boat, together with provisions to sustain their miserable lives through the winter. This spectacle of charity, he further says, so moved the noble heart of the com-

---

[1] *Briefe Intelligence from Virginia by Letters.* See Purchas, IV. 1808. Compare Poutrincourt's letter to Lescarbot, in Lescarbot, (1618,) 684. Also, *Plainte du Sieur de Poutrincourt devant le Juge de l'Admirauté de Guyenne*, Lescarbot, 687.

mander, that he closed his ears to all the promptings of foreign and domestic malice.[1]

The English had scarcely re-embarked, when Biencourt arrived with his followers, and beheld the scene of destruction. Hopelessly outnumbered, he tried to lure Argall and some of his officers into an ambuscade, but they would not be entrapped. Biencourt now asked for an interview. The word of honor was mutually given, and the two chiefs met in a meadow not far from the demolished dwellings. An anonymous English writer says that Biencourt offered to transfer his allegiance to King James, on condition of being permitted to remain at Port Royal and carry on the fur-trade under a guaranty of English protection, but that Argall would not listen to his overtures.[2] The interview proved a stormy one.

---

[1] " Ie ne sçay qui secourut tant à propos le Iesuite en ce danger que sa simplicité. Car tout de mesme que s'il eust esté bien fauorisé et qu'il eust peu beaucoup enuers ledit Anglois, il se mit à genoux deuant le Capitaine par deux diuerses fois et a deux diuerses occasions, à celle fin de le flechir à misericorde enuers les François du dit Port Royal esgarés par les bois et pour luy persuader de leur laisser quelques viures, leur chaloupe et quelqu' autre moyen de passer l'hyuer. Et voyez combien differentes petitions on faisoit audit Capitaine; car au mesme tempts que le P. Biard le supplioit ainsi pour les François, vn François crioit de loin, avec outrages et iniures, qu'il le falloit massacrer.

"Or Argal, qui est d'vn cœur noble, voyant ceste tant sincere affection du Iesuite, et de l'autre costé tant bestiale et enragée inhumanité de ce François, laquelle ne recognoissoit ny sa propre nation, ny bien-faicts, ny religion, ny estoit dompté par l'affliction et verges de Dieu, estima," etc. Biard, *Relation*, c. 29. He writes throughout in the third person.

[2] *Briefe Intelligence*, Purchas, IV. 1808.

Biard says that the Frenchmen vomited against him every species of malignant abuse. "In the mean time," he adds, "you will considerately observe to what madness the evil spirit exciteth those who sell themselves to him."[1]

According to Poutrincourt,[2] Argall admitted that the priest had urged him to attack Port Royal. Certain it is that Biencourt demanded his surrender, frankly declaring that he meant to hang him. "Whilest they were discoursing together," says the old English writer above mentioned, "one of the savages, rushing suddenly forth from the Woods, and licentiated to come neere, did after his manner, with such broken *French* as he had, earnestly mediate a peace, wondring why they that seemed to be of one Country should vse others with such hostilitie, and that with such a forme of habit and gesture as made them both to laugh."[3]

His work done, and, as he thought, the French settlements of Acadia effectually blotted out, Argall set sail for Virginia on the thirteenth of November. Scarcely was he at sea when a storm scattered the vessels. Of the smallest of the three nothing was ever heard. Argall, severely buffeted, reached his port in safety, having first, it is said, compelled the Dutch at Manhattan to acknowledge for a time the

---

[1] Biard, c. 29: "Cependant vous remarquerez sagement iusques à quelle rage le malin esprit agite ceux qui se vendent à luy."
[2] *Plainte du Sieur de Poutrincourt*, Lescarbot, (1618,) 689.
[3] Purchas, IV. 1808.

sovereignty of King James.[1] The captured ship of La Saussaye, with Biard and his colleague Quentin on board, was forced to yield to the fury of the western gales, and bear away for the Azores. To Biard the change of destination was not unwelcome. He stood in fear of the truculent Governor of Virginia, and his tempest-rocked slumbers were haunted with unpleasant visions of a rope's end.[2] It seems that some of the French at Port Royal, disappointed in their hope of hanging him, had commended him to Sir Thomas Dale as a proper subject for the gallows, drawing up a paper, signed by six of them, and containing allegations of a nature well fitted to kindle the wrath of that vehement official. The vessel was commanded by Turnel, Argall's lieutenant, apparently an officer of merit, a scholar and linguist. He had treated his prisoner with great kindness, because, says the latter, "he esteemed and loved him for his naïve simplicity and ingenuous candor."[3] But of late, thinking his kindness misplaced, he had changed it for an extreme coldness, preferring, in the words of Biard himself, "to think that the

---

[1] *Description of the Province of New Albion,* in *New York Historical Collections,* Second Series, I. 335. The statement is doubtful. It is supported, however, by the excellent authority of Dr. O'Callaghan, *History of New Netherland,* I. 69.

[2] "Le Mareschal Thomas Deel (que vous avez ouy estre fort aspre en ses humeurs) . . . attendoit en bon deuotion le Pere Biard pour luy tost accourcir les voyages, luy faisant trouuer au milieu d'une eschelle le bout du monde." Biard, *Relation,* c. 30, 33.

[3] ". . . il avoit faict estat de le priser et l'aymer pour sa naïfue simplicité et ouuerte candeur." *Ibid.,* c. 30.

Jesuit had lied, rather than so many who accused him."[1]

Water ran low, provisions began to fail, and they eked out their meagre supply by butchering the horses taken at Port Royal. At length they came within sight of Fayal, when a new terror seized the minds of the two Jesuits. Might not the Englishmen fear that their prisoners would denounce them to the fervent Catholics of that island as pirates and sacrilegious kidnappers of priests? From such hazard the escape was obvious. What more simple than to drop the priests into the sea?[2] In truth, the English had no little dread of the results of conference between the Jesuits and the Portuguese authorities of Fayal; but the conscience or humanity of Turnel revolted at the expedient which awakened such apprehension in the troubled mind of Biard. He contented himself with requiring that the two priests should remain hidden while the ship lay off the port: Biard does not say that he enforced the demand either by threats or by the imposition of oaths. He and his companion, however, rigidly complied with it, lying close in the hold or under the boats, while suspicious officials searched the ship, — a proof, he triumphantly declares, of the audacious

---

[1] ". . . il aimoit mieux croire que le Iesuite fust menteur que non pas tant d'autres qui l'accusoyent." *Ibid*.

[2] " Ce souci nous inquiétait fort. Qu'allaient-ils faire? Nous jetteraient-ils à l'eau? " *Lettre du P. Biard au T. R. P. Claude Aquaviva, Amiens, 26 Mai*, 1614, in Carayon, 106. Like all Biard's letters to Aquaviva, this is translated from the original Latin.

malice which has asserted it as a tenet of Rome that no faith need be kept with heretics.

Once more at sea, Turnel shaped his course for home, having, with some difficulty, gained a supply of water and provisions at Fayal. All was now harmony between him and his prisoners. When he reached Pembroke, in Wales, the appearance of the vessel — a French craft in English hands — again drew upon him the suspicion of piracy. The Jesuits, dangerous witnesses among the Catholics of Fayal, could at the worst do little harm with the Vice-Admiral at Pembroke. To him, therefore, he led the prisoners, in the sable garb of their order, now much the worse for wear, and commended them as persons without reproach, "wherein," adds the modest father, "he spoke the truth."[1] The result of their evidence was, we are told, that Turnel was henceforth treated, not as a pirate, but, according to his deserts, as an honorable gentleman. This interview led to a meeting with certain dignitaries of the Anglican Church, who, much interested in an encounter with Jesuits in their robes, were filled, says Biard, with wonder and admiration at what they were told of their conduct.[2] He explains that these churchmen differ widely in form and doctrine from the English Calvinists, who, he says, are called Puritans; and he adds that they are superior in every

[1] ". . . gens irreprochables, ce disoit-il, et disoit vray." Baird, *Relation*, c. 32.
[2] ". . . et les ministres en demonstroyent grands signes estonnement et d'admiration." *Ibid.*, c. 31.

respect to these, whom they detest as an execrable pest.[1]

Biard was sent to Dover and thence to Calais, returning, perhaps, to the tranquil honors of his chair of theology at Lyons. La Saussaye, La Motte, Fleury, and other prisoners were at various times sent from Virginia to England, and ultimately to France. Madame de Guercheville, her pious designs crushed in the bud, seems to have gained no further satisfaction than the restoration of the vessel. The French ambassador complained of the outrage, but answer was postponed; and, in the troubled state of France, the matter appears to have been dropped.[2]

Argall, whose violent and crafty character was offset by a gallant bearing and various traits of martial virtue, became Deputy-Governor of Virginia, and, under a military code, ruled the colony with a rod of iron. He enforced the observance of Sunday with an edifying rigor. Those who absented themselves from church were, for the first offence, imprisoned for the night, and reduced to slavery for a week; for the second offence, enslaved a month; and for the third, a year. Nor was he less strenuous in his devotion to mammon. He enriched himself by extortion and wholesale peculation; and his audacious dexterity, aided by the countenance of the Earl of Warwick, who is said to have had a trading con-

[1] ". . . et les detestent comme peste execrable." *Ibid.*, c. 32.
[2] *Order of Council respecting certain claims against Capt. Argall*, etc. *Answer to the preceding Order.* See *Colonial Documents of New York*, III. 1, 2.

nection with him, thwarted all the efforts of the company to bring him to account. In 1623, he was knighted by the hand of King James.[1]

Early in the spring following the English attack, Poutrincourt came to Port Royal. He found the place in ashes, and his unfortunate son, with the men under his command, wandering houseless in the forests. They had passed a winter of extreme misery, sustaining their wretched existence with roots, the buds of trees, and lichens peeled from the rocks.

Despairing of his enterprise, Poutrincourt returned to France. In the next year, 1615, during the civil disturbances which followed the marriage of the King, command was given him of the royal forces destined for the attack on Méry; and here, happier in his death than in his life, he fell, sword in hand.[2]

In spite of their reverses, the French kept hold on Acadia.[3] Biencourt, partially at least, rebuilt Port Royal; while winter after winter the smoke of fur traders' huts curled into the still, sharp air of these

[1] Argall's history may be gleaned from Purchas, Smith, Stith, Gorges, Beverly, etc. An excellent summary will be found in Belknap's *American Biography*, and a briefer one in Allen's.

[2] *Nobilissimi Herois Potrincurtii Epitaphium*, Lescarbot (1618), 694. He took the town, but was killed immediately after by a treacherous shot, in the fifty-eighth year of his age. He was buried on his barony of St. Just.

[3] According to Biard, more than five hundred French vessels sailed annually, at this time, to America, for the whale and cod fishery and the fur-trade.

frosty wilds, till at length, with happier auspices, plans of settlement were resumed.[1]

Rude hands strangled the "Northern Paraguay" in its birth. Its beginnings had been feeble, but behind were the forces of a mighty organization, at once devoted and ambitious, enthusiastic and calculating. Seven years later the "Mayflower" landed her emigrants at Plymouth. What would have been the issues had the zeal of the pious lady of honor preoccupied New England with a Jesuit colony?

In an obscure stroke of lawless violence began the strife of France and England, Protestantism and Rome, which for a century and a half shook the struggling communities of North America, and closed at last in the memorable triumph on the Plains of Abraham.

---

[1] There is an autograph letter in the Archives de la Marine from Biencourt, — who had succeeded to his father's designation, — written at Port Royal in September, 1618, and addressed "aux Autorités de la Ville de Paris," in which he urges upon them the advantages of establishing fortified posts in Acadia, thus defending it against incursions of the English, who had lately seized a French trader from Dieppe, and insuring the continuance and increase of the traffic in furs, from which the city of Paris derived such advantages. Moreover, he adds, it will serve as an asylum for the indigent and suffering of the city, to their own great benefit and the advantage of the municipality, who will be relieved of the burden of their maintenance. It does not appear that the city responded to his appeal.

CHAPTER IX.

1608, 1609.

CHAMPLAIN AT QUEBEC.

A NEW ENTERPRISE. — THE ST. LAWRENCE. — CONFLICT WITH BASQUES. — TADOUSSAC. — QUEBEC FOUNDED. — CONSPIRACY. — WINTER. — THE MONTAGNAIS. — SPRING. — PROJECTS OF EXPLORATION.

A LONELY ship sailed up the St. Lawrence. The white whales floundering in the Bay of Tadoussac, and the wild duck diving as the foaming prow drew near, — there was no life but these in all that watery solitude, twenty miles from shore to shore. The ship was from Honfleur, and was commanded by Samuel de Champlain. He was the Æneas of a destined people, and in her womb lay the embryo life of Canada.

De Monts, after his exclusive privilege of trade was revoked and his Acadian enterprise ruined, had, as we have seen, abandoned it to Poutrincourt. Perhaps would it have been well for him had he abandoned with it all Transatlantic enterprises; but the passion for discovery and the noble ambition of founding colonies had taken possession of his mind. These, rather than a mere hope of gain, seem to have been his controlling motives; yet the profits of the fur-trade were vital to the new designs he was meditating, to meet the heavy outlay they demanded, and he solicited and obtained a fresh monopoly of the traffic for one year.[1]

Champlain was, at the time, in Paris; but his unquiet thoughts turned westward. He was enamoured of the New World, whose rugged charms had seized his fancy and his heart; and as explorers of Arctic seas have pined in their repose for polar ice and snow, so did his restless thoughts revert to the fog-wrapped coasts, the piny odors of forests, the noise of waters, the sharp and piercing sunlight, so dear to his remembrance. He longed to unveil the mystery of that boundless wilderness, and plant the Catholic faith and the power of France amid its ancient barbarism.

Five years before, he had explored the St. Lawrence as far as the rapids above Montreal. On its banks, as he thought, was the true site for a settlement, — a fortified post, whence, as from a secure basis, the waters of the vast interior might be traced back towards their sources, and a western route discovered to China and Japan. For the fur-trade, too, the innumerable streams that descended to the great river might all be closed against foreign intrusion by a single fort at some commanding point, and made tributary to a rich and permanent commerce; while — and this was nearer to his heart, for he had often been heard to say that the saving of a soul was worth more than the conquest of an empire — countless

[1] See the patent in Champlain (1613), 163.

savage tribes, in the bondage of Satan, might by the same avenues be reached and redeemed.

De Monts embraced his views; and, fitting out two ships, gave command of one to the elder Pontgravé, of the other to Champlain. The former was to trade with the Indians and bring back the cargo of furs which, it was hoped, would meet the expense of the voyage. To Champlain fell the harder task of settlement and exploration.

Pontgravé, laden with goods for the Indian trade of Tadoussac, sailed from Honfleur on the fifth of April, 1608. Champlain, with men, arms, and stores for the colony, followed, eight days later. On the fifteenth of May he was on the Grand Bank; on the thirtieth he passed Gaspé, and on the third of June neared Tadoussac. No living thing was to be seen. He anchored, lowered a boat, and rowed into the port, round the rocky point at the southeast, then, from the fury of its winds and currents, called La Pointe de Tous les Diables.[1] There was life enough within, and more than he cared to find. In the still anchorage under the cliffs lay Pontgravé's vessel, and at her side another ship, which proved to be a Basque fur-trader.

Pontgravé, arriving a few days before, had found himself anticipated by the Basques, who were busied in a brisk trade with bands of Indians cabined along the borders of the cove. He displayed the royal

[1] Champlain (1613), 166. Also called La Pointe aux Rochers. Ibid. (1632), 119.

letters, and commanded a cessation of the prohibited traffic; but the Basques proved refractory, declared that they would trade in spite of the King, fired on Pontgravé with cannon and musketry, wounded him and two of his men, and killed a third. They then boarded his vessel, and carried away all his cannon, small arms, and ammunition, saying that they would restore them when they had finished their trade and were ready to return home.

Champlain found his comrade on shore, in a disabled condition. The Basques, though still strong enough to make fight, were alarmed for the consequences of their conduct, and anxious to come to terms. A peace, therefore, was signed on board their vessel; all differences were referred to the judgment of the French courts, harmony was restored, and the choleric strangers betook themselves to catching whales.

This port of Tadoussac was long the centre of the Canadian fur-trade. A desolation of barren mountains closes round it, betwixt whose ribs of rugged granite, bristling with savins, birches, and firs, the Saguenay rolls its gloomy waters from the northern wilderness. Centuries of civilization have not tamed the wildness of the place; and still, in grim repose, the mountains hold their guard around the waveless lake that glistens in their shadow, and doubles, in its sullen mirror, crag, precipice, and forest.

Near the brink of the cove or harbor where the vessels lay, and a little below the mouth of a brook which formed one of the outlets of this small lake, stood the remains of the wooden barrack built by Chauvin eight years before. Above the brook were the lodges of an Indian camp,[1] — stacks of poles covered with birch-bark. They belonged to an Algonquin horde, called *Montagnais*, denizens of surrounding wilds, and gatherers of their only harvest, — skins of the moose, caribou, and bear; fur of the beaver, marten, otter, fox, wild-cat, and lynx. Nor was this all, for there were intermediate traders betwixt the French and the shivering bands who roamed the weary stretch of stunted forest between the head-waters of the Saguenay and Hudson's Bay. Indefatigable canoe-men, in their birchen vessels, light as egg-shells, they threaded the devious tracks of countless rippling streams, shady by-ways of the forest, where the wild duck scarcely finds depth to swim; then descended to their mart along those scenes of picturesque yet dreary grandeur which steam has made familiar to modern tourists. With slowly moving paddles, they glided beneath the cliff whose shaggy brows frown across the zenith, and whose base the deep waves wash with a hoarse and hollow cadence; and they passed the sepulchral Bay of the Trinity, dark as the tide of Acheron, — a sanctuary of solitude and silence: depths which, as the fable runs, no sounding line can fathom, and heights at whose dizzy verge the wheeling eagle seems a speck.[2]

[1] *Plan du Port de Tadoussac*, Champlain (1613), 172.
[2] Bouchette estimates the height of these cliffs at eighteen hundred

Peace being established with the Basques, and the wounded Pontgravé busied, as far as might be, in transferring to the hold of his ship the rich lading of the Indian canoes, Champlain spread his sails, and again held his course up the St. Lawrence. Far to the south, in sun and shadow, slumbered the woody mountains whence fell the countless springs of the St. John, behind tenantless shores, now white with glimmering villages, — La Chenaie, Granville, Kamouraska, St. Roche, St. Jean, Vincelot, Berthier. But on the north the jealous wilderness still asserts its sway, crowding to the river's verge its walls, domes, and towers of granite; and, to this hour, its solitude is scarcely broken.

Above the point of the Island of Orleans, a constriction of the vast channel narrows it to less than a mile, with the green heights of Point Levi on one side, and on the other the cliffs of Quebec.[1] Here,

feet. They overhang the river and bay. The scene is one of the most remarkable on the continent.

[1] The origin of this name has been disputed, but there is no good ground to doubt its Indian origin, which is distinctly affirmed by Champlain and Lescarbot. Charlevoix, *Fastes Chronologiques* (1608), derives it from the Algonquin word *Quebeio*, or *Quelibec*, signifying a *narrowing* or *contracting* (*rétrécissement*). A half-breed Algonquin told Garneau that the word *Quebec*, or *Ouabec*, means *a strait*. The same writer was told by M. Malo, a missionary among the Micmacs, a branch of the Algonquins, that in their dialect the word *Kibec* had the same meaning. Martin says, "Les Algonquins l'appellent *Ouabec*, et les Micmacs *Kebèque*, c'est à dire, 'là où la rivière est fermée.'" (Martin's *Bressani*, App., 326.) The derivations given by La Potherie, Le Beau, and others, are purely fanciful. The circumstance of the word *Quebec* being found engraved on the ancient seal of Lord Suffolk (see Hawkins, *Picture of Quebec*) can only be regarded as a curious

a small stream, the St. Charles, enters the St. Lawrence, and in the angle betwixt them rises the promontory, on two sides a natural fortress. Between the cliffs and the river lay a strand covered with walnuts and other trees. From this strand, by a rough passage gullied downward from the place where Prescott Gate now guards the way, one might climb the heights to the broken plateau above, now burdened with its ponderous load of churches, convents, dwellings, ramparts, and batteries. Thence, by a gradual ascent, the rock sloped upward to its highest summit, Cape Diamond,[1] looking down on the St. Lawrence from a height of three hundred and fifty feet. Here the citadel now stands; then the fierce sun fell on the bald, baking rock, with its crisped mosses and parched lichens. Two centuries and a half have quickened the solitude with swarming life, covered the deep bosom of the river with barge and steamer and gliding sail, and reared cities and villages on the site of forests; but nothing can destroy the surpassing grandeur of the scene.

On the strand between the water and the cliffs Champlain's axemen fell to their work. They were pioneers of an advancing host, — advancing, it is

---

coincidence. In Cartier's times the site of Quebec was occupied by a tribe of the Iroquois race, who called their village *Stadaconé*. The Hurons called it, says Sagard, *Atou-ta-requee*. In the modern Huron dialect, *Tiatou-ta-riti* means *the narrows*.

[1] Champlain calls Cape Diamond Mont du Gas (Guast), from the family name of De Monts. He gives the name of Cape Diamond to l'ointe à Puiseaux. See Map of Quebec (1613).

true, with feeble and uncertain progress, — priests, soldiers, peasants, feudal scutcheons, royal insignia: not the Middle Age, but engendered of it by the stronger life of modern centralization, sharply stamped with a parental likeness, heir to parental weakness and parental force.

In a few weeks a pile of wooden buildings rose on the brink of the St. Lawrence, on or near the site of the market-place of the Lower Town of Quebec.[1] The pencil of Champlain, always regardless of proportion and perspective, has preserved its likeness. A strong wooden wall, surmounted by a gallery loop-holed for musketry, enclosed three buildings, containing quarters for himself and his men, together with a courtyard, from one side of which rose a tall dove-cot, like a belfry. A moat surrounded the whole, and two or three small cannon were planted on salient platforms towards the river. There was a large storehouse near at hand, and a part of the adjacent ground was laid out as a garden.

In this garden Champlain was one morning directing his laborers, when Têtu, his pilot, approached him with an anxious countenance, and muttered a request to speak with him in private. Champlain assenting, they withdrew to the neighboring woods, when the pilot disburdened himself of his secret. One Antoine Natel, a locksmith, smitten by conscience or fear, had revealed to him a conspiracy to murder his commander and deliver Quebec into the

[1] Compare Faribault, *Voyages de Découverte au Canada*, 105.

hands of the Basques and Spaniards then at Tadoussac. Another locksmith, named Duval, was author of the plot, and, with the aid of three accomplices, had befooled or frightened nearly all the company into taking part in it. Each was assured that he should make his fortune, and all were mutually pledged to poniard the first betrayer of the secret. The critical point of their enterprise was the killing of Champlain. Some were for strangling him, some for raising a false alarm in the night and shooting him as he came out from his quarters.

Having heard the pilot's story, Champlain, remaining in the woods, desired his informant to find Antoine Natel, and bring him to the spot. Natel soon appeared, trembling with excitement and fear, and a close examination left no doubt of the truth of his statement. A small vessel, built by Pontgravé at Tadoussac, had lately arrived, and orders were now given that it should anchor close at hand. On board was a young man in whom confidence could be placed. Champlain sent him two bottles of wine, with a direction to tell the four ringleaders that they had been given him by his Basque friends at Tadoussac, and to invite them to share the good cheer. They came aboard in the evening, and were seized and secured. "Voyla donc mes galants bien estonnez," writes Champlain.

It was ten o'clock, and most of the men on shore were asleep. They were wakened suddenly, and told of the discovery of the plot and the arrest of the ringleaders. Pardon was then promised them, and they were dismissed again to their beds, greatly relieved; for they had lived in trepidation, each fearing the other. Duval's body, swinging from a gibbet, gave wholesome warning to those he had seduced; and his head was displayed on a pike, from the highest roof of the buildings, food for birds and a lesson to sedition. His three accomplices were carried by Pontgravé to France, where they made their atonement in the galleys.[1]

It was on the eighteenth of September that Pontgravé set sail, leaving Champlain with twenty-eight men to hold Quebec through the winter. Three weeks later, and shores and hills glowed with gay prognostics of approaching desolation, — the yellow and scarlet of the maples, the deep purple of the ash, the garnet hue of young oaks, the crimson of the tupelo at the water's edge, and the golden plumage of birch saplings in the fissures of the cliff. It was a short-lived beauty. The forest dropped its festal robes. Shrivelled and faded, they rustled to the earth. The crystal air and laughing sun of October passed away, and November sank upon the shivering waste, chill and sombre as the tomb.

A roving band of Montagnais had built their huts near the buildings, and were busying themselves with their autumn eel-fishery, on which they greatly relied to sustain their miserable lives through the winter. Their slimy harvest being gathered, and

[1] Lescarbot (1612), 623; Purchas, IV. 1642.

duly smoked and dried, they gave it for safe-keeping to Champlain, and set out to hunt beavers. It was deep in the winter before they came back, reclaimed their eels, built their birch cabins again, and disposed themselves for a life of ease, until famine or their enemies should put an end to their enjoyments. These were by no means without alloy. While, gorged with food, they lay dozing on piles of branches in their smoky huts, where, through the crevices of the thin birch bark, streamed in a cold capable at times of congealing mercury, their slumbers were beset with nightmare visions of Iroquois forays, scalpings, butcherings, and burnings. As dreams were their oracles, the camp was wild with fright. They sent out no scouts and placed no guard; but, with each repetition of these nocturnal terrors, they came flocking in a body to beg admission within the fort. The women and children were allowed to enter the yard and remain during the night, while anxious fathers and jealous husbands shivered in the darkness without.

On one occasion, a group of wretched beings was seen on the farther bank of the St. Lawrence, like wild animals driven by famine to the borders of the settler's clearing. The river was full of drifting ice, and there was no crossing without risk of life. The Indians, in their desperation, made the attempt; and midway their canoes were ground to atoms among the tossing masses. Agile as wild-cats, they all leaped upon a huge raft of ice, the squaws carrying their children on their shoulders, a feat at which Champlain marvelled when he saw their starved and emaciated condition. Here they began a wail of despair; when happily the pressure of other masses thrust the sheet of ice against the northern shore. They landed and soon made their appearance at the fort, worn to skeletons and horrible to look upon. The French gave them food, which they devoured with a frenzied avidity, and, unappeased, fell upon a dead dog left on the snow by Champlain for two months past as a bait for foxes. They broke this carrion into fragments, and thawed and devoured it, to the disgust of the spectators, who tried vainly to prevent them.

This was but a severe access of the periodical famine which, during winter, was a normal condition of the Algonquin tribes of Acadia and the Lower St. Lawrence, who, unlike the cognate tribes of New England, never tilled the soil, or made any reasonable provision against the time of need.

One would gladly know how the founders of Quebec spent the long hours of their first winter; but on this point the only man among them, perhaps, who could write, has not thought it necessary to enlarge. He himself beguiled his leisure with trapping foxes, or hanging a dead dog from a tree and watching the hungry martens in their efforts to reach it. Towards the close of winter, all found abundant employment in nursing themselves or their neighbors, for the inevitable scurvy broke out with virulence.

At the middle of May, only eight men of the twenty-eight were alive, and of these half were suffering from disease.[1]

This wintry purgatory wore away; the icy stalactites that hung from the cliffs fell crashing to the earth; the clamor of the wild geese was heard; the bluebirds appeared in the naked woods; the water-willows were covered with their soft caterpillar-like blossoms; the twigs of the swamp maple were flushed with ruddy bloom; the ash hung out its black tufts; the shad-bush seemed a wreath of snow; the white stars of the bloodroot gleamed among dank, fallen leaves; and in the young grass of the wet meadows the marsh-marigolds shone like spots of gold.

Great was the joy of Champlain when, on the fifth of June, he saw a sailboat rounding the Point of Orleans, betokening that the spring had brought with it the longed for succors. A son-in-law of Pontgravé, named Marais, was on board, and he reported that Pontgravé was then at Tadoussac, where he had lately arrived. Thither Champlain hastened, to take counsel with his comrade. His constitution or his courage had defied the scurvy. They met, and it was determined betwixt them, that, while Pontgravé remained in charge of Quebec, Champlain should enter at once on his long-meditated explorations, by which, like La Salle seventy years later, he had good hope of finding a way to China.

But there was a lion in the path. The Indian

[1] Champlain (1613), 205.

tribes, to whom peace was unknown, infested with their scalping parties the streams and pathways of the forest, and increased tenfold its inseparable risks. The after career of Champlain gives abundant proof that he was more than indifferent to all such chances; yet now an expedient for evading them offered itself, so consonant with his instincts that he was glad to accept it.

During the last autumn, a young chief from the banks of the then unknown Ottawa had been at Quebec; and, amazed at what he saw, he had begged Champlain to join him in the spring against his enemies. These enemies were a formidable race of savages, — the Iroquois, or Five Confederate Nations, who dwelt in fortified villages within limits now embraced by the State of New York, and who were a terror to all the surrounding forests. They were deadly foes of their kindred the Hurons, who dwelt on the lake which bears their name, and were allies of Algonquin bands on the Ottawa.[1] All alike were tillers of the soil, living at ease when compared with the famished Algonquins of the Lower St. Lawrence.

By joining these Hurons and Algonquins against their Iroquois enemies, Champlain might make him-

[1] The tribes east of the Mississippi, between the latitudes of Lake Superior and of the Ohio, were divided, with slight exceptions, into two groups or families, distinguished by a radical difference of language. One of these families of tribes is called *Algonquin*, from the name of a small Indian community on the Ottawa. The other is called the *Huron-Iroquois*, from the names of its two principal members.

self the indispensable ally and leader of the tribes of Canada, and at the same time fight his way to discovery in regions which otherwise were barred against him. From first to last it was the policy of France in America to mingle in Indian politics, hold the balance of power between adverse tribes, and envelop in the network of her power and diplomacy the remotest hordes of the wilderness. Of this policy the Father of New France may perhaps be held to have set a rash and premature example. Yet while he was apparently following the dictates of his own adventurous spirit, it became evident, a few years later, that under his thirst for discovery and spirit of knight-errantry lay a consistent and deliberate purpose. That it had already assumed a definite shape is not likely; but his after course makes it plain that, in embroiling himself and his colony with the most formidable savages on the continent, he was by no means acting so recklessly as at first sight would appear.

CHAPTER X.

1609.

LAKE CHAMPLAIN.

CHAMPLAIN JOINS A WAR PARTY. — PREPARATION. — DEPARTURE. — THE RIVER RICHELIEU. — THE SPIRITS CONSULTED. — DISCOVERY OF LAKE CHAMPLAIN. — BATTLE WITH THE IROQUOIS. — FATE OF PRISONERS. — PANIC OF THE VICTORS.

IT was past the middle of June, and the expected warriors from the upper country had not come, — a delay which seems to have given Champlain little concern, for, without waiting longer, he set out with no better allies than a band of Montagnais. But, as he moved up the St. Lawrence, he saw, thickly clustered in the bordering forest, the lodges of an Indian camp, and, landing, found his Huron and Algonquin allies. Few of them had ever seen a white man, and they surrounded the steel-clad strangers in speechless wonder. Champlain asked for their chief, and the staring throng moved with him towards a lodge where sat, not one chief, but two; for each band had its own. There were feasting, smoking, and speeches; and, the needful ceremony over, all descended together to Quebec; for the strangers were bent on seeing those wonders of architecture, the fame of which had pierced the recesses of their forests.

On their arrival, they feasted their eyes and glutted their appetites; yelped consternation at the sharp explosions of the arquebuse and the roar of the cannon; pitched their camps, and bedecked themselves for their war-dance. In the still night, their fire glared against the black and jagged cliff, and the fierce red light fell on tawny limbs convulsed with frenzied gestures and ferocious stampings; on contorted visages, hideous with paint; on brandished weapons, stone war-clubs, stone hatchets, and stone-pointed lances; while the drum kept up its hollow boom, and the air was split with mingled yells.

The war-feast followed, and then all embarked together. Champlain was in a small shallop, carrying, besides himself, eleven men of Pontgravé's party, including his son-in-law Marais and the pilot La Routte. They were armed with the arquebuse, — a matchlock or firelock somewhat like the modern carbine, and from its shortness not ill suited for use in the forest. On the twenty-eighth of June[1] they spread their sails and held their course against the current, while around them the river was alive with canoes, and hundreds of naked arms plied the paddle with a steady, measured sweep. They crossed the Lake of St. Peter, threaded the devious channels among its many islands, and reached at last the

[1] Champlain's dates, in this part of his narrative, are exceedingly careless and confused, May and June being mixed indiscriminately.

mouth of the Rivière des Iroquois, since called the Richelieu, or the St. John.[1] Here, probably on the site of the town of Sorel, the leisurely warriors encamped for two days, hunted, fished, and took their ease, regaling their allies with venison and wildfowl. They quarrelled, too; three fourths of their number seceded, took to their canoes in dudgeon, and paddled towards their homes, while the rest pursued their course up the broad and placid stream.

Walls of verdure stretched on left and right. Now, aloft in the lonely air rose the cliffs of Belœil, and now, before them, framed in circling forests, the Basin of Chambly spread its tranquil mirror, glittering in the sun. The shallop outsailed the canoes. Champlain, leaving his allies behind, crossed the basin and tried to pursue his course; but, as he listened in the stillness, the unwelcome noise of rapids reached his ear, and, by glimpses through the dark foliage of the Islets of St. John he could see the gleam of snowy foam and the flash of hurrying waters. Leaving the boat by the shore in charge of four men, he went with Marais, La Routte, and five others, to explore the wild before him. They pushed their way through the damps and shadows of the wood, through thickets and tangled vines, over mossy rocks and mouldering logs. Still the hoarse surging of the rapids followed them; and when, parting the screen of foliage, they looked out upon the river, they saw it thick set with rocks where, plunging over

---

[1] Also called the Chambly, the St. Louis, and the Sorel.

ledges, gurgling under drift-logs, darting along clefts, and boiling in chasms, the angry waters filled the solitude with monotonous ravings.[1]

Champlain retraced his steps. He had learned the value of an Indian's word. His allies had promised him that his boat could pass unobstructed throughout the whole journey. "It afflicted me," he says, "and troubled me exceedingly to be obliged to return without having seen so great a lake, full of fair islands and bordered with the fine countries which they had described to me."

When he reached the boat, he found the whole savage crew gathered at the spot. He mildly rebuked their bad faith, but added, that, though they had deceived him, he, as far as might be, would fulfil his pledge. To this end, he directed Marais, with the boat and the greater part of the men, to return to Quebec, while he, with two who offered to follow him, should proceed in the Indian canoes.

The warriors lifted their canoes from the water, and bore them on their shoulders half a league through the forest to the smoother stream above. Here the chiefs made a muster of their forces, counting twenty-four canoes and sixty warriors. All embarked again, and advanced once more, by marsh, meadow, forest, and scattered islands, — then full of game, for it was an uninhabited land, the war-path and battle-ground of hostile tribes. The warriors observed a certain

[1] In spite of the changes of civilization, the tourist, with Champlain's journal in his hand, can easily trace each stage of his progress.

system in their advance. Some were in front as a vanguard: others formed the main body; while an equal number were in the forests on the flanks and rear, hunting for the subsistence of the whole; for, though they had a provision of parched maize pounded into meal, they kept it for use when, from the vicinity of the enemy, hunting should become impossible.

Late in the day they landed and drew up their canoes, ranging them closely, side by side. Some stripped sheets of bark, to cover their camp sheds; others gathered wood, the forest being full of dead, dry trees; others felled the living trees, for a barricade. They seem to have had steel axes, obtained by barter from the French; for in less than two hours they had made a strong defensive work, in the form of a half-circle, open on the river side, where their canoes lay on the strand, and large enough to enclose all their huts and sheds.[1] Some of their number had gone forward as scouts, and, returning, reported no signs of an enemy. This was the extent of their precaution, for they placed no guard, but all, in full security, stretched themselves to sleep, — a vicious custom from which the lazy warrior of the forest rarely departs.

They had not forgotten, however, to consult their

---

[1] Such extempore works of defence are still used among some tribes of the remote West. The author has twice seen them, made of trees piled together as described by Champlain, probably by war parties of the Crow or Snake Indians.

Champlain, usually too concise, is very minute in his description of the march and encampment.

oracle. The medicine-man pitched his magic lodge in the woods, formed of a small stack of poles, planted in a circle and brought together at the tops like stacked muskets. Over these he placed the filthy deer-skins which served him for a robe, and, creeping in at a narrow opening, hid himself from view. Crouched in a ball upon the earth, he invoked the spirits in mumbling inarticulate tones; while his naked auditory, squatted on the ground like apes, listened in wonder and awe. Suddenly, the lodge moved, rocking with violence to and fro, — by the power of the spirits, as the Indians thought, while Champlain could plainly see the tawny fist of the medicine-man shaking the poles. They begged him to keep a watchful eye on the peak of the lodge, whence fire and smoke would presently issue; but with the best efforts of his vision, he discovered none. Meanwhile the medicine-man was seized with such convulsions, that, when his divination was over, his naked body streamed with perspiration. In loud, clear tones, and in an unknown tongue, he invoked the spirit, who was understood to be present in the form of a stone, and whose feeble and squeaking accents were heard at intervals, like the wail of a young puppy.[1]

[1] This mode of divination was universal among the Algonquin tribes, and is not extinct to this day among their roving Northern bands. Le Jeune, Lafitau, and other early Jesuit writers, describe it with great minuteness. The former (*Relation*, 1634) speaks of an audacious conjurer, who, having invoked the Manitou, or spirit, killed him with a hatchet. To all appearance he was a stone, which, however, when struck with the hatchet, proved to be full of flesh and blood. A kindred superstition prevails among the Crow Indians.

In this manner they consulted the spirit — as Champlain thinks, the Devil — at all their camps. His replies, for the most part, seem to have given them great content; yet they took other measures, of which the military advantages were less questionable. The principal chief gathered bundles of sticks, and, without wasting his breath, stuck them in the earth in a certain order, calling each by the name of some warrior, a few taller than the rest representing the subordinate chiefs. Thus was indicated the position which each was to hold in the expected battle. All gathered round and attentively studied the sticks, ranged like a child's wooden soldiers, or the pieces on a chessboard; then, with no further instruction, they formed their ranks, broke them, and reformed them again and again with excellent alacrity and skill.

Again the canoes advanced, the river widening as they went. Great islands appeared, leagues in extent, — Isle à la Motte, Long Island, Grande Isle; channels where ships might float and broad reaches of water stretched between them, and Champlain entered the lake which preserves his name to posterity. Cumberland Head was passed, and from the opening of the great channel between Grande Isle and the main he could look forth on the wilderness sea. Edged with woods, the tranquil flood spread southward beyond the sight. Far on the left rose the forest ridges of the Green Mountains, and on the right the Adirondacks, — haunts in these later years of amateur sportsmen from counting-rooms or college halls. Then the Iroquois made them their hunting-ground; and beyond, in the valleys of the Mohawk, the Onondaga, and the Genesee, stretched the long line of their five cantons and palisaded towns.

At night they encamped again. The scene is a familiar one to many a tourist; and perhaps, standing at sunset on the peaceful strand, Champlain saw what a roving student of this generation has seen on those same shores, at that same hour, — the glow of the vanished sun behind the western mountains, darkly piled in mist and shadow along the sky; near at hand, the dead pine, mighty in decay, stretching its ragged arms athwart the burning heaven, the crow perched on its top like an image carved in jet; and aloft, the nighthawk, circling in his flight, and, with a strange whirring sound, diving through the air each moment for the insects he makes his prey.

The progress of the party was becoming dangerous. They changed their mode of advance and moved only in the night. All day they lay close in the depth of the forest, sleeping, lounging, smoking tobacco of their own raising, and beguiling the hours, no doubt, with the shallow banter and obscene jesting with which knots of Indians are wont to amuse their leisure. At twilight they embarked again, paddling their cautious way till the eastern sky began to redden. Their goal was the rocky promontory where Fort Ticonderoga was long afterward built. Thence, they would pass the outlet of Lake George, and launch their canoes again on that Como of the wilderness, whose waters, limpid as a fountain-head, stretched far southward between their flanking mountains. Landing at the future site of Fort William Henry, they would carry their canoes through the forest to the river Hudson, and, descending it, attack perhaps some outlying town of the Mohawks. In the next century this chain of lakes and rivers became the grand highway of savage and civilized war, linked to memories of momentous conflicts.

The allies were spared so long a progress. On the morning of the twenty-ninth of July, after paddling all night, they hid as usual in the forest on the western shore, apparently between Crown Point and Ticonderoga. The warriors stretched themselves to their slumbers, and Champlain, after walking till nine or ten o'clock through the surrounding woods, returned to take his repose on a pile of spruce-boughs. Sleeping, he dreamed a dream, wherein he beheld the Iroquois drowning in the lake; and, trying to rescue them, he was told by his Algonquin friends that they were good for nothing, and had better be left to their fate. For some time past he had been beset every morning by his superstitious allies, eager to learn about his dreams; and, to this moment, his unbroken slumbers had failed to furnish the desired prognostics. The announcement of this auspicious vision filled the crowd with joy, and at nightfall they embarked, flushed with anticipated victories.[1]

[1] The power of dreams among Indians in their primitive condition can scarcely be over-estimated. Among the ancient Hurons and

ENCOUNTER WITH THE IROQUOIS.

It was ten o'clock in the evening, when, near a projecting point of land, which was probably Ticonderoga, they descried dark objects in motion on the lake before them. These were a flotilla of Iroquois canoes, heavier and slower than theirs, for they were made of oak bark.[1] Each party saw the other, and the mingled war-cries pealed over the darkened water. The Iroquois, who were near the shore, having no stomach for an aquatic battle, landed, and, making night hideous with their clamors, began to barricade themselves. Champlain could see them in the woods, laboring like beavers, hacking down trees with iron axes taken from the Canadian tribes in war, and with stone hatchets of their own making. The allies remained on the lake, a bowshot from the hostile barricade, their canoes made fast together by poles lashed across. All night they

cognate tribes, they were the universal authority and oracle; but while a dreamer of reputation had unlimited power, the dream of a *vaurien* was held in no account. There were professed interpreters of dreams. Brébeuf, *Rel. des Hurons*, 117. A man, dreaming that he had killed his wife, made it an excuse for killing her in fact. All these tribes, including the Iroquois, had a stated game called *Ononhara*, or the dreaming game, in which dreams were made the pretext for the wildest extravagances. See Lafitau, Charlevoix, Sagard, Brébeuf, etc.

[1] Champlain (1613), 232. Probably a mistake; the Iroquois canoes were usually of elm bark. The paper-birch was used wherever it could be had, being incomparably the best material. All the tribes, from the mouth of the Saco northward and eastward, and along the entire northern portion of the valley of the St. Lawrence and the Great Lakes, used the birch. The best substitutes were elm and spruce. The birch bark, from its laminated texture, could be peeled at any time; the others only when the sap was in motion.

danced with as much vigor as the frailty of their vessels would permit, their throats making amends for the enforced restraint of their limbs. It was agreed on both sides that the fight should be deferred till daybreak; but meanwhile a commerce of abuse, sarcasm, menace, and boasting gave unceasing exercise to the lungs and fancy of the combatants, — "much," says Champlain, "like the besiegers and besieged in a beleaguered town."

As day approached, he and his two followers put on the light armor of the time. Champlain wore the doublet and long hose then in vogue. Over the doublet he buckled on a breastplate, and probably a back-piece, while his thighs were protected by cuisses of steel, and his head by a plumed casque. Across his shoulder hung the strap of his bandoleer, or ammunition-box; at his side was his sword, and in his hand his arquebuse.[1] Such was the equipment of this ancient Indian-fighter, whose exploits date eleven years before the landing of the Puritans at Plymouth, and sixty-six years before King Philip's War.

Each of the three Frenchmen was in a separate canoe, and, as it grew light, they kept themselves hidden, either by lying at the bottom, or covering themselves with an Indian robe. The canoes approached the shore, and all landed without opposi-

[1] Champlain, in his rude drawing of the battle (ed. 1613), portrays himself and his equipment with sufficient distinctness. Compare plates of the weapons and armor of the period in Meyrick, *Ancient Armor*, and Susane, *Histoire de l'Ancienne Infanterie Française.*

tion at some distance from the Iroquois, whom they presently could see filing out of their barricade, — tall, strong men, some two hundred in number, the boldest and fiercest warriors of North America. They advanced through the forest with a steadiness which excited the admiration of Champlain. Among them could be seen three chiefs, made conspicuous by their tall plumes. Some bore shields of wood and hide, and some were covered with a kind of armor made of tough twigs interlaced with a vegetable fibre supposed by Champlain to be cotton.[1]

The allies, growing anxious, called with loud cries for their champion, and opened their ranks that he might pass to the front. He did so, and, advancing before his red companions in arms, stood revealed to the gaze of the Iroquois, who, beholding the warlike apparition in their path, stared in mute amazement. "I looked at them," says Champlain, "and they looked at me. When I saw them getting ready to shoot their arrows at us, I levelled my arquebuse, which I had loaded with four balls, and aimed straight at one of the three chiefs. The shot brought down two, and wounded another. On this, our Indians set up such a yelling that one could not have heard a

[1] According to Lafitau, both bucklers and breastplates were in frequent use among the Iroquois. The former were very large and made of cedar wood covered with interwoven thongs of hide. The kindred nation of the Hurons, says Sagard (*Voyage des Hurons*, 126–206), carried large shields, and wore greaves for the legs and cuirasses made of twigs interwoven with cords. His account corresponds with that of Champlain, who gives a wood-cut of a warrior thus armed.

thunder-clap, and all the while the arrows flew thick on both sides. The Iroquois were greatly astonished and frightened to see two of their men killed so quickly, in spite of their arrow-proof armor. As I was reloading, one of my companions fired a shot from the woods, which so increased their astonishment that, seeing their chiefs dead, they abandoned the field and fled into the depth of the forest." The allies dashed after them. Some of the Iroquois were killed, and more were taken. Camp, canoes, provisions, all were abandoned, and many weapons flung down in the panic flight. The victory was complete.

At night, the victors led out one of the prisoners, told him that he was to die by fire, and ordered him to sing his death-song if he dared. Then they began the torture, and presently scalped their victim alive,[1] when Champlain, sickening at the sight, begged leave to shoot him. They refused, and he turned away in anger and disgust; on which they called him back and told him to do as he pleased. He turned again, and a shot from his arquebuse put the wretch out of misery.

[1] It has been erroneously asserted that the practice of scalping did not prevail among the Indians before the advent of Europeans. In 1535, Cartier saw five scalps at Quebec, dried and stretched on hoops. In 1564, Laudonnière saw them among the Indians of Florida. The Algonquins of New England and Nova Scotia were accustomed to cut off and carry away the head, which they afterwards scalped. Those of Canada, it seems, sometimes scalped dead bodies on the field. The Algonquin practice of carrying off heads as trophies is mentioned by Lalemant, Roger Williams, Lescarbot, and Champlain. Compare *Historical Magazine*, First Series, V. 253.

The scene filled him with horror; but a few months later, on the Place de la Grève at Paris, he might have witnessed tortures equally revolting and equally vindictive, inflicted on the regicide Ravaillac by the sentence of grave and learned judges.

The allies made a prompt retreat from the scene of their triumph. Three or four days brought them to the mouth of the Richelieu. Here they separated; the Hurons and Algonquins made for the Ottawa, their homeward route, each with a share of prisoners for future torments. At parting, they invited Champlain to visit their towns and aid them again in their wars, an invitation which this paladin of the woods failed not to accept.

The companions now remaining to him were the Montagnais. In their camp on the Richelieu, one of them dreamed that a war party of Iroquois was close upon them; on which, in a torrent of rain, they left their huts, paddled in dismay to the islands above the Lake of St. Peter, and hid themselves all night in the rushes. In the morning they took heart, emerged from their hiding-places, descended to Quebec, and went thence to Tadoussac, whither Champlain accompanied them. Here the squaws, stark naked, swam out to the canoes to receive the heads of the dead Iroquois, and, hanging them from their necks, danced in triumph along the shore. One of the heads and a pair of arms were then bestowed on Champlain, — touching memorials of gratitude, which, however, he was by no means to keep for himself, but to present to the King.

Thus did New France rush into collision with the redoubted warriors of the Five Nations. Here was the beginning, and in some measure doubtless the cause, of a long suite of murderous conflicts, bearing havoc and flame to generations yet unborn. Champlain had invaded the tiger's den; and now, in smothered fury, the patient savage would lie biding his day of blood.

CHAPTER XI.

1610–1612.

WAR. — TRADE. — DISCOVERY.

CHAMPLAIN AT FONTAINEBLEAU. — CHAMPLAIN ON THE ST. LAWRENCE. — ALARM. — BATTLE. — WAR PARTIES. — ICEBERGS. — ADVENTURERS. — CHAMPLAIN AT MONTREAL. — RETURN TO FRANCE. — THE COMTE DE SOISSONS. — THE PRINCE DE CONDÉ.

CHAMPLAIN and Pontgravé returned to France, while Pierre Chauvin of Dieppe held Quebec in their absence. The King was at Fontainebleau, — it was a few months before his assassination, — and here Champlain recounted his adventures, to the great satisfaction of the lively monarch. He gave him also, not the head of the dead Iroquois, but a belt wrought in embroidery of dyed quills of the Canada porcupine, together with two small birds of scarlet plumage, and the skull of a gar-fish.

De Monts was at court, striving for a renewal of his monopoly. His efforts failed; on which, with great spirit but little discretion, he resolved to push his enterprise without it. Early in the spring of 1610, the ship was ready, and Champlain and Pontgravé were on board, when a violent illness seized the former, reducing him to the most miserable of all conflicts, the battle of the eager spirit against the treacherous and failing flesh. Having partially recovered, he put to sea, giddy and weak, in wretched plight for the hard career of toil and battle which the New World offered him. The voyage was prosperous, no other mishap occurring than that of an ardent youth of St. Malo, who drank the health of Pontgravé with such persistent enthusiasm that he fell overboard and was drowned.

There were ships at Tadoussac, fast loading with furs; and boats, too, higher up the river, anticipating the trade, and draining De Monts's resources in advance. Champlain, who was left free to fight and explore wherever he should see fit, had provided, to use his own phrase, "two strings to his bow." On the one hand, the Montagnais had promised to guide him northward to Hudson's Bay; on the other, the Hurons were to show him the Great Lakes, with the mines of copper on their shores; and to each the same reward was promised, — to join them against the common foe, the Iroquois. The rendezvous was at the mouth of the river Richelieu. Thither the Hurons were to descend in force, together with Algonquins of the Ottawa; and thither Champlain now repaired, while around his boat swarmed a multitude of Montagnais canoes, filled with warriors whose lank hair streamed loose in the wind.

There is an island in the St. Lawrence near the mouth of the Richelieu. On the nineteenth of June it was swarming with busy and clamorous savages, —

Champlain's Montagnais allies, cutting down the trees and clearing the ground for a dance and a feast; for they were hourly expecting the Algonquin warriors, and were eager to welcome them with befitting honors. But suddenly, far out on the river, they saw an advancing canoe. Now on this side, now on that, the flashing paddles urged it forward as if death were on its track; and as it drew near, the Indians on board cried out that the Algonquins were in the forest, a league distant, engaged with a hundred warriors of the Iroquois, who, outnumbered, were fighting savagely within a barricade of trees.

The air was split with shrill outcries. The Montagnais snatched their weapons, — shields, bows, arrows, war-clubs, sword-blades made fast to poles, — and ran headlong to their canoes, impeding each other in their haste, screeching to Champlain to follow, and invoking with no less vehemence the aid of certain fur-traders, just arrived in four boats from below. These, as it was not their cue to fight, lent them a deaf ear; on which, in disgust and scorn, they paddled off, calling to the recusants that they were women, fit for nothing but to make war on beaver-skins.

Champlain and four of his men were in the canoes. They shot across the intervening water, and, as their prows grated on the pebbles, each warrior flung down his paddle, snatched his weapons, and ran into the woods. The five Frenchmen followed, striving vainly to keep pace with the naked, light-limbed rabble, bounding like shadows through the forest. They quickly disappeared. Even their shrill cries grew faint, till Champlain and his men, discomforted and vexed, found themselves deserted in the midst of a swamp. The day was sultry, the forest air heavy, close, and filled with hosts of mosquitoes, "so thick," says the chief sufferer, "that we could scarcely draw breath, and it was wonderful how cruelly they persecuted us."[1] Through black mud, spongy moss, water knee-deep, over fallen trees, among slimy logs and entangling roots, tripped by vines, lashed by recoiling boughs, panting under their steel head-pieces and heavy corselets, the Frenchmen struggled on, bewildered and indignant. At length they descried two Indians running in the distance, and shouted to them in desperation, that, if they wanted their aid, they must guide them to the enemy.

At length they could hear the yells of the combatants; there was light in the forest before them, and they issued into a partial clearing made by the Iroquois axemen near the river. Champlain saw their barricade. Trees were piled into a circular breastwork, trunks, boughs, and matted foliage forming a strong defence, within which the Iroquois stood savagely at bay. Around them flocked the allies, half hidden in the edges of the forest, like hounds around a wild boar, eager, clamorous, yet

[1] " . . . quantité de mousquites, qui estoient si espoisses qu'elles ne nous permettoient point presque de reprendre nostre halaine, tant elles nous persécutoient, et si cruellement que c'estoit chose estrange." Champlain (1613), 250.

afraid to rush in. They had attacked, and had met a bloody rebuff. All their hope was now in the French; and when they saw them, a yell arose from hundreds of throats that outdid the wilderness voices whence its tones were borrowed, — the whoop of the horned owl, the scream of the cougar, the howl of starved wolves on a winter night. A fierce response pealed from the desperate band within; and, amid a storm of arrows from both sides, the Frenchmen threw themselves into the fray, firing at random through the fence of trunks, boughs, and drooping leaves, with which the Iroquois had encircled themselves. Champlain felt a stone-headed arrow splitting his ear and tearing through the muscles of his neck. He drew it out, and, the moment after, did a similar office for one of his men. But the Iroquois had not recovered from their first terror at the arquebuse; and when the mysterious and terrible assailants, clad in steel and armed with thunder-bolts, ran up to the barricade, thrust their pieces through the openings, and shot death among the crowd within, they could not control their fright, but with every report threw themselves flat on the ground. Animated with unwonted valor, the allies, covered by their large shields, began to drag out the felled trees of the barricade, while others, under Champlain's direction, gathered at the edge of the forest, preparing to close the affair with a final rush. New actors soon appeared on the scene. These were a boat's crew of the fur-traders under a young man of St. Malo, one Des

Prairies, who, when he heard the firing, could not resist the impulse to join the fight. On seeing them, Champlain checked the assault, in order, as he says, that the new-comers might have their share in the sport. The traders opened fire, with great zest and no less execution; while the Iroquois, now wild with terror, leaped and writhed to dodge the shot which tore through their frail armor of twigs. Champlain gave the signal; the crowd ran to the barricade, dragged down the boughs or clambered over them, and bore themselves, in his own words, "so well and manfully," that, though scratched and torn by the sharp points, they quickly forced an entrance. The French ceased their fire, and, followed by a smaller body of Indians, scaled the barricade on the farther side. Now, amid howlings, shouts, and screeches, the work was finished. Some of the Iroquois were cut down as they stood, hewing with their war-clubs, and foaming like slaughtered tigers; some climbed the barrier and were killed by the furious crowd without; some were drowned in the river; while fifteen, the only survivors, were made prisoners. "By the grace of God," writes Champlain, "behold the battle won!" Drunk with ferocious ecstasy, the conquerors scalped the dead and gathered fagots for the living; while some of the fur-traders, too late to bear part in the fight, robbed the carcasses of their blood-bedrenched robes of beaver-skin amid the derision of the surrounding Indians.[1]

[1] Champlain (1613), 254. This narrative, like most others, is much abridged in the edition of 1632.

That night, the torture fires blazed along the shore. Champlain saved one prisoner from their clutches, but nothing could save the rest. One body was quartered and eaten.[1] "As for the rest of the prisoners," says Champlain, "they were kept to be put to death by the women and girls, who in this respect are no less inhuman than the men, and, indeed, much more so; for by their subtlety they invent more cruel tortures, and take pleasure in it."

On the next day, a large band of Hurons appeared at the rendezvous, greatly vexed that they had come too late. The shores were thickly studded with Indian huts, and the woods were full of them. Here were warriors of three designations, including many subordinate tribes, and representing three grades of savage society, — the Hurons, the Algonquins of the Ottawa, and the Montagnais; afterwards styled by a Franciscan friar, than whom few men better knew them, the nobles, the burghers, and the peasantry and paupers of the forest.[2] Many of them, from the remote interior, had never before seen a white man;

---

[1] Traces of cannibalism may be found among most of the North American tribes, though they are rarely very conspicuous. Sometimes the practice arose, as in the present instance, from revenge or ferocity; sometimes it bore a religious character, as with the Miamis, among whom there existed a secret religious fraternity of man-eaters; sometimes the heart of a brave enemy was devoured in the idea that it made the eater brave. This last practice was common. The ferocious threat, used in speaking of an enemy, "I will eat his heart," is by no means a mere figure of speech. The roving hunter-tribes, in their winter wanderings, were not infrequently impelled to cannibalism by famine.

[2] Sagard, *Voyage des Hurons*, 184.

and, wrapped like statues in their robes, they stood gazing on the French with a fixed stare of wild and wondering eyes.

Judged by the standard of Indian war, a heavy blow had been struck on the common enemy. Here were hundreds of assembled warriors; yet none thought of following up their success. Elated with unexpected fortune, they danced and sang; then loaded their canoes, hung their scalps on poles, broke up their camps, and set out triumphant for their homes. Champlain had fought their battles, and now might claim, on their part, guidance and escort to the distant interior. Why he did not do so is scarcely apparent. There were cares, it seems, connected with the very life of his puny colony, which demanded his return to France. Nor were his anxieties lessened by the arrival of a ship from his native town of Brouage, with tidings of the King's assassination. Here was a death-blow to all that had remained of De Monts's credit at court; while that unfortunate nobleman, like his old associate, Poutrincourt, was moving with swift strides toward financial ruin. With the revocation of his monopoly, fur-traders had swarmed to the St. Lawrence. Tadoussac was full of them, and for that year the trade was spoiled. Far from aiding to support a burdensome enterprise of colonization, it was in itself an occasion of heavy loss.

Champlain bade farewell to his garden at Quebec, where maize, wheat, rye, and barley, with vegetables of all kinds, and a small vineyard of native grapes, — for he was a zealous horticulturist,[1] — held forth a promise which he was not to see fulfilled. He left one Du Parc in command, with sixteen men, and, sailing on the eighth of August, arrived at Honfleur, with no worse accident than that of running over a sleeping whale near the Grand Bank.

With the opening spring he was afloat again. Perils awaited him worse than those of Iroquois tomahawks; for, approaching Newfoundland, the ship was entangled for days among drifting fields and bergs of ice. Escaping at length, she arrived at Tadoussac on the thirteenth of May, 1611. She had anticipated the spring. Forests and mountains, far and near, all were white with snow. A principal object with Champlain was to establish such relations with the great Indian communities of the interior as to secure to De Monts and his associates the advantage of trade with them; and to this end he now repaired to Montreal, a position in the gateway, as it were, of their yearly descents of trade or war. On arriving, he began to survey the ground for the site of a permanent post.

A few days convinced him, that, under the present system, all his efforts would be vain. Wild reports of the wonders of New France had gone abroad, and a crowd of hungry adventurers had hastened to the land of promise, eager to grow rich, they scarcely

[1] During the next year, he planted roses around Quebec. Champlain (1613), 313.

knew how, and soon to return disgusted. A fleet of
boats and small vessels followed in Champlain's wake.
Within a few days, thirteen of them arrived at Montreal, and more soon appeared. He was to break the
ground; others would reap the harvest. Travel, discovery, and battle, all must inure to the profit, not
of the colony, but of a crew of greedy traders.

Champlain, however, chose the site and cleared
the ground for his intended post. It was immediately above a small stream, now running under arches
of masonry, and entering the St. Lawrence at Point
Callières, within the modern city. He called it
Place Royale;[1] and here, on the margin of the river,
he built a wall of bricks made on the spot, in order
to measure the destructive effects of the "ice-shove"
in the spring.

Now, down the surges of St. Louis, where the
mighty floods of the St. Lawrence, contracted to a
narrow throat, roll in fury among their sunken rocks,
— here, through foam and spray and the roar of the
angry torrent, a fleet of birch canoes came dancing
like dry leaves on the froth of some riotous brook.
They bore a band of Hurons first at the rendezvous.
As they drew near the landing, all the fur-traders'
boats blazed out a clattering fusillade, which was
designed to bid them welcome, but in fact terrified
many of them to such a degree that they scarcely dared
to come ashore. Nor were they reassured by the

[1] The mountain being Mont Royal (Montreal). The Hospital of
the Gray Nuns was built on a portion of Champlain's Place Royale.

bearing of the disorderly crowd, who, in jealous competition for their beaver-skins, left them not a moment's peace, and outraged all their notions of decorum. More soon appeared, till hundreds of warriors were encamped along the shore, all restless, suspicious, and alarmed. Late one night they awakened Champlain. On going with them to their camp, he found chiefs and warriors in solemn conclave around the glimmering firelight. Though they were fearful of the rest, their trust in him was boundless. "Come to our country, buy our beaver, build a fort, teach us the true faith, do what you will, but do not bring this crowd with you." The idea had seized them that these lawless bands of rival traders, all well armed, meant to plunder and kill them. Champlain assured them of safety, and the whole night was consumed in friendly colloquy. Soon afterward, however, the camp broke up, and the uneasy warriors removed to the borders of the Lake of St. Louis, placing the rapids betwixt themselves and the objects of their alarm. Here Champlain visited them, and hence these intrepid canoe-men, kneeling in their birchen egg-shells, carried him homeward down the rapids, somewhat, as he admits, to the discomposure of his nerves.[1]

[1] The first white man to descend the rapids of St. Louis was a youth named Louis, who, on the 10th of June, 1611, went with two Indians to shoot herons on an island, and was drowned on the way down; the second was a young man who in the summer before had gone with the Hurons to their country, and who returned with them on the 13th of June; the third was Champlain himself.

The great gathering dispersed: the traders descended to Tadoussac, and Champlain to Quebec; while the Indians went, some to their homes, some to fight the Iroquois. A few months later, Champlain was in close conference with De Monts at Pons, a place near Rochelle, of which the latter was governor. The last two years had made it apparent, that, to keep the colony alive and maintain a basis for those discoveries on which his heart was bent, was impossible without a change of system. De Monts, engrossed with the cares of his government, placed all in the hands of his associate; and Champlain, fully empowered to act as he should judge expedient, set out for Paris. On the way, Fortune, at one stroke, wellnigh crushed him and New France together; for his horse fell on him, and he narrowly escaped with life. When he was partially recovered, he resumed his journey, pondering on means of rescue for the fading colony. A powerful protector must be had, — a great name to shield the enterprise from assaults and intrigues of jealous rival interests. On reaching Paris he addressed himself to a prince of the blood, Charles de Bourbon, Comte de Soissons; described New France, its resources, and its boundless extent; urged the need of unfolding a mystery pregnant perhaps with results of the deepest moment; laid before him maps and memoirs, and begged him to become the guardian of this new world. The royal consent being obtained, the Comte de Soissons became Lieutenant-General for the King in New France, with vice-regal powers. These, in turn, he conferred upon Champlain, making him his lieutenant, with full control over the trade in furs at and above Quebec, and with power to associate with himself such persons as he saw fit, to aid in the exploration and settlement of the country.[1]

Scarcely was the commission drawn when the Comte de Soissons, attacked with fever, died, — to the joy of the Breton and Norman traders, whose jubilation, however, found a speedy end. Henri de Bourbon, Prince de Condé, first prince of the blood, assumed the vacant protectorship. He was grandson of the gay and gallant Condé of the civil wars, was father of the great Condé, the youthful victor of Rocroy, and was husband of Charlotte de Montmorency, whose blond beauties had fired the inflammable heart of Henry the Fourth. To the unspeakable wrath of that keen lover, the prudent Condé fled with his bride, first to Brussels, and then to Italy; nor did he return to France till the regicide's knife had put his jealous fears to rest.[2] After his return, he began to intrigue against the court. He was a man of common abilities, greedy of money and power, and scarcely seeking even the decency of a pretext

---

[1] *Commission de Monseigneur le Comte de Soissons donnée au Sieur de Champlein*, 15 *Oct.*, 1612. See Champlain (1632), 231, and *Mémoires des Commissaires*, II. 451.

[2] The anecdote, as told by the Princess herself to her wandering court during the romantic campaigning of the Fronde, will be found in the curious *Mémoires de Lenet*.

to cover his mean ambition.[1] His chief honor — an honor somewhat equivocal — is, as Voltaire observes, to have been father of the great Condé. Busy with his intrigues, he cared little for colonies and discoveries; and his rank and power were his sole qualifications for his new post.

In Champlain alone was the life of New France. By instinct and temperament he was more impelled to the adventurous toils of exploration than to the duller task of building colonies. The profits of trade had value in his eyes only as means to these ends, and settlements were important chiefly as a base of discovery. Two great objects eclipsed all others, — to find a route to the Indies, and to bring the heathen tribes into the embraces of the Church, since, while he cared little for their bodies, his solicitude for their souls knew no bounds.

It was no part of his plan to establish an odious monopoly. He sought rather to enlist the rival traders in his cause; and he now, in concurrence with De Monts, invited them to become sharers in the traffic, under certain regulations, and on condition of aiding in the establishment and support of the colony. The merchants of St. Malo and Rouen accepted the terms, and became members of the new company; but the intractable heretics of Rochelle, refractory in commerce as in religion, kept aloof, and preferred the chances of an illicit trade. The pros-

---

[1] *Mémoires de Madame de Motteville, passim* ; Sismondi, *Histoire des Français*, XXIV., XXV., *passim*.

pects of New France were far from flattering; for little could be hoped from this unwilling league of selfish traders, each jealous of the rest. They gave the Prince of Condé large gratuities to secure his countenance and support. The hungry viceroy took them, and with these emoluments his interest in the colony ended.

CHAPTER XII.

1612, 1613.

THE IMPOSTOR VIGNAU.

ILLUSIONS.— A PATH TO THE NORTH SEA. — THE OTTAWA.— FOREST TRAVELLERS. — INDIAN FEAST. — THE IMPOSTOR EXPOSED. — RETURN TO MONTREAL.

THE arrangements just indicated were a work of time. In the summer of 1612, Champlain was forced to forego his yearly voyage to New France; nor, even in the following spring, were his labors finished and the rival interests brought to harmony. Meanwhile, incidents occurred destined to have no small influence on his movements. Three years before, after his second fight with the Iroquois, a young man of his company had boldly volunteered to join the Indians on their homeward journey, and winter among them. Champlain gladly assented, and in the following summer the adventurer returned. Another young man, one Nicolas de Vignau, next offered himself; and he also, embarking in the Algonquin canoes, passed up the Ottawa, and was seen no more for a twelvemonth. In 1612 he reappeared in Paris, bringing a tale of wonders; for, says Champlain, "he was the most impudent liar that has been seen for many a day." He averred that at the sources of the Ottawa he had found a great lake; that he had crossed it, and discovered a river flowing northward; that he had descended this river, and reached the shores of the sea; that here he had seen the wreck of an English ship, whose crew, escaping to land, had been killed by the Indians; and that this sea was distant from Montreal only seventeen days by canoe. The clearness, consistency, and apparent simplicity of his story deceived Champlain, who had heard of a voyage of the English to the northern seas, coupled with rumors of wreck and disaster,[1] and was thus confirmed in his belief of Vignau's honesty. The Maréchal de Brissac, the President Jeannin, and other persons of eminence about the court, greatly interested by these dexterous fabrications, urged Champlain to follow up without delay a discovery which promised results so important; while he, with the Pacific, Japan, China, the Spice Islands, and India stretching in flattering vista before his fancy, entered with eagerness on the chase of this illusion. Early in the spring of 1613 the unwearied voyager crossed the Atlantic, and sailed up the St. Lawrence. On Monday, the twenty-seventh of May, he left the Island of St. Helen, opposite Montreal, with four Frenchmen, one of whom was Nicolas de Vignau, and one Indian, in two small canoes. They passed

[1] Evidently the voyage of Henry Hudson in 1610–12, when that navigator, after discovering Hudson's Strait, lost his life through a mutiny. Compare Jérémie, *Relation*, in *Recueil de Voyages au Nord*, VI.

the swift current at St. Ann's, crossed the Lake of Two Mountains, and advanced up the Ottawa till the rapids of Carillon and the Long Saut checked their course. So dense and tangled was the forest, that they were forced to remain in the bed of the river, trailing their canoes along the bank with cords, or pushing them by main force up the current. Champlain's foot slipped; he fell in the rapids, two boulders, against which he braced himself, saving him from being swept down, while the cord of the canoe, twisted round his hand, nearly severed it. At length they reached smoother water, and presently met fifteen canoes of friendly Indians. Champlain gave them the most awkward of his Frenchmen and took one of their number in return, — an exchange greatly to his profit.

All day they plied their paddles, and when night came they made their camp-fire in the forest. He who now, when two centuries and a half are passed, would see the evening bivouac of Champlain, has but to encamp, with Indian guides, on the upper waters of this same Ottawa, or on the borders of some lonely river of New Brunswick or of Maine.

Day dawned. The east glowed with tranquil fire, that pierced with eyes of flame the fir-trees whose jagged tops stood drawn in black against the burning heaven. Beneath, the glossy river slept in shadow, or spread far and wide in sheets of burnished bronze; and the white moon, paling in the face of day, hung like a disk of silver in the western sky. Now a fervid light touched the dead top of the hemlock, and creeping downward bathed the mossy beard of the patriarchal cedar, unstirred in the breathless air; now a fiercer spark beamed from the east; and now, half risen on the sight, a dome of crimson fire, the sun blazed with floods of radiance across the awakened wilderness.

The canoes were launched again, and the voyagers held their course. Soon the still surface was flecked with spots of foam; islets of froth floated by, tokens of some great convulsion. Then, on their left, the falling curtain of the Rideau shone like silver betwixt its bordering woods, and in front, white as a snow-drift, the cataracts of the Chaudière barred their way. They saw the unbridled river careering down its sheeted rocks, foaming in unfathomed chasms, wearying the solitude with the hoarse outcry of its agony and rage.

On the brink of the rocky basin where the plunging torrent boiled like a caldron, and puffs of spray sprang out from its concussion like smoke from the throat of a cannon, Champlain's two Indians took their stand, and, with a loud invocation, threw tobacco into the foam, — an offering to the local spirit, the Manitou of the cataract.[1]

[1] An invariable custom with the upper Indians on passing this place. When many were present, it was attended with solemn dances and speeches, a contribution of tobacco being first taken on a dish. It was thought to insure a safe voyage; but was often an occasion of disaster, since hostile war parties, lying in ambush at the spot, would surprise and kill the votaries of the Manitou in the very presence of their

They shouldered their canoes over the rocks, and through the woods; then launched them again, and, with toil and struggle, made their amphibious way, pushing dragging, lifting, paddling, shoving with poles; till, when the evening sun poured its level rays across the quiet Lake of the Chaudière, they landed, and made their camp on the verge of a woody island.

Day by day brought a renewal of their toils. Hour by hour, they moved prosperously up the long windings of the solitary stream; then, in quick succession, rapid followed rapid, till the bed of the Ottawa seemed a slope of foam. Now, like a wall bristling at the top with woody islets, the Falls of the Chats faced them with the sheer plunge of their sixteen cataracts; now they glided beneath overhanging cliffs, where, seeing but unseen, the crouched wild-cat eyed them from the thicket; now through the maze of water-girded rocks, which the white cedar and the spruce clasped with serpent-like roots, or among islands where old hemlocks darkened the water with deep green shadow. Here, too, the rock-maple reared its verdant masses, the beech its glistening leaves and clean, smooth stem, and behind, stiff and sombre, rose the balsam-fir. Here in the tortuous channels the muskrat swam and plunged, and the splashing wild duck dived beneath the alders or among the red and matted roots of thirsty water-

guardian. It is on the return voyage that Champlain particularly describes the sacrifice.

willows. Aloft, the white-pine towered above a sea of verdure; old fir-trees, hoary and grim, shaggy with pendent mosses, leaned above the stream, and beneath, dead and submerged, some fallen oak thrust from the current its bare, bleached limbs, like the skeleton of a drowned giant. In the weedy cove stood the moose, neck-deep in water to escape the flies, wading shoreward, with glistening sides, as the canoes drew near, shaking his broad antlers and writhing his hideous nostril, as with clumsy trot he vanished in the woods.

In these ancient wilds, to whose ever verdant antiquity the pyramids are young and Nineveh a mushroom of yesterday; where the sage wanderer of the Odyssey, could he have urged his pilgrimage so far, would have surveyed the same grand and stern monotony, the same dark sweep of melancholy woods, — here, while New England was a solitude, and the settlers of Virginia scarcely dared venture inland beyond the sound of a cannon-shot, Champlain was planting on shores and islands the emblems of his faith. Of the pioneers of the North American forests, his name stands foremost on the list. It was he who struck the deepest and boldest strokes into the heart of their pristine barbarism. At Chantilly, at Fontainebleau, Paris, in the cabinets of princes and of royalty itself, mingling with the proud vanities of the court; then lost from sight in the depths of Canada, the companion of savages, sharer of their toils, privations, and battles, more hardy, patient, and bold than they, — such, for successive years, were the alternations of this man's life.

To follow on his trail once more. His Indians said that the rapids of the river above were impassable. Nicolas de Vignau affirmed the contrary; but, from the first, Vignau had been found always in the wrong. His aim seems to have been to involve his leader in difficulties, and disgust him with a journey which must soon result in exposing the imposture which had occasioned it. Champlain took counsel of the Indians. The party left the river, and entered the forest.

"We had a hard march," says Champlain. "I carried for my share of the luggage three arquebuses, three paddles, my overcoat, and a few *bagatelles*. My men carried a little more than I did, and suffered more from the mosquitoes than from their loads. After we had passed four small ponds and advanced two leagues and a half, we were so tired that we could go no farther, having eaten nothing but a little roasted fish for nearly twenty-four hours. So we stopped in a pleasant place enough by the edge of a pond, and lighted a fire to drive off the mosquitoes, which plagued us beyond all description; and at the same time we set our nets to catch a few fish."

On the next day they fared still worse, for their way was through a pine forest where a tornado had passed, tearing up the trees and piling them one upon another in a vast "windfall," where boughs, roots, and trunks were mixed in confusion. Sometimes they climbed over and sometimes crawled through these formidable barricades, till, after an exhausting march, they reached the banks of Muskrat Lake, by the edge of which was an Indian settlement.[1]

This neighborhood was the seat of the principal Indian population of the river,[2] and, as the canoes advanced, unwonted signs of human life could be seen on the borders of the lake. Here was a rough clearing. The trees had been burned; there was a rude and desolate gap in the sombre green of the pine forest. Dead trunks, blasted and black with fire,

[1] In 1867 a man in the employ of Captain Overman found, on the line of march followed by Champlain from the pond where he passed the night to Muskrat Lake, a brass astrolabe bearing the date 1603. As the astrolabe, an antiquated instrument for taking latitudes, was not many years after Champlain's day superseded by the quadrant, at least so far as French usage was concerned, the conjecture is admissible that this one was dropped by him. See a pamphlet by A. J. Russell, *Champlain's Astrolabe* (Montreal, 1879), and another by O. H. Marshall, *Discovery of an Astrolabe supposed to have been lost by Champlain* (New York, 1879).

[2] Usually called *Algoumequins* or *Algonquins*, by Champlain and other early writers, — a name now always used in a generic sense to designate a large family of cognate tribes, speaking languages radically similar, and covering a vast extent of country.

The Algonquins of the Isle des Allumettes and its neighborhood are most frequently mentioned by the early writers as *la Nation de l'Isle*. Lalemant (*Relation des Hurons*, 1639) calls them *Ehonkeronons*. Vimont (*Relation*, 1640) calls them *Kichesipirini*. The name *Algonquin* was used generically as early as the time of Sagard, whose *Histoire du Canada* appeared in 1636. Champlain always limits it to the tribes of the Ottawa.

Isle des Allumettes was called Isle du Borgne, from a renowned one-eyed chief who made his abode here, and who, after greatly exasperating the Jesuits by his evil courses, at last became a convert and died in the faith. They regarded the people of this island as the haughtiest of all the tribes. Le Jeune, *Relation* (1636), 230.

stood grimly upright amid the charred stumps and prostrate bodies of comrades half consumed. In the intervening spaces, the soil had been feebly scratched with hoes of wood or bone, and a crop of maize was growing, now some four inches high.[1] The dwellings of these slovenly farmers, framed of poles covered with sheets of bark, were scattered here and there, singly or in groups, while their tenants were running to the shore in amazement. The chief, Nibachis, offered the calumet, then harangued the crowd: "These white men must have fallen from the clouds. How else could they have reached us through the woods and rapids which even we find it hard to pass? The French chief can do anything. All that we have heard of him must be true." And they hastened to regale the hungry visitors with a repast of fish.

Champlain asked for guidance to the settlements above. It was readily granted. Escorted by his friendly hosts, he advanced beyond the foot of Muskrat Lake, and, landing, saw the unaccustomed sight of pathways through the forest. They led to the clearings and cabins of a chief named Tessouat, who, amazed at the apparition of the white strangers, exclaimed that he must be in a dream.[2] Next, the

---

[1] Champlain, *Quatriesme Voyage*, 29. This is a pamphlet of fifty-two pages, containing the journal of his voyage of 1613, and apparently published at the close of that year.

[2] Tessouat's village seems to have been on the lower Lac des Allumettes, a wide expansion of that arm of the Ottawa which flows along the southern side of Isle des Allumettes. Champlain, perhaps from the loss of his astrolabe, is wrong, by one degree, in his reckoning of

voyagers crossed to the neighboring island, then deeply wooded with pine, elm, and oak. Here were more desolate clearings, more rude cornfields and bark-built cabins. Here, too, was a cemetery, which excited the wonder of Champlain, for the dead were better cared for than the living. Each grave was covered with a double row of pieces of wood, inclined like a roof till they crossed at the ridge, along which was laid a thick tablet of wood, meant apparently either to bind the whole together or protect it from rain. At one end stood an upright tablet, or flattened post, rudely carved with an intended representation of the features of the deceased. If a chief, the head was adorned with a plume. If a warrior, there were figures near it of a shield, a lance, a war-club, and a bow and arrows; if a boy, of a small bow and one arrow; and if a woman or a girl, of a kettle, an earthen pot, a wooden spoon, and a paddle. The whole was decorated with red and yellow paint; and beneath slept the departed, wrapped in a robe of skins, his earthly treasures about him, ready for use in the land of souls.

Tessouat was to give a *tabagie*, or solemn feast, in honor of Champlain, and the chiefs and elders of the island were invited. Runners were sent to summon the guests from neighboring hamlets; and, on the morrow, Tessouat's squaws swept his cabin for the

the latitude, 47° for 46°. Tessouat was father, or predecessor, of the chief Le Borgne, whose Indian name was the same. See note 2, *ante*, p. 201.

festivity. Then Champlain and his Frenchmen were seated on skins in the place of honor, and the naked guests appeared in quick succession, each with his wooden dish and spoon, and each ejaculating his guttural salute as he stooped at the low door. The spacious cabin was full. The congregated wisdom and prowess of the nation sat expectant on the bare earth. Each long, bare arm thrust forth its dish in turn as the host served out the banquet, in which, as courtesy enjoined, he himself was to have no share. First, a mess of pounded maize, in which were boiled, without salt, morsels of fish and dark scraps of meat; then, fish and flesh broiled on the embers, with a kettle of cold water from the river. Champlain, in wise distrust of Ottawa cookery, confined himself to the simpler and less doubtful viands. A few minutes, and all alike had vanished. The kettles were empty. Then pipes were filled and touched with fire brought in by the squaws, while the young men who had stood thronged about the entrance now modestly withdrew, and the door was closed for counsel.[1]

First, the pipes were passed to Champlain. Then, for full half an hour, the assembly smoked in silence. At length, when the fitting time was come, he

[1] Champlain's account of this feast (*Quatriesme Voyage*, 32) is unusually minute and graphic. In every particular — excepting the pounded maize — it might, as the writer can attest from personal experience, be taken as the description of a similar feast among some of the tribes of the Far West at the present day, — as, for example, one of the remoter bands of the Dacotah, a race radically distinct from the Algonquin.

addressed them in a speech in which he declared, that, moved by affection for them, he visited their country to see its richness and its beauty, and to aid them in their wars; and he now begged them to furnish him with four canoes and eight men, to convey him to the country of the Nipissings, a tribe dwelling northward on the lake which bears their name.[1]

His audience looked grave, for they were but cold and jealous friends of the Nipissings. For a time they discoursed in murmuring tones among themselves, all smoking meanwhile with redoubled vigor. Then Tessouat, chief of these forest republicans, rose and spoke in behalf of all: —

"We always knew you for our best friend among the Frenchmen. We love you like our own children. But why did you break your word with us last year when we all went down to meet you at Montreal, to give you presents and go with you to war? You were not there, but other Frenchmen were there who abused us. We will never go again. As for the four canoes, you shall have them if you insist upon it; but it grieves us to think of the hardships you

---

[1] The *Nebecerini* of Champlain, called also *Nipissingues, Nipissiriniens, Nibissiriniens, Bissiriniens, Epiciriniens*, by various early French writers. They are the *Askikouanheronons* of Lalemant, who borrowed the name from the Huron tongue, and were also called *Sorciers* from their ill repute as magicians. They belonged, like the Ottawas, to the great Algouquin family, and are considered by Charlevoix (*Journal Historique*, 186) as alone preserving the original type of that race and language. They had, however, borrowed certain usages from their Huron neighbors.

must endure. The Nipissings have weak hearts. They are good for nothing in war, but they kill us with charms, and they poison us. Therefore we are on bad terms with them. They will kill you, too."

Such was the pith of Tessouat's discourse, and at each clause the conclave responded in unison with an approving grunt.

Champlain urged his petition; sought to relieve their tender scruples in his behalf; assured them that he was charm-proof, and that he feared no hardships. At length he gained his point. The canoes and the men were promised, and, seeing himself as he thought on the highway to his phantom Northern Sea, he left his entertainers to their pipes, and with a light heart issued from the close and smoky den to breathe the fresh air of the afternoon. He visited the Indian fields, with their young crops of pumpkins, beans, and French peas, — the last a novelty obtained from the traders.[1] Here, Thomas, the interpreter, soon joined him with a countenance of ill news. In the absence of Champlain, the assembly had reconsidered their assent. The canoes were denied.

With a troubled mind he hastened again to the hall of council, and addressed the naked senate in terms better suited to his exigencies than to their dignity: —

[1] " Pour passer le reste du jour, je fus me pourmener par les jardins, qui n'estoient remplis que de quelques citronilles, phasioles, et de nos pois, qu'il commencent à cultiver, où Thomas, mon truchement, qui entendoit fort bien la langue, me vint trouver," etc. Champlain (1632). Lib. IV. c. 2.

"I thought you were men; I thought you would hold fast to your word: but I find you children, without truth. You call yourselves my friends, yet you break faith with me. Still I would not incommode you; and if you cannot give me four canoes, two will serve."¹

The burden of the reply was, rapids, rocks, cataracts, and the wickedness of the Nipissings. "We will not give you the canoes, because we are afraid of losing you," they said.

"This young man," rejoined Champlain, pointing to Vignau, who sat by his side, "has been to their country, and did not find the road or the people so bad as you have said."

"Nicolas," demanded Tessouat, "did you say that you had been to the Nipissings?"

The impostor sat mute for a time, and then replied, "Yes, I have been there."

Hereupon an outcry broke from the assembly, and they turned their eyes on him askance, "as if," says Champlain, "they would have torn and eaten him."

"You are a liar," returned the unceremonious host; "you know very well that you slept here among my children every night, and got up again every morning; and if you ever went to the Nipissings, it must have been when you were asleep. How can you be so impudent as to lie to your chief, and so

---

¹ "... et leur dis, que je les avois jusques à ce jour estimez hommes, et veritables, et que maintenant ils ce monstroient enfants et mensongers," etc. Champlain (1632), Lib. IV. c. 2.

wicked as to risk his life among so many dangers? He ought to kill you with tortures worse than those with which we kill our enemies." [1]

Champlain urged him to reply, but he sat motionless and dumb. Then he led him from the cabin, and conjured him to declare if in truth he had seen this sea of the north. Vignau, with oaths, affirmed that all he had said was true. Returning to the council, Champlain repeated the impostor's story — how he had seen the sea, the wreck of an English ship, the heads of eighty Englishmen, and an English boy, prisoner among the Indians.

At this, an outcry rose louder than before, and the Indians turned in ire upon Vignau.

"You are a liar." "Which way did you go?" "By what rivers?" "By what lakes?" "Who went with you?"

Vignau had made a map of his travels, which Champlain now produced, desiring him to explain it to his questioners; but his assurance failed him, and he could not utter a word.

Champlain was greatly agitated. His heart was in the enterprise, his reputation was in a measure at

---

[1] "Alors Tessouat ... luy dit en son langage: Nicolas, est-il vray que tu as dit avoir esté aux Nebecerini? Il fut longtemps sans parler, puis il leur dit en leur langue, qu'il parloit aucunement: Ouy j'y ay esté. Aussitost ils le regardèrent de travers, et se jettant sur luy, comme s'ils l'eussent voulu manger ou deschirer, firent de grands cris, et Tessouat luy dit : Tu es un asseuré menteur: tu sçais bien que tous les soirs tu couchois à mes costez avec mes enfants, et tous les matins tu t'y levois: si tu as esté vers ces peuples, ç'a esté en dormant," etc. Champlain (1632), Lib. IV. c. 2.

stake; and now, when he thought his triumph so near, he shrank from believing himself the sport of an impudent impostor. The council broke up, — the Indians displeased and moody, and he, on his part, full of anxieties and doubts.

"I called Vignau to me in presence of his companions," he says. "I told him that the time for deceiving me was ended; that he must tell me whether or not he had really seen the things he had told of; that I had forgotten the past, but that, if he continued to mislead me, I would have him hanged without mercy."

Vignau pondered for a moment; then fell on his knees, owned his treachery, and begged forgiveness. Champlain broke into a rage, and, unable, as he says, to endure the sight of him, ordered him from his presence, and sent the interpreter after him to make further examination. Vanity, the love of notoriety, and the hope of reward, seem to have been his inducements; for he had in fact spent a quiet winter in Tessouat's cabin, his nearest approach to the northern sea; and he had flattered himself that he might escape the necessity of guiding his commander to this pretended discovery. The Indians were somewhat exultant.

"Why did you not listen to chiefs and warriors, instead of believing the lies of this fellow?" And they counselled Champlain to have him killed at once, adding, "Give him to us, and we promise you that he shall never lie again."

No motive remaining for farther advance, the party set out on their return, attended by a fleet of forty canoes bound to Montreal[1] for trade. They passed the perilous rapids of the Calumet, and were one night encamped on an island, when an Indian, slumbering in an uneasy posture, was visited with a nightmare. He leaped up with a yell, screamed that somebody was killing him, and ran for refuge into the river. Instantly all his companions sprang to their feet, and, hearing in fancy the Iroquois war-whoop, took to the water, splashing, diving, and wading up to their necks, in the blindness of their fright. Champlain and his Frenchmen, roused at the noise, snatched their weapons and looked in vain for an enemy. The panic-stricken warriors, reassured at length, waded crestfallen ashore, and the whole ended in a laugh.

At the Chaudière, a contribution of tobacco was collected on a wooden platter, and, after a solemn harangue, was thrown to the guardian Manitou. On the seventeenth of June they approached Montreal, where the assembled traders greeted them with discharges of small arms and cannon. Here, among the rest, was Champlain's lieutenant, Du Parc, with his men, who had amused their leisure with hunting, and were revelling in a sylvan abundance, while their baffled chief, with worry of mind, fatigue of body, and a Lenten diet of half-cooked fish, was grievously

---

[1] The name is used here for distinctness. The locality is indicated by Champlain as *Le Saut*, from the Saut St. Louis, immediately above.

fallen away in flesh and strength. He kept his word with De Vignau, left the scoundrel unpunished, bade farewell to the Indians, and, promising to rejoin them the next year, embarked in one of the trading-ships for France.

CHAPTER XIII.

1615.

DISCOVERY OF LAKE HURON.

RELIGIOUS ZEAL OF CHAMPLAIN. — RÉCOLLET FRIARS. — ST. FRAN-
CIS. — EXPLORATION AND WAR. — LE CARON ON THE OTTAWA. —
CHAMPLAIN REACHES LAKE HURON. — THE HURON TOWNS. —
MASS IN THE WILDERNESS.

IN New France, spiritual and temporal interests were inseparably blended, and, as will hereafter appear, the conversion of the Indians was used as a means of commercial and political growth. But, with the single-hearted founder of the colony, considerations of material advantage, though clearly recognized, were no less clearly subordinate. He would fain rescue from perdition a people living, as he says, "like brute beasts, without faith, without law, without religion, without God." While the want of funds and the indifference of his merchant associates, who as yet did not fully see that their trade would find in the missions its surest ally, were threatening to wreck his benevolent schemes, he found a kindred spirit in his friend Houël, secretary to the King, and comptroller-general of the salt-works of Brouage. Near this town was a convent of

Récollet friars, some of whom were well known to Houël. To them he addressed himself; and several of the brotherhood, "inflamed," we are told, "with charity," were eager to undertake the mission. But the Récollets, mendicants by profession, were as weak in resources as Champlain himself. He repaired to Paris, then filled with bishops, cardinals, and nobles, assembled for the States-General. Responding to his appeal, they subscribed fifteen hundred livres for the purchase of vestments, candles, and ornaments for altars. The King gave letters patent in favor of the mission, and the Pope gave it his formal authorization. By this instrument the papacy in the person of Paul the Fifth virtually repudiated the action of the papacy in the person of Alexander the Sixth, who had proclaimed all America the exclusive property of Spain.[1]

The Récollets form a branch of the great Franciscan Order, founded early in the thirteenth century by Saint Francis of Assisi. Saint, hero, or madman, according to the point of view from which he is regarded, he belonged to an era of the Church when the tumult of invading heresies awakened in her defence a band of impassioned champions, widely different from the placid saints of an earlier age. He was very young when dreams and voices began to reveal to him his vocation, and kindle his high-wrought nature to sevenfold heat. Self-respect,

[1] The papal brief and the royal letter are in Sagard, *Histoire de la Nouvelle France*, and Le Clerc, *Établissement de la Foy*.

natural affection, decency, became in his eyes but stumbling-blocks and snares. He robbed his father to build a church; and, like so many of the Roman Catholic saints, confounded filth with humility, exchanged clothes with beggars, and walked the streets of Assisi in rags amid the hootings of his townsmen. He vowed perpetual poverty and perpetual beggary, and, in token of his renunciation of the world, stripped himself naked before the Bishop of Assisi, and then begged of him in charity a peasant's mantle. Crowds gathered to his fervid and dramatic eloquence. His handful of disciples multiplied, till Europe became thickly dotted with their convents. At the end of the eighteenth century, the three Orders of Saint Francis numbered a hundred and fifteen thousand friars and twenty-eight thousand nuns. Four popes, forty-five cardinals, and forty-six canonized martyrs were enrolled on their record, besides about two thousand more who had shed their blood for the faith.[1] Their missions embraced nearly all the known world; and, in 1621, there were in Spanish America alone five hundred Franciscan convents.[2]

In process of time the Franciscans had relaxed their ancient rigor; but much of their pristine spirit still subsisted in the Récollets, a reformed branch of the Order, sometimes known as Franciscans of the Strict Observance.

[1] Helyot, *Histoire des Ordres Religieux et Militaires*, devotes his seventh volume (ed. 1792) to the Franciscans and Jesuits. He draws largely from the great work of Wadding on the Franciscans.

[2] Le Clerc, *Établissement de la Foy*, I. 33-52.

Four of their number were named for the mission of New France, — Denis Jamay, Jean Dolbeau, Joseph le Caron, and the lay brother Pacifique du Plessis. "They packed their church ornaments," says Champlain, "and we, our luggage." All alike confessed their sins, and, embarking at Honfleur, reached Quebec at the end of May, 1615. Great was the perplexity of the Indians as the apostolic mendicants landed beneath the rock. Their garb was a form of that common to the brotherhood of Saint Francis, consisting of a rude garment of coarse gray cloth, girt at the waist with the knotted cord of the Order, and furnished with a peaked hood, to be drawn over the head. Their naked feet were shod with wooden sandals, more than an inch thick.[1]

Their first care was to choose a site for their convent, near the fortified dwellings and storehouses built by Champlain. This done, they made an altar, and celebrated the first mass ever said in Canada. Dolbeau was the officiating priest; all New France kneeled on the bare earth around him, and cannon from the ship and the ramparts hailed the mystic rite.[2] Then, in imitation of the Apostles, they took counsel together, and assigned to each his province in the vast field of their mission, — to Le Caron the Hurons, and to Dolbeau the Montagnais; while

[1] An engraving of their habit will be found in Helyot (1792).
[2] *Lettre du P. Jean Dolbeau au P. Didace David, son ami; de Quebec le 20 Juillet*, 1615. See Le Clerc, *Établissement de la Foy*, I. 62.

Jamay and Du Plessis were to remain for the present near Quebec.

Dolbeau, full of zeal, set out for his post, and in the next winter tried to follow the roving hordes of Tadoussac to their frozen hunting-grounds. He was not robust, and his eyes were weak. Lodged in a hut of birch bark, full of abominations, dogs, fleas, stench, and all uncleanness, he succumbed at length to the smoke, which had wellnigh blinded him, forcing him to remain for several days with his eyes closed.[1] After debating within himself whether God required of him the sacrifice of his sight, he solved his doubts with a negative, and returned to Quebec, only to depart again with opening spring on a tour so extensive that it brought him in contact with outlying bands of the Esquimaux.[2] Meanwhile Le Caron had long been absent on a more noteworthy mission.

While his brethren were building their convent and garnishing their altar at Quebec, the ardent friar had hastened to the site of Montreal, then thronged with a savage concourse come down for the yearly trade. He mingled with them, studied their manners, tried to learn their languages, and, when Champlain and Pontgravé arrived, declared his purpose of wintering in their villages. Dissuasion availed nothing. "What," he demanded, "are privations to him whose life is devoted to perpetual poverty, and who has no ambition but to serve God?"

---

[1] Sagard, *Hist. de la Nouvelle France*, 26.
[2] Le Clerc, *Établissement de la Foy*, I. 71.

The assembled Indians were more eager for temporal than for spiritual succor, and beset Champlain with clamors for aid against the Iroquois. He and Pontgravé were of one mind. The aid demanded must be given, and that from no motive of the hour, but in pursuance of a deliberate policy. It was evident that the innumerable tribes of New France, otherwise divided, were united in a common fear and hate of these formidable bands, who, in the strength of their fivefold league, spread havoc and desolation through all the surrounding wilds. It was the aim of Champlain, as of his successors, to persuade the threatened and endangered hordes to live at peace with each other, and to form against the common foe a virtual league, of which the French colony would be the heart and the head, and which would continually widen with the widening area of discovery. With French soldiers to fight their battles, French priests to baptize them, and French traders to supply their increasing wants, their dependence would be complete. They would become assured tributaries to the growth of New France. It was a triple alliance of soldier, priest, and trader. The soldier might be a roving knight, and the priest a martyr and a saint; but both alike were subserving the interests of that commerce which formed the only solid basis of the colony. The scheme of English colonization made no account of the Indian tribes. In the scheme of French colonization they were all in all.

In one point the plan was fatally defective, since it

involved the deadly enmity of a race whose character and whose power were as yet but ill understood, — the fiercest, boldest, most politic, and most ambitious savages to whom the American forest has ever given birth.

The chiefs and warriors met in council, — Algonquins of the Ottawa, and Hurons from the borders of the great Fresh-Water Sea. Champlain promised to join them with all the men at his command, while they, on their part, were to muster without delay twenty-five hundred warriors for an inroad into the country of the Iroquois. He descended at once to Quebec for needful preparation; but when, after a short delay, he returned to Montreal, he found, to his chagrin, a solitude. The wild concourse had vanished; nothing remained but the skeleton poles of their huts, the smoke of their fires, and the refuse of their encampments. Impatient at his delay, they had set out for their villages, and with them had gone Father Joseph le Caron.

Twelve Frenchmen, well armed, had attended him. Summer was at its height, and as his canoe stole along the bosom of the glassy river, and he gazed about him on the tawny multitude whose fragile craft covered the water like swarms of gliding insects, he thought, perhaps, of his whitewashed cell in the convent of Brouage, of his book, his table, his rosary, and all the narrow routine of that familiar life from which he had awakened to contrasts so startling. That his progress up the Ottawa was far from being an excursion of pleasure is attested by his letters, fragments of which have come down to us.

"It would be hard to tell you," he writes to a friend, "how tired I was with paddling all day, with all my strength, among the Indians; wading the rivers a hundred times and more, through the mud and over the sharp rocks that cut my feet; carrying the canoe and luggage through the woods to avoid the rapids and frightful cataracts; and half starved all the while, for we had nothing to eat but a little *sagamite*, a sort of porridge of water and pounded maize, of which they gave us a very small allowance every morning and night. But I must needs tell you what abundant consolation I found under all my troubles; for when one sees so many infidels needing nothing but a drop of water to make them children of God, one feels an inexpressible ardor to labor for their conversion, and sacrifice to it one's repose and life."[1]

Another Récollet, Gabriel Sagard, followed the same route in similar company a few years later, and has left an account of his experience, of which Le Caron's was the counterpart. Sagard reckons from

---

[1] ". . . Car helas quand on voit un si grand nombre d'Infidels, et qu'il ne tient qu'à une goutte d'eau pour les rendre enfans de Dieu, on ressent je ne sçay quelle ardeur de travailler à leur conversion et d'y sacrifier son repos et sa vie." Le Caron, in Le Clerc, I. 74. Le Clerc, usually exact, affixes a wrong date to Le Caron's departure, which took place, not in the autumn, but about the first of July, Champlain following on the ninth. Of Champlain the editions consulted have been those of 1620 and 1627, the narrative being abridged in the edition of 1632. Compare Sagard, *Histoire de la Nouvelle France*.

eighty to a hundred waterfalls and rapids in the course of the journey, and the task of avoiding them by pushing through the woods was the harder for him because he saw fit to go barefoot, "in imitation of our seraphic father, Saint Francis." "We often came upon rocks, mudholes, and fallen trees, which we had to scramble over, and sometimes we must force our way with head and hands through dense woods and thickets, without road or path. When the time came, my Indians looked for a good place to pass the night. Some went for dry wood; others for poles to make a shed; others kindled a fire, and hung the kettle to a stick stuck aslant in the ground; and others looked for two flat stones to bruise the Indian corn, of which they make sagamite."

This sagamite was an extremely thin porridge; and, though scraps of fish were now and then boiled in it, the friar pined away daily on this weak and scanty fare, which was, moreover, made repulsive to him by the exceeding filthiness of the cookery. Nevertheless, he was forced to disguise his feelings. "One must always keep a smiling, modest, contented face, and now and then sing a hymn, both for his own consolation and to please and edify the savages, who take a singular pleasure in hearing us sing the praises of our God. Among all his trials, none afflicted him so much as the flies and mosquitoes. "If I had not kept my face wrapped in a cloth, I am almost sure they would have blinded me, so pestiferous and poisonous are the bites of these little demons.

They make one look like a leper, hideous to the sight.
I confess that this is the worst martyrdom I suffered
in this country; hunger, thirst, weariness, and fever
are nothing to it. These little beasts not only persecute you all day, but at night they get into your eyes
and mouth, crawl under your clothes, or stick their
long stings through them, and make such a noise
that it distracts your attention, and prevents you
from saying your prayers." He reckons three or four
kinds of them, and adds, that in the Montagnais
country there is still another kind, so small that they
can hardly be seen, but which "bite like devils'
imps." The sportsman who has bivouacked in the
woods of Maine will at once recognize the minute
tormentors there known as "no-see-'ems."

While through tribulations like these Le Caron
made his way towards the scene of his apostleship,
Champlain was following on his track. With two
canoes, ten Indians, Étienne Brulé his interpreter,
and another Frenchman, he pushed up the Ottawa
till he reached the Algonquin villages which had
formed the term of his former journeying. He passed
the two lakes of the Allumettes; and now, for twenty
miles, the river stretched before him, straight as the
bee can fly, deep, narrow, and black, between its
mountain shores. He passed the rapids of the
Joachims and the Caribou, the Rocher Capitaine, and
the Deux Rivières, and reached at length the tributary waters of the Mattawan. He turned to the left,
ascended this little stream forty miles or more, and,

crossing a portage track, well trodden, reached the margin of Lake Nipissing. The canoes were launched again, and glided by leafy shores and verdant islands till at length appeared signs of human life and clusters of bark lodges, half hidden in the vastness of the woods. It was the village of an Algonquin band, called the Nipissings, — a race so beset with spirits, infested by demons, and abounding in magicians, that the Jesuits afterwards stigmatized them as "the Sorcerers." In this questionable company Champlain spent two days, feasted on fish, deer, and bears. Then, descending to the outlet of the lake, he steered his canoes westward down the current of French River.

Days passed, and no sign of man enlivened the rocky desolation. Hunger was pressing them hard, for the ten gluttonous Indians had devoured already nearly all their provision for the voyage, and they were forced to subsist on the blueberries and wild raspberries that grew abundantly in the meagre soil, when suddenly they encountered a troop of three hundred savages, whom, from their strange and startling mode of wearing their hair, Champlain named the *Cheveux Relevés*. "Not one of our courtiers," he says, "takes so much pains in dressing his locks." Here, however, their care of the toilet ended; for, though tattooed on various parts of the body, painted, and armed with bows, arrows, and shields of bison-hide, they wore no clothing whatever. Savage as was their aspect, they were busied in the pacific task of gathering blueberries for their winter store. Their demeanor was friendly; and from them the voyager learned that the great lake of the Hurons was close at hand.[1]

Now, far along the western sky was traced the watery line of that inland ocean, and, first of white men except the Friar Le Caron, Champlain beheld the "Mer Douce," the Fresh-Water Sea of the Hurons. Before him, too far for sight, lay the spirit-haunted Manitoualins, and, southward, spread the vast bosom of the Georgian Bay. For more than a hundred miles, his course was along its eastern shores, among islets countless as the sea-sands, — an archipelago of rocks worn for ages by the wash of waves. He crossed Byng Inlet, Franklin Inlet, Parry Sound, and the wider bay of Matchedash, and seems to have landed at the inlet now called Thunder Bay, at the entrance of the Bay of Matchedash, and a little west of the Harbor of Penetanguishine.

An Indian trail led inland, through woods and thickets, across broad meadows, over brooks, and

[1] These savages belonged to a numerous Algonquin tribe who occupied a district west and southwest of the Nottawassaga Bay of Lake Huron, within the modern counties of Bruce and Grey, Canada West. Sagard speaks of meeting a party of them near the place where they were met by Champlain. Sagard, *Grand Voyage du Pays des Hurons*, 77. The Hurons called them *Ondataouaouat* or *Ondatahouat*, whence the name *Outaouat* (Ottawa), which is now commonly used to designate a particular tribe, or group of tribes, but which the French often employed as a generic term for all the Algonquin tribes of the Upper Lakes. It is written in various forms by French and English writers, as *Outouais, Outaouaks, Tawaas, Oadawwaus, Outavies, Outaouacs, Utawas, Ottawwawwug, Outtoaets, Outtawaats, Attawawas*.

along the skirts of green acclivities. To the eye of Champlain, accustomed to the desolation he had left behind, it seemed a land of beauty and abundance. He reached at last a broad opening in the forest, with fields of maize, pumpkins ripening in the sun, patches of sunflowers, from the seeds of which the Indians made hair-oil, and, in the midst, the Huron town of Otouacha. In all essential points, it resembled that which Cartier, eighty years before, had seen at Montreal, — the same triple palisade of crossed and intersecting trunks, and the same long lodges of bark, each containing several families. Here, within an area of thirty or forty miles, was the seat of one of the most remarkable savage communities on the continent. By the Indian standard, it was a mighty nation; yet the entire Huron population did not exceed that of a third or fourth class American city.[1]

To the south and southeast lay other tribes of kindred race and tongue, all stationary, all tillers of the soil, and all in a state of social advancement when compared with the roving bands of Eastern Canada: the Neutral Nation[2] west of the Niagara,

[1] Champlain estimates the number of Huron villages at seventeen or eighteen. Le Jeune, Sagard, and Lalemant afterwards reckoned them at from twenty to thirty-two. Le Clerc, following Le Caron, makes the population about ten thousand souls; but several later observers, as well as Champlain himself, set it at above thirty thousand.

[2] A warlike people, called Neutral from their neutrality between the Hurons and the Iroquois, which did not save them from sharing the destruction which overwhelmed the former.

and the Eries and Andastes in Western New York
and Pennsylvania; while from the Genesee eastward
to the Hudson lay the banded tribes of the Iroquois,
leading members of this potent family, deadly foes of
their kindred, and at last their destroyers.

In Champlain the Hurons saw the champion who
was to lead them to victory. There was bountiful
feasting in his honor in the great lodge at Otouacha;
and other welcome, too, was tendered, of which the
Hurons were ever liberal, but which, with all
courtesy, was declined by the virtuous Champlain.
Next, he went to Carmaron, a league distant, and
then to Touaguainchain and Tequenonquihaye; till
at length he reached Carhagouha, with its triple
palisade thirty-five feet high. Here he found Le
Caron. The Indians, eager to do him honor, were
building for him a bark lodge in the neighboring
forest, fashioned like their own, but much smaller.
In it the friar made an altar, garnished with those
indispensable decorations which he had brought with
him through all the vicissitudes of his painful journeying;
and hither, night and day, came a curious
multitude to listen to his annunciation of the new
doctrine. It was a joyful hour when he saw Champlain
approach his hermitage; and the two men embraced
like brothers long sundered.

The twelfth of August was a day evermore marked
with white in the friar's calendar. Arrayed in
priestly vestments, he stood before his simple altar;
behind him his little band of Christians, — the twelve

Frenchmen who had attended him, and the two who had followed Champlain. Here stood their devout and valiant chief, and, at his side, that pioneer of pioneers, Étienne Brulé, the interpreter.' The Host was raised aloft; the worshippers kneeled. Then their rough voices joined in the hymn of praise, *Te Deum laudamus;* and then a volley of their guns proclaimed the triumph of the faith to the *okies*, the *manitous*, and all the brood of anomalous devils who had reigned with undisputed sway in these wild realms of darkness. The brave friar, a true soldier of the Church, had led her forlorn hope into the fastnesses of hell; and now, with contented heart, he might depart in peace, for he had said the first mass in the country of the Hurons.

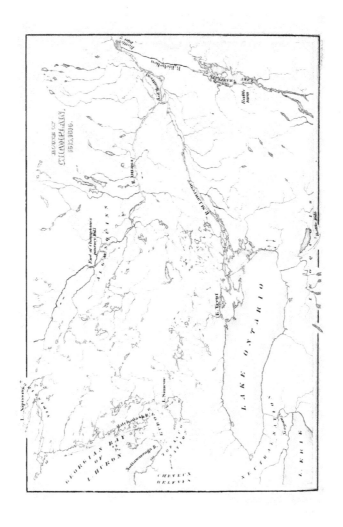

CHAPTER XIV.

1615, 1616.

THE GREAT WAR PARTY.

MUSTER OF WARRIORS. — DEPARTURE. — THE RIVER TRENT. — LAKE ONTARIO. — THE IROQUOIS TOWN. — ATTACK. — REPULSE. — CHAMPLAIN WOUNDED. — RETREAT. — ADVENTURES OF ÉTIENNE BRULÉ. — WINTER HUNT. — CHAMPLAIN LOST IN THE FOREST. — MADE UMPIRE OF INDIAN QUARRELS.

THE lot of the favored guest of an Indian camp or village is idleness without repose, for he is never left alone, with the repletion of incessant and inevitable feasts. Tired of this inane routine, Champlain, with some of his Frenchmen, set forth on a tour of observation. Journeying at their ease by the Indian trails, they visited, in three days, five palisaded villages. The country delighted them, with its meadows, its deep woods, its pine and cedar thickets, full of hares and partridges, its wild grapes and plums, cherries, crab-apples, nuts, and raspberries. It was the seventeenth of August when they reached the Huron metropolis, Cahiagué, in the modern township of Orillia, three leagues west of the river Severn, by which Lake Simcoe pours its waters into the bay of Matchedash. A shrill clamor of rejoicing, the fixed stare of wondering squaws, and the screaming flight

of terrified children hailed the arrival of Champlain.
By his estimate, the place contained two hundred
lodges; but they must have been relatively small,
since, had they been of the enormous capacity sometimes
found in these structures, Cahiagué alone would
have held the whole Huron population. Here was
the chief rendezvous, and the town swarmed with
gathering warriors. There was cheering news; for
an allied nation, called Carantouans, probably identical
with the Andastes, had promised to join the
Hurons in the enemy's country, with five hundred
men.[1] Feasts and the war-dance consumed the days,
till at length the tardy bands had all arrived; and,
shouldering their canoes and scanty baggage, the
naked host set forth.

At the outlet of Lake Simcoe they all stopped to
fish, — their simple substitute for a commissariat.
Hence, too, the intrepid Étienne Brulé, at his own
request, was sent with twelve Indians to hasten forward
the five hundred allied warriors, — a dangerous
venture, since his course must lie through the borders
of the Iroquois.

He set out on the eighth of September, and on the
morning of the tenth, Champlain, shivering in his
blanket, awoke to see the meadows sparkling with an
early frost, soon to vanish under the bright autumnal
sun. The Huron fleet pursued its course along Lake

---

[1] Champlain (1627), 31. While the French were aiding the Hurons
against the Iroquois, the Dutch on the Hudson aided the Iroquois against
this nation of allies, who captured three Dutchmen, but are said to have
set them free in the belief that they were French. Ibid.

Simcoe, across the portage to Balsam or Sturgeon Lake, and down the chain of lakes which form the sources of the river Trent. As the long line of canoes moved on its way, no human life was seen, no sign of friend or foe; yet at times, to the fancy of Champlain, the borders of the stream seemed decked with groves and shrubbery by the hands of man, and the walnut trees, laced with grape-vines, seemed decorations of a pleasure-ground.

They stopped and encamped for a deer-hunt. Five hundred Indians, in line, like the skirmishers of an army advancing to battle, drove the game to the end of a woody point; and the canoe-men killed them with spears and arrows as they took to the river. Champlain and his men keenly relished the sport, but paid a heavy price for their pleasure. A Frenchman, firing at a buck, brought down an Indian, and there was need of liberal gifts to console the sufferer and his friends.

The canoes now issued from the mouth of the Trent. Like a flock of venturous wild-fowl, they put boldly out upon Lake Ontario, crossed it in safety, and landed within the borders of New York, on or near the point of land west of Hungry Bay. After hiding their light craft in the woods, the warriors took up their swift and wary march, filing in silence between the woods and the lake, for four leagues along the strand. Then they struck inland, threaded the forest, crossed the outlet of Lake Oneida, and after a march of four days, were deep within the limits of the Iroquois. On the ninth of October some of their scouts met a fishing-party of this people, and captured them, — eleven in number, men, women, and children. They were brought to the camp of the exultant Hurons. As a beginning of the jubilation, a chief cut off a finger of one of the women, but desisted from further torturing on the angry protest of Champlain, reserving that pleasure for a more convenient season.

On the next day they reached an open space in the forest. The hostile town was close at hand, surrounded by rugged fields with a slovenly and savage cultivation. The young Hurons in advance saw the Iroquois at work among the pumpkins and maize, gathering their rustling harvest. Nothing could restrain the hare-brained and ungoverned crew. They screamed their war-cry and rushed in; but the Iroquois snatched their weapons, killed and wounded five or six of the assailants, and drove back the rest discomfited. Champlain and his Frenchmen were forced to interpose; and the report of their pieces from the border of the woods stopped the pursuing enemy, who withdrew to their defences, bearing with them their dead and wounded.[1]

It appears to have been a fortified town of the Onondagas, the central tribe of the Iroquois confederacy, standing, there is some reason to believe, within

[1] Le Clerc (I. 79-87) gives a few particulars not mentioned by Champlain, whose account will be found in the editions of 1620, 1627, and 1632.

the limits of Madison County, a few miles south of Lake Oneida.[1] Champlain describes its defensive works as much stronger than those of the Huron villages. They consisted of four concentric rows of palisades, formed of trunks of trees, thirty feet high, set aslant in the earth, and intersecting each other near the top, where they supported a kind of gallery, well defended by shot-proof timber, and furnished with wooden gutters for quenching fire. A pond or lake, which washed one side of the palisade, and was led by sluices within the town, gave an ample supply of water, while the galleries were well provided with magazines of stones.

Champlain was greatly exasperated at the desultory and futile procedure of his Huron allies. Against his advice, they now withdrew to the distance of a cannon-shot from the fort, and encamped in the forest, out of sight of the enemy. "I was moved," he says, "to speak to them roughly and harshly enough, in

[1] Champlain calls the tribe *Antouoronons, Antouhonorons,* or *Entouhonorons.* I at first supposed them to be the Senecas, but further inquiry leads me to believe that they were the Onondagas. Mr. O. H. Marshall thinks that the town was on Lake Onondaga, and supports his opinion in an excellent article in the *Magazine of American History.* General John S. Clark has, however, shown that the site of an ancient Indian fort on Nichols Pond, in the town of Fenner, Madison County, fulfils the conditions sufficiently to give some countenance to the supposition of its identity with that described by Champlain. A plan of the locality was kindly sent me by Mr. L. W. Ledyard, and another by Rev. W. M. Beauchamp, whose careful examination of the spot confirms but partially the conclusions of General Clark. Champlain's drawing of the fort was clearly made from memory, and contains obvious inaccuracies.

order to incite them to do their duty; for I foresaw that if things went according to their fancy, nothing but harm could come of it, to their loss and ruin." He proceeded, therefore, to instruct them in the art of war.

In the morning, aided doubtless by his ten or twelve Frenchmen, they set themselves with alacrity to their prescribed task. A wooden tower was made, high enough to overlook the palisade, and large enough to shelter four or five marksmen. Huge wooden shields, or movable parapets, like the mantelets of the Middle Ages, were also constructed. Four hours sufficed to finish the work, and then the assault began. Two hundred of the strongest warriors dragged the tower forward, and planted it within a pike's length of the palisade. Three arquebusiers mounted to the top, where, themselves well sheltered, they opened a raking fire along the galleries, now thronged with wild and naked defenders. But nothing could restrain the ungovernable Hurons. They abandoned their mantelets, and, deaf to every command, swarmed out like bees upon the open field, leaped, shouted, shrieked their war-cries, and shot off their arrows; while the Iroquois, yelling defiance from their ramparts, sent back a shower of stones and arrows in reply. A Huron, bolder than the rest, ran forward with firebrands to burn the palisade, and others followed with wood to feed the flame. But it was stupidly kindled on the leeward side, without the protecting shields designed to cover it;

and torrents of water, poured down from the gutters above, quickly extinguished it. The confusion was redoubled. Champlain strove in vain to restore order. Each warrior was yelling at the top of his throat, and his voice was drowned in the outrageous din. Thinking, as he says, that his head would split with shouting, he gave over the attempt, and busied himself and his men with picking off the Iroquois along their ramparts.

The attack lasted three hours, when the assailants fell back to their fortified camp, with seventeen warriors wounded. Champlain, too, had received an arrow in the knee, and another in the leg, which, for the time, disabled him. He was urgent, however, to renew the attack; while the Hurons, crestfallen and disheartened, refused to move from their camp unless the five hundred allies, for some time expected, should appear. They waited five days in vain, beguiling the interval with frequent skirmishes, in which they were always worsted; then began hastily to retreat, carrying their wounded in the centre, while the Iroquois, sallying from their stronghold, showered arrows on their flanks and rear. The wounded, Champlain among the rest, after being packed in baskets made on the spot, were carried each on the back of a strong warrior, "bundled in a heap," says Champlain, "doubled and strapped together after such a fashion that one could move no more than an infant in swaddling-clothes. The pain is extreme, as I can truly say from experience, having been carried several days in this way, since I could not stand, chiefly on account of the arrow-wound I had got in the knee. I never was in such torment in my life, for the pain of the wound was nothing to that of being bound and pinioned on the back of one of our savages. I lost patience, and as soon as I could bear my weight I got out of this prison, or rather out of hell."[1]

At length the dismal march was ended. They reached the spot where their canoes were hidden, found them untouched, embarked, and recrossed to the northern shore of Lake Ontario. The Hurons had promised Champlain an escort to Quebec; but as the chiefs had little power, in peace or war, beyond that of persuasion, each warrior found good reasons for refusing to lend his canoe. Champlain, too, had lost prestige. The "man with the iron breast" had proved not inseparably wedded to victory; and though the fault was their own, yet not the less was the lustre of their hero tarnished. There was no alternative. He must winter with the Hurons. The great war party broke into fragments, each band betaking itself to its hunting-ground. A chief named Durantal, or Darontal,[2] offered Champlain the shelter of his lodge, and he was glad to accept it.

Meanwhile, Étienne Brulé had found cause to rue

---

[1] Champlain (1627), 46. In the edition of 1632 there are some omissions and verbal changes in this part of the narrative.

[2] Champlain, with his usual carelessness, calls him by either name indifferently.

the hour when he undertook his hazardous mission to the Carantouan allies. Three years passed before Champlain saw him. It was in the summer of 1618, that, reaching the Saut St. Louis, he there found the interpreter, his hands and his swarthy face marked with traces of the ordeal he had passed. Brulé then told him his story.

He had gone, as already mentioned, with twelve Indians, to hasten the march of the allies, who were to join the Hurons before the hostile town. Crossing Lake Ontario, the party pushed onward with all speed, avoiding trails, threading the thickest forests and darkest swamps, for it was the land of the fierce and watchful Iroquois. They were well advanced on their way when they saw a small party of them crossing a meadow, set upon them, surprised them, killed four, and took two prisoners, whom they led to Carantouan, — a palisaded town with a population of eight hundred warriors, or about four thousand souls. The dwellings and defences were like those of the Hurons, and the town seems to have stood on or near the upper waters of the Susquehanna. They were welcomed with feasts, dances, and an uproar of rejoicing. The five hundred warriors prepared to depart; but, engrossed by the general festivity, they prepared so slowly, that, though the hostile town was but three days distant, they found on reaching it that the besiegers were gone. Brulé now returned with them to Carantouan, and, with enterprise worthy of his commander, spent the winter in a tour of exploration. Descending a river, evidently the Susquehanna, he followed it to its junction with the sea, through territories of populous tribes, at war the one with the other. When, in the spring, he returned to Carantouan, five or six of the Indians offered to guide him towards his countrymen. Less fortunate than before, he encountered on the way a band of Iroquois, who, rushing upon the party, scattered them through the woods. Brulé ran like the rest. The cries of pursuers and pursued died away in the distance. The forest was silent around him. He was lost in the shady labyrinth. For three or four days he wandered, helpless and famished, till at length he found an Indian foot-path, and, choosing between starvation and the Iroquois, desperately followed it to throw himself on their mercy. He soon saw three Indians in the distance, laden with fish newly caught, and called to them in the Huron tongue, which was radically similar to that of the Iroquois. They stood amazed, then turned to fly; but Brulé, gaunt with famine, flung down his weapons in token of friendship. They now drew near, listened to the story of his distress, lighted their pipes, and smoked with him; then guided him to their village, and gave him food.

A crowd gathered about him. "Whence do you come? Are you not one of the Frenchmen, the men of iron, who make war on us?"

Brulé answered that he was of a nation better than the French, and fast friends of the Iroquois.

His incredulous captors tied him to a tree, tore out his beard by handfuls, and burned him with firebrands, while their chief vainly interposed in his behalf. He was a good Catholic, and wore an *Agnus Dei* at his breast. One of his torturers asked what it was, and thrust out his hand to take it.

"If you touch it," exclaimed Brulé, "you and all your race will die."

The Indian persisted. The day was hot, and one of those thunder-gusts which often succeed the fierce heats of an American midsummer was rising against the sky. Brulé pointed to the inky clouds as tokens of the anger of his God. The storm broke, and, as the celestial artillery boomed over their darkening forests, the Iroquois were stricken with a superstitious terror. They all fled from the spot, leaving their victim still bound fast, until the chief who had endeavored to protect him returned, cut the cords, led him to his lodge, and dressed his wounds. Thenceforth there was neither dance nor feast to which Brulé was not invited; and when he wished to return to his countrymen, a party of Iroquois guided him four days on his way. He reached the friendly Hurons in safety, and joined them on their yearly descent to meet the French traders at Montreal.[1]

[1] The story of Étienne Brulé, whose name may possibly allude to the fiery ordeal through which he had passed, is in Champlain's narrative of his voyage of 1618. It will be found in the edition of 1627, but is omitted in the condensed edition of 1632. It is also told by Sagard.

Brulé met a lamentable fate. In 1632 he was treacherously murdered by Hurons at one of their villages near Penetanguishine.

Brulé's adventures find in some points their counterpart in those of his commander on the winter hunting-grounds of his Huron allies. As we turn the ancient, worm-eaten page which preserves the simple record of his fortunes, a wild and dreary scene rises before the mind, — a chill November air, a murky sky, a cold lake, bare and shivering forests, the earth strewn with crisp brown leaves, and, by the water-side, the bark sheds and smoking camp-fires of a band of Indian hunters. Champlain was of the party. There was ample occupation for his gun, for the morning was vocal with the clamor of wild-fowl, and his evening meal was enlivened by the rueful music of the wolves. It was a lake north or northwest of the site of Kingston. On the borders of a neighboring river, twenty-five of the Indians had been busied ten days in preparing for their annual deer-hunt. They planted posts interlaced with boughs in two straight converging lines, each extending more than half a mile through forests and swamps. At the angle where they met was made a strong enclosure like a pound. At dawn of day the hunters spread themselves through the woods, and advanced with shouts, clattering of sticks, and howlings like those

---

Several years after, when the Huron country was ravaged and half depopulated by an epidemic, the Indians believed that it was caused by the French in revenge for his death, and a renowned sorcerer averred that he had seen a sister of the murdered man flying over their country, breathing forth pestilence and death. Le Jeune, *Relation*, 1633, 34; Brébeuf, *Relation des Hurons*, 1635, 28; 1637, 160, 167 (Quebec, 1858).

of wolves, driving the deer before them into the enclosure, where others lay in wait to despatch them with arrows and spears.

Champlain was in the woods with the rest, when he saw a bird whose novel appearance excited his attention; and, gun in hand, he went in pursuit. The bird, flitting from tree to tree, lured him deeper and deeper into the forest; then took wing and vanished. The disappointed sportsman tried to retrace his steps. But the day was clouded, and he had left his pocket-compass at the camp. The forest closed around him, trees mingled with trees in endless confusion. Bewildered and lost, he wandered all day, and at night slept fasting at the foot of a tree. Awaking, he wandered on till afternoon, when he reached a pond slumbering in the shadow of the woods. There were water-fowl along its brink, some of which he shot, and for the first time found food to allay his hunger. He kindled a fire, cooked his game, and, exhausted, blanketless, drenched by a cold rain, made his prayer to Heaven, and again lay down to sleep. Another day of blind and weary wandering succeeded, and another night of exhaustion. He had found paths in the wilderness, but they were not made by human feet. Once more roused from his shivering repose, he journeyed on till he heard the tinkling of a little brook, and bethought him of following its guidance, in the hope that it might lead him to the river where the hunters were now encamped. With toilsome steps he followed the infant stream, now lost beneath the decaying masses of fallen trunks or the impervious intricacies of matted "windfalls," now stealing through swampy thickets or gurgling in the shade of rocks, till it entered at length, not into the river, but into a small lake. Circling around the brink, he found the point where the brook ran out and resumed its course. Listening in the dead stillness of the woods, a dull, hoarse sound rose upon his ear. He went forward, listened again, and could plainly hear the plunge of waters. There was light in the forest before him, and, thrusting himself through the entanglement of bushes, he stood on the edge of a meadow. Wild animals were here of various kinds; some skulking in the bordering thickets, some browsing on the dry and matted grass. On his right rolled the river, wide and turbulent, and along its bank he saw the portage path by which the Indians passed the neighboring rapids. He gazed about him. The rocky hills seemed familiar to his eye. A clew was found at last; and, kindling his evening fire, with grateful heart he broke a long fast on the game he had killed. With the break of day he descended at his ease along the bank, and soon descried the smoke of the Indian fires curling in the heavy morning air against the gray borders of the forest. The joy was great on both sides. The Indians had searched for him without ceasing; and from that day forth his host, Durantal, would never let him go into the forest alone.

They were thirty-eight days encamped on this

nameless river, and killed in that time a hundred and twenty deer. Hard frosts were needful to give them passage over the land of lakes and marshes that lay between them and the Huron towns. Therefore they lay waiting till the fourth of December; when the frost came, bridged the lakes and streams, and made the oozy marsh as firm as granite. Snow followed, powdering the broad wastes with dreary white. Then they broke up their camp, packed their game on sledges or on their shoulders, tied on their snowshoes, and began their march. Champlain could scarcely endure his load, though some of the Indians carried a weight fivefold greater. At night, they heard the cleaving ice uttering its strange groans of torment, and on the morrow there came a thaw. For four days they waded through slush and water up to their knees; then came the shivering northwest wind, and all was hard again. In nineteen days they reached the town of Cahiagué, and, lounging around their smoky lodge-fires, the hunters forgot the hardships of the past.

For Champlain there was no rest. A double motive urged him, — discovery, and the strengthening of his colony by widening its circle of trade. First, he repaired to Carhagouha; and here he found the friar, in his hermitage, still praying, preaching, making catechisms, and struggling with the manifold difficulties of the Huron tongue. After spending several weeks together, they began their journeyings, and in three days reached the chief village of the

Nation of Tobacco, a powerful tribe akin to the Hurons, and soon to be incorporated with them.[1] The travellers visited seven of their towns, and then passed westward to those of the people whom Champlain calls the *Cheveux Relevés*, and whom he commends for neatness and ingenuity no less than he condemns them for the nullity of their summer attire.[2] As the strangers passed from town to town, their arrival was everywhere the signal of festivity. Champlain exchanged pledges of amity with his hosts, and urged them to come down with the Hurons to the yearly trade at Montreal.

Spring was now advancing, and, anxious for his colony, he turned homeward, following that long circuit of Lake Huron and the Ottawa which Iroquois hostility made the only practicable route. Scarcely had he reached the Nipissings, and gained from them a pledge to guide him to that delusive northern sea which never ceased to possess his thoughts, when evil news called him back in haste to the Huron towns. A band of those Algonquins who dwelt on the great island in the Ottawa had spent the winter encamped near Cahiagué, whose inhabitants made them a present of an Iroquois prisoner, with the friendly intention that they should enjoy the pleasure of torturing him. The Algonquins, on the contrary, fed, clothed, and adopted him. On this, the donors,

---

[1] The Dionondadies, Petuneux, or Nation of Tobacco, had till recently, according to Lalemant, been at war with the Hurons.

[2] See *ante*, p. 222.

in a rage, sent a warrior to kill the Iroquois. He stabbed him, accordingly, in the midst of the Algonquin chiefs, who in requital killed the murderer. Here was a *casus belli* involving most serious issues for the French, since the Algonquins, by their position on the Ottawa, could cut off the Hurons and all their allies from coming down to trade. Already a fight had taken place at Cahiagué; the principal Algonquin chief had been wounded, and his band forced to purchase safety by a heavy tribute of wampum [1] and a gift of two female prisoners.

All eyes turned to Champlain as umpire of the quarrel. The great council-house was filled with Huron and Algonquin chiefs, smoking with that immobility of feature beneath which their race often hide a more than tiger-like ferocity. The umpire addressed the assembly, enlarged on the folly of falling to blows between themselves when the common enemy stood ready to devour them both, extolled the advantages of the French trade and alliance, and, with zeal not wholly disinterested, urged them to shake hands like brothers. The friendly counsel was accepted, the pipe of peace was smoked, the storm dispelled, and the commerce of New France rescued from a serious peril.[2]

[1] Wampum was a sort of beads, of several colors, made originally by the Indians from the inner portion of certain shells, and afterwards by the French of porcelain and glass. It served a treble purpose, — that of currency, decoration, and record. Wrought into belts of various devices, each having its significance, it preserved the substance of treaties and compacts from generation to generation.

[2] Champlain (1627), 63-72.

Once more Champlain turned homeward, and with him went his Huron host, Durantal. Le Caron had preceded him; and, on the eleventh of July, the fellow-travellers met again in the infant capital of Canada. The Indians had reported that Champlain was dead, and he was welcomed as one risen from the grave. The friars, who were all here, chanted lauds in their chapel, with a solemn mass and thanksgiving. To the two travellers, fresh from the hardships of the wilderness, the hospitable board of Quebec, the kindly society of countrymen and friends, the adjacent gardens, — always to Champlain an object of especial interest, — seemed like the comforts and repose of home.

The chief Durantal found entertainment worthy of his high estate. The fort, the ship, the armor, the plumes, the cannon, the marvellous architecture of the houses and barracks, the splendors of the chapel, and above all the good cheer outran the boldest excursion of his fancy; and he paddled back at last to his lodge in the woods, bewildered with astonishment and admiration.

CHAPTER XV.

1616-1627.

HOSTILE SECTS.—RIVAL INTERESTS.

QUEBEC.—TADOUSSAC.— EMBARRASSMENTS OF CHAMPLAIN.— MONT- MORENCY. — MADAME DE CHAMPLAIN. — DISORDER AND DANGER. —THE DUC DE VENTADOUR. — THE JESUITS. — CATHOLICS AND HERETICS. — RICHELIEU. — THE HUNDRED ASSOCIATES.

AT Quebec the signs of growth were faint and few. By the water-side, under the cliff, the so-called "habitation," built in haste eight years before, was already tottering, and Champlain was forced to rebuild it. On the verge of the rock above, where now are seen the buttresses of the demolished castle of St. Louis, he began, in 1620, a fort, behind which were fields and a few buildings. A mile or more distant, by the bank of the St. Charles, where the General Hospital now stands, the Récollets, in the same year, built for themselves a small stone house, with ditches and outworks for defence; and here they began a farm, the stock consisting of several hogs, a pair of asses, a pair of geese, seven pairs of fowls, and four pairs of ducks.[1] The only other

[1] *Lettre du P. Denis Jamet*, 15 Aout, 1620, in Sagard, *Histoire du Canada*, 58.

agriculturist in the colony was Louis Hébert, who had come to Canada in 1617 with a wife and three children, and who made a house for himself on the rock, at a little distance from Champlain's fort.

Besides Quebec, there were the three trading-stations of Montreal, Three Rivers, and Tadoussac, occupied during a part of the year. Of these, Tadoussac was still the most important. Landing here from France in 1617, the Récollet Paul Huet said mass for the first time in a chapel built of branches, while two sailors standing beside him waved green boughs to drive off the mosquitoes. Thither afterward came Brother Gervais Mohier, newly arrived in Canada; and meeting a crowd of Indians in festal attire, he was frightened at first, suspecting that they might be demons. Being invited by them to a feast, and told that he must not decline, he took his place among a party of two hundred, squatted about four large kettles full of fish, bear's meat, pease, and plums, mixed with figs, raisins, and biscuit procured at great cost from the traders, the whole boiled together and well stirred with a canoe-paddle. As the guest did no honor to the portion set before him, his entertainers tried to tempt his appetite with a large lump of bear's fat, a supreme luxury in their eyes. This only increased his embarrassment, and he took a hasty leave, uttering the ejaculation, "Ho, ho, ho!" which, as he had been correctly informed, was the proper mode of acknowledgment to the master of the feast.

A change had now begun in the life of Champlain. His forest rovings were over. To battle with savages and the elements was more congenial with his nature than to nurse a puny colony into growth and strength; yet to each task he gave himself with the same strong devotion.

His difficulties were great. Quebec was half trading-factory, half mission. Its permanent inmates did not exceed fifty or sixty persons, — fur-traders, friars, and two or three wretched families, who had no inducement, and little wish, to labor. The fort is facetiously represented as having two old women for garrison, and a brace of hens for sentinels.[1] All was discord and disorder. Champlain was the nominal commander; but the actual authority was with the merchants, who held, excepting the friars, nearly everybody in their pay. Each was jealous of the other, but all were united in a common jealousy of Champlain. The few families whom they brought over were forbidden to trade with the Indians, and compelled to sell the fruits of their labor to the agents of the company at a low, fixed price, receiving goods in return at an inordinate valuation. Some of the merchants were of Rouen, some of St. Malo; some were Catholics, some were Huguenots. Hence unceasing bickerings. All exercise of the Reformed religion, on land or water, was prohibited within the limits of New France; but the Huguenots set the prohibition at naught, roaring their heretical psalmody

[1] *Advis au Roy sur les Affaires de la Nouvelle France*, 7.

with such vigor from their ships in the river that the unhallowed strains polluted the ears of the Indians on shore. The merchants of Rochelle, who had refused to join the company, carried on a bold illicit traffic along the borders of the St. Lawrence, endangering the colony by selling fire-arms to the Indians, eluding pursuit, or, if hard pressed, showing fight; and this was a source of perpetual irritation to the incensed monopolists.[1]

The colony could not increase. The company of merchants, though pledged to promote its growth, did what they could to prevent it. They were fur-traders, and the interests of the fur-trade are always opposed to those of settlement and population. They feared, too, and with reason, that their monopoly might be suddenly revoked, like that of De Monts, and they thought only of making profit from it while it lasted. They had no permanent stake in the country; nor had the men in their employ, who formed nearly all the scanty population of Canada. Few, if any, of these had brought wives to the colony, and none of them thought of cultivating the soil. They formed a floating population, kept from starving by yearly supplies from France.

Champlain, in his singularly trying position, displayed a mingled zeal and fortitude. He went every

---

[1] Champlain, 1627 and 1632, *passim*; Sagard, *Hist. du Canada*, *passim*; Le Clerc, *Établissement de la Foy*, cc. 4-7; *Advis au Roy sur les Affaires de la Nouvelle France; Décret de Prise de Corps d'Hébert; Plainte de la Nouvelle France à la France sa Germaine*, *passim*.

year to France, laboring for the interests of the colony. To throw open the trade to all competitors was a measure beyond the wisdom of the times; and he hoped only to bind and regulate the monopoly so as to make it subserve the generous purpose to which he had given himself. The imprisonment of Condé was a source of fresh embarrassment; but the young Duc de Montmorency assumed his place, purchasing from him the profitable lieutenancy of New France for eleven thousand crowns, and continuing Champlain in command. Champlain had succeeded in binding the company of merchants with new and more stringent engagements; and, in the vain belief that these might not be wholly broken, he began to conceive fresh hopes for the colony. In this faith he embarked with his wife for Quebec in the spring of 1620; and, as the boat drew near the landing, the cannon welcomed her to the rock of her banishment. The buildings were falling to ruin; rain entered on all sides; the courtyard, says Champlain, was as squalid and dilapidated as a grange pillaged by soldiers. Madame de Champlain was still very young. If the Ursuline tradition is to be trusted, the Indians, amazed at her beauty and touched by her gentleness, would have worshipped her as a divinity. Her husband had married her at the age of twelve;[1] when, to his horror, he presently discovered that she was infected with the heresies of her

[1] *Contrat de Mariage de Samuel de Champlain,* 27 *Dec.,* 1610. Charavay, *Documents Inédits sur Samuel de Champlain.*

father, a disguised Huguenot. He addressed himself
at once to her conversion, and his pious efforts were
something more than successful. During the four
years which she passed in Canada, her zeal, it is true,
was chiefly exercised in admonishing Indian squaws
and catechising their children; but, on her return to
France, nothing would content her but to become a
nun. Champlain refused; but, as she was childless,
he at length consented to a virtual though not formal
separation. After his death she gained her wish,
became an Ursuline nun, founded a convent of that
order at Meaux, and died with a reputation almost
saintly.[1]

At Quebec, matters grew from bad to worse. The
few emigrants, with no inducement to labor, fell into
a lazy apathy, lounging about the trading-houses,
gaming, drinking when drink could be had, or roving
into the woods on vagabond hunting excursions.
The Indians could not be trusted. In the year 1617
they had murdered two men near the end of the
Island of Orleans. Frightened at what they had
done, and incited perhaps by other causes, the
Montagnais and their kindred bands mustered at
Three Rivers to the number of eight hundred,
resolved to destroy the French. The secret was
betrayed; and the childish multitude, naked and
famishing, became suppliants to their intended victims
for the means of life. The French, themselves at

[1] *Extraits des Chroniques de l'Ordre des Ursulines, Journal de Quebec,*
10 *Mars,* 1855.

the point of starvation, could give little or nothing. An enemy far more formidable awaited them; and now were seen the fruits of Champlain's intermeddling in Indian wars. In the summer of 1622, the Iroquois descended upon the settlement. A strong party of their warriors hovered about Quebec, but, still fearful of the arquebuse, forbore to attack it, and assailed the Récollet convent on the St. Charles. The prudent friars had fortified themselves. While some prayed in the chapel, the rest, with their Indian converts, manned the walls. The Iroquois respected their palisades and demi-lunes, and withdrew, after burning two Huron prisoners.

Yielding at length to reiterated complaints, the Viceroy Montmorency suppressed the company of St. Malo and Rouen, and conferred the trade of New France, burdened with similar conditions destined to be similarly broken, on two Huguenots, William and Émery de Caen.[1] The change was a signal for fresh disorders. The enraged monopolists refused to yield. The rival traders filled Quebec with their quarrels; and Champlain, seeing his authority set at naught, was forced to occupy his newly built fort with a band of armed followers. The evil rose to such a pitch that he joined with the Récollets and the better-disposed among the colonists in sending one of the friars to lay their grievances before the King. The dispute was compromised by a temporary union of

[1] *Lettre de Montmorency à Champlain*, 2 *Février*, 1621; Paris Documents in archives of Massachusetts, I. 493.

the two companies, together with a variety of *arrêts* and regulations, suited, it was thought, to restore tranquillity.[1]

A new change was at hand. Montmorency, tired of his viceroyalty, which gave him ceaseless annoyance, sold it to his nephew, Henri de Lévis, Duc de Ventadour. It was no worldly motive which prompted this young nobleman to assume the burden of fostering the infancy of New France. He had retired from the court, and entered into holy orders. For trade and colonization he cared nothing; the conversion of infidels was his sole care. The Jesuits had the keeping of his conscience, and in his eyes they were the most fitting instruments for his purpose. The Récollets, it is true, had labored with an unflagging devotion. The six friars of their Order — for this was the number which the Calvinist Caen had bound himself to support — had established five distinct missions, extending from Acadia to the borders of Lake Huron; but the field was too vast for their powers. Ostensibly by a spontaneous movement of their own, but in reality, it is probable, under influences brought to bear on them from without, the Récollets applied for the assistance of the Jesuits, who, strong in resources as in energy, would not be compelled to rest on the reluctant support of Huguenots. Three of their brotherhood — Charles

[1] *Le Roy à Champlain*, 20 *Mars*, 1622; Champlain (1632, Seconde Partie), Livre I.; Le Clerc, *Établissement de la Foy*, c. 6; Sagard, *Histoire du Canada*, Livre I. c. 7.

Lalemant, Enemond Masse, and Jean de Brébeuf — accordingly embarked; and, fourteen years after Biard and Masse had landed in Acadia, Canada beheld for the first time those whose names stand so prominent in her annals, — the mysterious followers of Loyola. Their reception was most inauspicious. Champlain was absent. Caen would not lodge them in the fort; the traders would not admit them to their houses. Nothing seemed left for them but to return as they came; when a boat, bearing several Récollets, approached the ship to proffer them the hospitalities of the convent on the St. Charles.[1] They accepted the proffer, and became guests of the charitable friars, who nevertheless entertained a lurking jealousy of these formidable co-workers.

The Jesuits soon unearthed and publicly burnt a libel against their Order belonging to some of the traders. Their strength was soon increased. The Fathers Noirot and De la Noue landed, with twenty laborers, and the Jesuits were no longer houseless.[2] Brébeuf set forth for the arduous mission of the Hurons; but on arriving at Trois Rivières he learned that one of his Franciscan predecessors, Nicolas Viel, had recently been drowned by Indians of that tribe,

[1] Le Clerc, *Établissement de la Foy*, I. 310; *Lalemant à Champlain, 28 Juillet*, 1625, in Le Clerc, I. 313; Lalemant, *Relation*, 1625, in *Mercure Français*, XIII.

[2] Lalemant, in a letter dated 1 August, 1626, says that at that time there were only forty-three Frenchmen at Quebec. The Jesuits employed themselves in confessing them, preaching two sermons a month, studying the Indian languages, and cultivating the ground, as a preparation for more arduous work. See Carayon, *Première Mission*, 117.

in the rapid behind Montreal, known to this day as the Saut au Récollet. Less ambitious for martyrdom than he afterwards approved himself, he postponed his voyage to a more auspicious season. In the following spring he renewed the attempt, in company with De la Noue and one of the friars. The Indians, however, refused to receive him into their canoes, alleging that his tall and portly frame would overset them; and it was only by dint of many presents that their pretended scruples could be conquered. Brébeuf embarked with his companions, and, after months of toil, reached the barbarous scene of his labors, his sufferings, and his death.

Meanwhile the Viceroy had been deeply scandalized by the contumacious heresy of Émery de Caen, who not only assembled his Huguenot sailors at prayers, but forced Catholics to join them. He was ordered thenceforth to prohibit his crews from all praying and psalm-singing on the river St. Lawrence. The crews revolted, and a compromise was made. It was agreed that for the present they might pray, but not sing.[1] "A bad bargain," says the pious Champlain, "but we made the best of it we could." Caen, enraged at the Viceroy's reproofs, lost no opportunity to vent his spleen against the Jesuits, whom he cordially hated.

Eighteen years had passed since the founding of

---

[1] ". . . en fin, fut accordé qu'ils ne chanteroient point les Pseaumes, mais qu'ils s'assembleroient pour faire leur prières." Champlain (1632, Seconde Partie), 108.

Quebec, and still the colony could scarcely be said to exist but in the founder's brain. Those who should have been its support were engrossed by trade or propagandism. Champlain might look back on fruitless toils, hopes deferred, a life spent seemingly in vain. The population of Quebec had risen to a hundred and five persons, men, women, and children. Of these, one or two families only had learned to support themselves from the products of the soil. All withered under the monopoly of the Caens.[1] Champlain had long desired to rebuild the fort, which was weak and ruinous; but the merchants would not grant the men and means which, by their charter, they were bound to furnish. At length, however, his urgency in part prevailed, and the work began to advance. Meanwhile the Caens and their associates had greatly prospered, paying, it is said, an annual dividend of forty per cent. In a single year they brought from Canada twenty-two thousand beaver-skins, though the usual number did not exceed twelve or fifteen thousand.[2]

While infant Canada was thus struggling into a half-stifled being, the foundation of a commonwealth destined to a marvellous vigor of development had been laid on the Rock of Plymouth. In their character, as in their destiny, the rivals were widely different; yet, at the outset, New England was unfaith-

---

[1] *Advis au Roy, passim; Plainte de la Nouvelle France.*

[2] Lalemant, *Relation*, 1625, in *Mercure Français*, XIII. The skins sold at a pistole each. The Caens employed forty men and upwards in Canada, besides a hundred and fifty in their ships.

ful to the principle of freedom. New England Protestantism appealed to Liberty, then closed the door against her; for all Protestantism is an appeal from priestly authority to the right of private judgment, and the New England Puritan, after claiming this right for himself, denied it to all who differed with him. On a stock of freedom he grafted a scion of despotism;[1] yet the vital juices of the root penetrated at last to the uttermost branches, and nourished them to an irrepressible strength and expansion. With New France it was otherwise. She was con-

[1] In Massachusetts, none but church-members could vote or hold office. In other words, the deputies to the General Court were deputies of churches, and the Governor and magistrates were church-members, elected by church-members. Church and State were not united: they were identified. A majority of the people, including men of wealth, ability, and character, were deprived of the rights of freemen because they were not church-members. When some of them petitioned the General Court for redress, they were imprisoned and heavily fined as guilty of sedition. Their sedition consisted in their proposing to appeal to Parliament, though it was then composed of Puritans. See Palfrey, *History of New England*, Vol. II. Ch. IV.

The New England Puritans were foes, not only of episcopacy, but of presbytery. But under their system of separate and independent churches, it was impossible to enforce the desired uniformity of doctrine. Therefore, while inveighing against English and Scottish presbytery, they established a virtual presbytery of their own. A distinction was made. The New England Synod could not *coerce* an erring church; it could only *advise* and *exhort*. This was clearly insufficient, and, accordingly, in cases of heresy and schism, the *civil power was invoked*. That is to say, the churches in their ecclesiastical capacity consigned doctrinal offenders for punishment to the same churches acting in a civil capacity, while they professed an abomination of presbytery because it endangered liberty of conscience. See *A Platform of Church Discipline, gather'd out of the Word of God and agreed upon by the Elders and Messengers of the Churches assembled in the Synod at Cambridge, in New England*, Ch. XVII. §§ 8, 9.

sistent to the last. Root, stem, and branch, she was the nursling of authority. Deadly absolutism blighted her early and her later growth. Friars and Jesuits, a Ventadour and a Richelieu, shaped her destinies. All that conflicted against advancing liberty — the centralized power of the crown and the tiara, the ultramontane in religion, the despotic in policy — found their fullest expression and most fatal exercise. Her records shine with glorious deeds, the self-devotion of heroes and of martyrs; and the result of all is disorder, imbecility, ruin.

The great champion of absolutism, Richelieu, was now supreme in France. His thin frame, pale cheek, and cold, calm eye, concealed an inexorable will and a mind of vast capacity, armed with all the resources of boldness and of craft. Under his potent agency, the royal power, in the weak hands of Louis the Thirteenth, waxed and strengthened daily, triumphing over the factions of the court, the turbulence of the Huguenots, the ambitious independence of the nobles, and all the elements of anarchy which, since the death of Henry the Fourth, had risen into fresh life. With no friends and a thousand enemies, disliked and feared by the pitiful King whom he served, making his tool by turns of every party and of every principle, he advanced by countless crooked paths towards his object, — the greatness of France under a concentrated and undivided authority.

In the midst of more urgent cares, he addressed himself to fostering the commercial and naval power.

Montmorency then held the ancient charge of Admiral of France. Richelieu bought it, suppressed it, and, in its stead, constituted himself Grand Master and Superintendent of Navigation and Commerce. In this new capacity, the mismanaged affairs of New France were not long concealed from him; and he applied a prompt and powerful remedy. The privileges of the Caens were annulled. A company was formed, to consist of a hundred associates, and to be called the Company of New France. Richelieu himself was the head, and the Maréchal Deffiat and other men of rank, besides many merchants and burghers of condition, were members.[1] The whole of New France, from Florida to the Arctic Circle, and from Newfoundland to the sources of the St. Lawrence and its tributary waters, was conferred on them forever, with the attributes of sovereign power. A perpetual monopoly of the fur-trade was granted them, with a monopoly of all other commerce within the limits of their government for fifteen years.[2] The trade of the colony was declared free, for the same period, from all duties and imposts. Nobles, officers, and ecclesiastics, members of the Company, might engage in commercial pursuits without derogating from the privileges of their order; and, in evidence of his good-will, the King gave them two ships of war, armed and equipped.

[1] *Noms, Surnoms, et Qualitez des Associez de la Compagnie de la Nouvelle France.*

[2] The whale and the cod fishery were, however, to remain open to all.

On their part, the Company were bound to convey to New France during the next year, 1628, two or three hundred men of all trades, and before the year 1643 to increase the number to four thousand persons,[1] of both sexes; to lodge and support them for three years; and, this time expired, to give them cleared lands for their maintenance. Every settler must be a Frenchman and a Catholic; and for every new settlement at least three ecclesiastics must be provided. Thus was New France to be forever free from the taint of heresy. The stain of her infancy was to be wiped away. Against the foreigner and the Huguenot the door was closed and barred. England threw open her colonies to all who wished to enter, — to the suffering and oppressed, the bold, active, and enterprising. France shut out those who wished to come, and admitted only those who did not, — the favored class who clung to the old faith and had no motive or disposition to leave their homes. English colonization obeyed a natural law, and sailed with wind and tide; French colonization spent its whole struggling existence in futile efforts to make head against them. The English colonist developed inherited freedom on a virgin soil; the French colonist was pursued across the Atlantic by a paternal despotism better in intention and more withering in effect

[1] Charlevoix erroneously says sixteen thousand. Compare *Acte pour l'Établissement de la Compagnie des Cent Associés*, in *Mercure Français*, XIV. Partie II. 232; *Édits et Ordonnances*, I. 5. The act of establishment was originally published in a small duodecimo volume, which differs, though not very essentially, from the copy in the *Mercure*.

than that which he left behind. If, instead of excluding Huguenots, France had given them an asylum in the west, and left them there to work out their own destinies, Canada would never have been a British province, and the United States would have shared their vast domain with a vigorous population of self-governing Frenchmen.

A trading company was now feudal proprietor of all domains in North America within the claim of France. Fealty and homage on its part, and on the part of the Crown the appointment of supreme judicial officers, and the confirmation of the titles of dukes, marquises, counts, and barons, were the only reservations. The King heaped favors on the new corporation. Twelve of the *bourgeois* members were ennobled; while artisans and even manufacturers were tempted, by extraordinary privileges, to emigrate to the New World. The associates, of whom Champlain was one, entered upon their functions with a capital of three hundred thousand livres.[1]

[1] *Articles et Conventions de Société et Compagnie,* in *Mercure Français,* XIV. Partie II. 250.

CHAPTER XVI.

1628, 1629.

THE ENGLISH AT QUEBEC.

REVOLT OF ROCHELLE. — WAR WITH ENGLAND. — THE ENGLISH ON THE ST. LAWRENCE. — BOLD ATTITUDE OF CHAMPLAIN. — THE FRENCH SQUADRON DESTROYED. — FAMINE. — RETURN OF THE ENGLISH. — QUEBEC SURRENDERED. — ANOTHER NAVAL BATTLE. — MICHEL. — CHAMPLAIN AT LONDON.

THE first care of the new Company was to succor Quebec, whose inmates were on the verge of starvation. Four armed vessels, with a fleet of transports commanded by Roquemont, one of the associates, sailed from Dieppe with colonists and supplies in April, 1628; but nearly at the same time another squadron, destined also for Quebec, was sailing from an English port. War had at length broken out in France. The Huguenot revolt had come to a head. Rochelle was in arms against the King; and Richelieu, with his royal ward, was beleaguering it with the whole strength of the kingdom. Charles the First of England, urged by the heated passions of Buckingham, had declared himself for the rebels, and sent a fleet to their aid. At home, Charles detested the followers of Calvin as dangerous to his own authority; abroad, he befriended them as dangerous to the authority of a rival. In France, Richelieu crushed Protestantism as a curb to the house of Bourbon; in Germany, he nursed and strengthened it as a curb to the house of Austria.

The attempts of Sir William Alexander to colonize Acadia had of late turned attention in England towards the New World; and on the breaking out of the war an expedition was set on foot, under the auspices of that singular personage, to seize on the French possessions in North America. It was a private enterprise, undertaken by London merchants, prominent among whom was Gervase Kirke, an Englishman of Derbyshire, who had long lived at Dieppe, and had there married a Frenchwoman.[1] Gervase Kirke and his associates fitted out three small armed ships, commanded respectively by his sons David, Lewis, and Thomas. Letters of marque were obtained from the King, and the adventurers were authorized to drive out the French from Acadia and Canada. Many Huguenot refugees were among the crews. Having been expelled from New France as settlers, the persecuted sect were returning as enemies. One Captain Michel, who had been in the service of the Caens, "a furious Calvinist,"[2] is said to have instigated the attempt, acting, it is affirmed, under the influence of one of his former employers.

[1] Henry Kirke, *First English Conquest of Canada* (1871), 27, 28, 206-208. David Kirke was knighted in Scotland. Hence he is said to have been Scotch by descent.

[2] Charlevoix, I. 171.

Meanwhile the famished tenants of Quebec were eagerly waiting the expected succor. Daily they gazed beyond Point Levi and along the channels of Orleans, in the vain hope of seeing the approaching sails. At length, on the ninth of July, two men, worn with struggling through forests and over torrents, crossed the St. Charles and mounted the rock. They were from Cape Tourmente, where Champlain had some time before established an outpost, and they brought news that, according to the report of Indians, six large vessels lay in the harbor of Tadoussac.[1] The friar Le Caron was at Quebec, and, with a brother Récollet, he went in a canoe to gain further intelligence. As the missionary scouts were paddling along the borders of the Island of Orleans, they met two canoes advancing in hot haste, manned by Indians, who with shouts and gestures warned them to turn back.

The friars, however, waited till the canoes came up, when they saw a man lying disabled at the bottom of one of them, his moustaches burned by the flash of the musket which had wounded him. He proved to be Foucher, who commanded at Cape Tourmente. On that morning, — such was the story of the fugitives, — twenty men had landed at that post from a small fishing-vessel. Being to all appearance French, they were hospitably received; but no sooner had they entered the houses than they began to pillage

[1] Champlain (1632, Seconde Partie), 152.

and burn all before them, killing the cattle, wounding the commandant, and making several prisoners.[1]

The character of the fleet at Tadoussac was now sufficiently clear. Quebec was incapable of defence. Only fifty pounds of gunpowder were left in the magazine; and the fort, owing to the neglect and ill-will of the Caens, was so wretchedly constructed, that, a few days before, two towers of the main building had fallen. Champlain, however, assigned to each man his post, and waited the result.[2] On the next afternoon, a boat was seen issuing from behind the Point of Orleans and hovering hesitatingly about the mouth of the St. Charles. On being challenged, the men on board proved to be Basque fishermen, lately captured by the English, and now sent by Kirke unwilling messengers to Champlain. Climbing the steep pathway to the fort, they delivered their letter, — a summons, couched in terms of great courtesy, to surrender Quebec. There was no hope but in courage. A bold front must supply the lack of batteries and ramparts; and Champlain dismissed the Basques with a reply, in which, with equal courtesy, he expressed his determination to hold his position to the last.[3]

All now stood on the watch, hourly expecting the enemy; when, instead of the hostile squadron, a small boat crept into sight, and one Desdames, with ten Frenchmen, landed at the storehouses. He

---

[1] Sagard, 919.   [2] 10 July, 1628.
[3] Sagard, 922; Champlain (1632, Seconde Partie), 157.

brought stirring news. The French commander, Roquemont, had despatched him to tell Champlain that the ships of the Hundred Associates were ascending the St. Lawrence, with reinforcements and supplies of all kinds. But on his way Desdames had seen an ominous sight, — the English squadron standing under full sail out of Tadoussac, and steering downwards as if to intercept the advancing succor. He had only escaped them by dragging his boat up the beach and hiding it; and scarcely were they out of sight when the booming of cannon told him that the fight was begun.

Racked with suspense, the starving tenants of Quebec waited the result; but they waited in vain. No white sail moved athwart the green solitudes of Orleans. Neither friend nor foe appeared; and it was not till long afterward that Indians brought them the tidings that Roquemont's crowded transports had been overpowered, and all the supplies destined to relieve their miseries sunk in the St. Lawrence or seized by the victorious English. Kirke, however, deceived by the bold attitude of Champlain, had been too discreet to attack Quebec, and after his victory employed himself in cruising for French fishing-vessels along the borders of the Gulf.

Meanwhile, the suffering at Quebec increased daily. Somewhat less than a hundred men, women, and children were cooped up in the fort, subsisting on a meagre pittance of pease and Indian corn. The garden of the Héberts, the only thrifty settlers, was ransacked for every root or seed that could afford nutriment. Months wore on, and in the spring the distress had risen to such a pitch that Champlain had wellnigh resolved to leave to the women, children, and sick the little food that remained, and with the able-bodied men invade the Iroquois, seize one of their villages, fortify himself in it, and sustain his followers on the buried stores of maize with which the strongholds of these provident savages were always furnished.

Seven ounces of pounded pease were now the daily food of each; and, at the end of May, even this failed. Men, women, and children betook themselves to the woods, gathering acorns and grubbing up roots. Those of the plant called Solomon's seal were most in request.[1] Some joined the Hurons or the Algonquins; some wandered towards the Abenakis of Maine; some descended in a boat to Gaspé, trusting to meet a French fishing-vessel. There was scarcely one who would not have hailed the English as deliverers. But the English had sailed home with their booty, and the season was so late that there was little prospect of their return. Forgotten alike by friends and foes, Quebec was on the verge of extinction.

On the morning of the nineteenth of July, an Indian, renowned as a fisher of eels, who had built his hut on the St. Charles, hard by the new dwelling of the Jesuits, came, with his usual imperturbability

[1] Sagard, 977.

of visage, to Champlain. He had just discovered three ships sailing up the south channel of Orleans. Champlain was alone. All his followers were absent, fishing or searching for roots. At about ten o'clock his servant appeared with four small bags of roots, and the tidings that he had seen the three ships a league off, behind Point Levi. As man after man hastened in, Champlain ordered the starved and ragged band, sixteen in all,[1] to their posts, whence with hungry eyes, they watched the English vessels anchoring in the basin below, and a boat with a white flag moving towards the shore. A young officer landed with a summons to surrender. The terms of capitulation were at length settled. The French were to be conveyed to their own country, and each soldier was allowed to take with him his clothes, and, in addition, a coat of beaver-skin.[2] On this some murmuring rose, several of those who had gone to the Hurons having lately returned with peltry of no small value. Their complaints were vain; and on the twentieth of July, amid the roar of cannon from the ships, Lewis Kirke, the Admiral's brother, landed at the head of his soldiers, and planted the cross of St. George where the followers of Wolfe again planted it a hundred and thirty years later. After inspecting the worthless fort, he repaired to the houses of the Récollets and Jesuits on the St.

[1] Champlain (1632, Seconde Partie), 267.
[2] *Articles granted to the Sieurs Champlain and Le Pont by Thomas Kearke*, 19 July, 1629.

Charles. He treated the former with great courtesy, but displayed against the latter a violent aversion, expressing his regret that he could not have begun his operations by battering their house about their ears. The inhabitants had no cause to complain of him. He urged the widow and family of the settler Hébert, the patriarch, as he has been styled, of New France, to remain and enjoy the fruits of their industry under English allegiance; and, as beggary in France was the alternative, his offer was accepted.

Champlain, bereft of his command, grew restless, and begged to be sent to Tadoussac, where the Admiral, David Kirke, lay with his main squadron, having sent his brothers Lewis and Thomas to seize Quebec. Accordingly, Champlain, with the Jesuits, embarking with Thomas Kirke, descended the river. Off Mal Bay a strange sail was seen. As she approached, she proved to be a French ship. In fact, she was on her way to Quebec with supplies, which, if earlier sent, would have saved the place. She had passed the Admiral's squadron in a fog; but here her good fortune ceased. Thomas Kirke bore down on her, and the cannonade began. The fight was hot and doubtful; but at length the French struck, and Kirke sailed into Tadoussac with his prize. Here lay his brother, the Admiral, with five armed ships.

The Admiral's two voyages to Canada were private ventures; and though he had captured nineteen fishing-vessels, besides Roquemont's eighteen transports and other prizes, the result had not answered his hopes. His mood, therefore, was far from benign, especially as he feared, that, owing to the declaration of peace, he would be forced to disgorge a part of his booty; yet, excepting the Jesuits, he treated his captives with courtesy, and often amused himself with shooting larks on shore in company with Champlain. The Huguenots, however, of whom there were many in his ships, showed an exceeding bitterness against the Catholics. Chief among them was Michel, who had instigated and conducted the enterprise, the merchant admiral being but an indifferent seaman. Michel, whose skill was great, held a high command and the title of Rear-Admiral. He was a man of a sensitive temperament, easily piqued on the point of honor. His morbid and irritable nerves were wrought to the pitch of frenzy by the reproaches of treachery and perfidy with which the French prisoners assailed him, while, on the other hand, he was in a state of continual rage at the fancied neglect and contumely of his English associates. He raved against Kirke, who, as he declared, treated him with an insupportable arrogance. "I have left my country," he exclaimed, "for the service of foreigners; and they give me nothing but ingratitude and scorn." His fevered mind, acting on his diseased body, often excited him to transports of fury, in which he cursed indiscriminately the people of St. Malo, against whom he had a grudge, and the Jesuits, whom he detested. On one occasion, Kirke was conversing with some of the latter.

"Gentlemen," he said, "your business in Canada was to enjoy what belonged to M. de Caen, whom you dispossessed."

"Pardon me, sir," answered Brébeuf, "we came purely for the glory of God, and exposed ourselves to every kind of danger to convert the Indians."

Here Michel broke in: "Ay, ay, convert the Indians! You mean, convert the beaver!"

"That is false!" retorted Brébeuf.

Michel raised his fist, exclaiming, "But for the respect I owe the General, I would strike you for giving me the lie."

Brébeuf, a man of powerful frame and vehement passions, nevertheless regained his practised self-command, and replied: "You must excuse me. I did not mean to give you the lie. I should be very sorry to do so. The words I used are those we use in the schools when a doubtful question is advanced, and they mean no offence. Therefore I ask you to pardon me."

Despite the apology, Michel's frenzied brain harped on the presumed insult, and he raved about it without ceasing.

"*Bon Dieu!*" said Champlain, "you swear well for a Reformer!"

"I know it," returned Michel; "I should be content if I had but struck that Jesuit who gave me the lie before my General."

At length, one of his transports of rage ended in a lethargy from which he never awoke. His funeral was conducted with a pomp suited to his rank; and, amid discharges of cannon whose dreary roar was echoed from the yawning gulf of the Saguenay, his body was borne to its rest under the rocks of Tadoussac. Good Catholics and good Frenchmen saw in his fate the immediate finger of Providence. "I do not doubt that his soul is in perdition," remarks Champlain, who, however, had endeavored to befriend the unfortunate man during the access of his frenzy.[1]

Having finished their carousings, which were profuse, and their trade with the Indians, which was not lucrative, the English steered down the St. Lawrence. Kirke feared greatly a meeting with Razilly, a naval officer of distinction,[2] who was to have sailed from France with a strong force to succor Quebec; but, peace having been proclaimed, the expedition had been limited to two ships under Captain Daniel. Thus Kirke, wilfully ignoring the treaty of peace, was left to pursue his depredations unmolested. Daniel, however, though too weak to cope with him, achieved a signal exploit. On the island of Cape Breton, near the site of Louisburg, he found an English fort, built two months before, under the auspices, doubtless, of Sir William Alexander. Daniel, regarding it as a bold encroachment on

[1] Champlain (1632, Seconde Partie), 256: "Je ne doute point qu'elle ne soit aux enfers." The dialogue above is literally translated. The Jesuits Le Jeune and Charlevoix tell the story with evident satisfaction.

[2] Claude de Razilly was one of three brothers, all distinguished in the marine service.

French territory, stormed it at the head of his pikemen, entered sword in hand, and took it with all its defenders.[1]

Meanwhile, Kirke with his prisoners was crossing the Atlantic. His squadron at length reached Plymouth, whence Champlain set out for London. Here he had an interview with the French ambassador, who, at his instance, gained from the King a promise, that, in pursuance of the terms of the treaty concluded in the previous April, New France should be restored to the French Crown.

It long remained a mystery why Charles consented to a stipulation which pledged him to resign so important a conquest. The mystery is explained by the recent discovery of a letter from the King to Sir Isaac Wake, his ambassador at Paris. The promised dowry of Queen Henrietta Maria, amounting to eight hundred thousand crowns, had been but half paid by the French government, and Charles, then at issue with his Parliament, and in desperate need of money, instructs his ambassador, that, when he receives the balance due, and not before, he is to give up to the French both Quebec and Port Royal, which had also been captured by Kirke. The letter was accompanied by "solemn instruments under our hand and seal" to make good the transfer on fulfilment of the condition. It was for a sum equal to about two hundred and

---

[1] *Relation du Voyage fait par le Capitaine Daniel;* Champlain (1632, Seconde Partie), 271. Captain Farrar, who commanded the fort, declares, however, that they were "treacherously surprised." *Petition of Captain Constance Farrar*, Dec., 1629.

forty thousand dollars that Charles entailed on Great Britain and her colonies a century of bloody wars. The Kirkes and their associates, who had made the conquest at their own cost, under the royal authority, were never reimbursed, though David Kirke received the honor of knighthood, which cost the King nothing.[1]

[1] *Charles I. to Sir Isaac Wake,* 12 June, 1631, printed in Brymner, *Report on Canadian Archives,* 1884, p. lx.

Before me is a copy of the original agreement for the restitution of Quebec and Port Royal, together with ships and goods taken after the peace. It is indorsed, *Articles arrestés entre les Députés des Deux Couronnes pour la Restitution des Choses qui ont été prinses depuis le Traicté de Paix fait entre elles;* 24 *Avril,* 1629. It was not till two years later that King Charles carried it into effect, on receiving the portion of the Queen. See also *Lettres de Chateauneuf, Ambassadeur de France, au Cardinal de Richelieu,* Nov., Dec., 1629, and *Memorial of the French Ambassador to King Charles,* Feb., 1630; *Lord Dorchester to Sir Isaac Wake,* 15 April, 1630; *Examination of Capt. David Kirke before Sir Henry Marten,* 27 May (?), 1631; *The King to Sir William Alexander,* 12 June, 1632; *Extrait concernant ce qui s'est passé dans l'Acadie et le Canada en* 1627 *et* 1628 *tiré d'un Requête du Chevalier Louis Kirk,* in *Mémoires des Commissaires,* II. 275; *Literæ continentes Promissionem Regis ad tradendum,* etc., in Hazard, I. 314; *Traité de Paix fait à Suze,* Ibid. 319; *Règlemens entre les Roys de France et d'Angleterre* in *Mercure Français,* XVIII. 39; Bushworth, II. 24; *Traité entre le Roi Louis XIII. et Charles I., Roi d'Angleterre, pour la Restitution de la Nouvelle France, l'Acadie, et Canada,* 29 *Mars,* 1632.

In the Archives des Affaires Étrangères is a letter, not signed, but evidently written by Champlain, apparently on the 16th of October, the day of his arrival in England. It gives a few details not in his printed narrative. It states that Lewis Kirke took two silver chalices from a chest of the Jesuits, on which the Jesuit Masse said, " Do not profane them, for they are sacred." " Profane them!" returned Kirke; "since you tell me that, I will keep them, which I would not have done otherwise. I take them because you believe in them, for I will have no idolatry."

CHAPTER XVII.

1632-1635.

DEATH OF CHAMPLAIN.

NEW FRANCE RESTORED TO THE FRENCH CROWN. — ZEAL OF CHAMPLAIN. — THE ENGLISH LEAVE QUEBEC. — RETURN OF JESUITS. — ARRIVAL OF CHAMPLAIN. — DAILY LIFE AT QUEBEC. — PROPAGANDISM. — POLICY AND RELIGION. — DEATH OF CHAMPLAIN.

ON Monday, the fifth of July, 1632, Émery de Caen anchored before Quebec. He was commissioned by the French Crown to reclaim the place from the English; to hold for one year a monopoly of the fur-trade, as an indemnity for his losses in the war; and, when this time had expired, to give place to the Hundred Associates of New France.[1]

By the convention of Suza, New France was to be restored to the French Crown; yet it had been matter of debate whether a fulfilment of this engagement was worth the demanding. That wilderness of woods and savages had been ruinous to nearly all connected with it. The Caens, successful at first, had suffered heavily in the end. The Associates were on the verge of bankruptcy. These deserts were useless unless peopled; and to people them would depopulate

[1] *Articles accordés au Sr. de Caen; Acte de Protestation du Sr. de Caen.*

France. Thus argued the inexperienced reasoners of the time, judging from the wretched precedents of Spanish and Portuguese colonization. The world had not as yet the example of an island kingdom, which, vitalized by a stable and regulated liberty, has peopled a continent and spread colonies over all the earth, gaining constantly new vigor with the matchless growth of its offspring.

On the other hand, honor, it was urged, demanded that France should be reinstated in the land which she had discovered and explored. Should she, the centre of civilization, remain cooped up within her own narrow limits, while rivals and enemies were sharing the vast regions of the West? The commerce and fisheries of New France would in time become a school for French sailors. Mines even now might be discovered; and the fur-trade, well conducted, could not but be a source of wealth. Disbanded soldiers and women from the streets might be shipped to Canada. Thus New France would be peopled and old France purified. A power more potent than reason reinforced such arguments. Richelieu seems to have regarded it as an act of personal encroachment that the subjects of a foreign crown should seize on the domain of a company of which he was the head; and it could not be supposed, that, with power to eject them, the arrogant minister would suffer them to remain in undisturbed possession.

A spirit far purer and more generous was active

in the same behalf. The character of Champlain belonged rather to the Middle Age than to the seventeenth century. Long toil and endurance had calmed the adventurous enthusiasm of his youth into a steadfast earnestness of purpose; and he gave himself with a loyal zeal and devotedness to the profoundly mistaken principles which he had espoused. In his mind, patriotism and religion were inseparably linked. France was the champion of Christianity, and her honor, her greatness, were involved in her fidelity to this high function. Should she abandon to perdition the darkened nations among whom she had cast the first faint rays of hope? Among the members of the Company were those who shared his zeal; and though its capital was exhausted, and many of the merchants were withdrawing in despair, these enthusiasts formed a subordinate association, raised a new fund, and embarked on the venture afresh.[1]

England, then, resigned her prize, and Caen was despatched to reclaim Quebec from the reluctant hands of Thomas Kirke. The latter, obedient to an order from the King of England, struck his flag, embarked his followers, and abandoned the scene of his conquest. Caen landed with the Jesuits, Paul le Jeune and Anne de la Noue. They climbed the steep stairway which led up the rock, and, as they reached the top, the dilapidated fort lay on their left, while farther on was the stone cottage of the Héberts, surrounded with its vegetable gardens, —

[1] *État de la dépense de la Compagnie de la Nouvelle France.*

1633.]   CHAMPLAIN RESUMES COMMAND.   277

the only thrifty spot amid a scene of neglect. But few Indians could be seen. True to their native instincts, they had, at first, left the defeated French and welcomed the conquerors. Their English partialities were, however, but short-lived. Their intrusion into houses and store-rooms, the stench of their tobacco, and their importunate begging, though before borne patiently, were rewarded by the newcomers with oaths and sometimes with blows. The Indians soon shunned Quebec, seldom approaching it except when drawn by necessity or a craving for brandy. This was now the case; and several Algonquin families, maddened with drink, were howling, screeching, and fighting within their bark lodges. The women were frenzied like the men. It was dangerous to approach the place unarmed.[1]

In the following spring, 1633, on the twenty-third of May, Champlain, commissioned anew by Richelieu, resumed command at Quebec in behalf of the Company.[2] Father le Jeune, Superior of the mission, was wakened from his morning sleep by the boom of the saluting cannon. Before he could sally forth, the convent door was darkened by the stately form of his brother Jesuit, Brébeuf, newly arrived; and the Indians who stood by uttered ejaculations of astonishment at the raptures of their greeting. The father hastened to the fort, and arrived in time to

[1] *Relation du Voyage fait à Canada pour la Prise de Possession du Fort de Quebec par les François* in *Mercure Français*, XVIII.

[2] *Voyage de Champlain* in *Mercure Français*, XIX.; *Lettre de Caen à . . .*

see a file of musketeers and pikemen mounting the pathway of the cliff below, and the heretic Caen resigning the keys of the citadel into the Catholic hands of Champlain. Le Jeune's delight exudes in praises of one not always a theme of Jesuit eulogy, but on whom, in the hope of a continuance of his favors, no praise could now be ill bestowed. "I sometimes think that this great man [Richelieu], who by his admirable wisdom and matchless conduct of affairs is so renowned on earth, is preparing for himself a dazzling crown of glory in heaven by the care he evinces for the conversion of so many lost infidel souls in this savage land. I pray affectionately for him every day," etc.[1]

For Champlain, too, he has praises which, if more measured, are at least as sincere. Indeed, the Father Superior had the best reason to be pleased with the temporal head of the colony. In his youth, Champlain had fought on the side of that more liberal and national form of Romanism of which the Jesuits were the most emphatic antagonists. Now, as Le Jeune tells us, with evident contentment, he chose him, the Jesuit, as director of his conscience. In truth, there were none but Jesuits to confess and absolve him; for the Récollets, prevented, to their deep chagrin, from returning to the missions they had founded, were seen no more in Canada, and the followers of Loyola were sole masters of the field.[2]

[1] Le Jeune, *Relation*, 1633, 26 (Quebec, 1858).
[2] *Mémoire faict en 1637 pour l'Affaire des Pères Récollectz* . . . *touchant le Droit qu'ils ont depuis l'An 1615 d'aller en Quanada. Mé-*

The manly heart of the commandant, earnest, zealous, and direct, was seldom chary of its confidence, or apt to stand too warily on its guard in presence of a profound art mingled with a no less profound sincerity.

A stranger visiting the fort of Quebec would have been astonished at its air of conventual decorum. Black Jesuits and scarfed officers mingled at Champlain's table. There was little conversation, but, in its place, histories and the lives of saints were read aloud, as in a monastic refectory.[1] Prayers, masses, and confessions followed one another with an edifying regularity, and the bell of the adjacent chapel, built by Champlain, rang morning, noon, and night. Godless soldiers caught the infection, and whipped themselves in penance for their sins. Debauched artisans outdid each other in the fury of their contrition. Quebec was become a mission. Indians gathered thither as of old, not from the baneful lure of brandy, for the traffic in it was no longer tolerated, but from the less pernicious attractions of gifts, kind words, and politic blandishments. To the vital principle of propagandism both the commercial and the military character were subordinated; or, to speak more justly, trade, policy, and military power leaned on the missions as their main support, the grand instrument of their extension. The missions were to explore the interior; the missions were to win over

moire instructif contenant la Conduite des Pères Récollects de Paris en leur Mission de Canada.

[1] Le Jeune, *Relation*, 1634, 2 (Quebec, 1858). Compare Du Creux, *Historia Canadensis*, 156.

the savage hordes at once to Heaven and to France. Peaceful, benign, beneficent, were the weapons of this conquest. France aimed to subdue, not by the sword, but by the cross; not to overwhelm and crush the nations she invaded, but to convert, civilize, and embrace them among her children.

And who were the instruments and the promoters of this proselytism, at once so devout and so politic? Who can answer? Who can trace out the crossing and mingling currents of wisdom and folly, ignorance and knowledge, truth and falsehood, weakness and force, the noble and the base, — can analyze a systematized contradiction, and follow through its secret wheels, springs, and levers a phenomenon of moral mechanism? Who can define the Jesuits? The story of their missions is marvellous as a tale of chivalry, or legends of the lives of saints. For many years, it was the history of New France and of the wild communities of her desert empire.

Two years passed. The mission of the Hurons was established, and here the indomitable Brébeuf, with a band worthy of him, toiled amid miseries and perils as fearful as ever shook the constancy of man; while Champlain at Quebec, in a life uneventful, yet harassing and laborious, was busied in the round of cares which his post involved.

Christmas day, 1635, was a dark day in the annals of New France. In a chamber of the fort, breathless and cold, lay the hardy frame which war, the wilderness, and the sea had buffeted so long in vain. After two months and a half of illness, Champlain, stricken with paralysis, at the age of sixty-eight, was dead. His last cares were for his colony and the succor of its suffering families. Jesuits, officers, soldiers, traders, and the few settlers of Quebec followed his remains to the church; Le Jeune pronounced his eulogy,[1] and the feeble community built a tomb to his honor.[2]

The colony could ill spare him. For twenty-seven years he had labored hard and ceaselessly for its welfare, sacrificing fortune, repose, and domestic peace to a cause embraced with enthusiasm and pursued with intrepid persistency. His character belonged partly to the past, partly to the present. The *preux chevalier*, the crusader, the romance-loving explorer, the curious, knowledge-seeking traveller, the practical navigator, all claimed their share in him. His views, though far beyond those of the mean spirits around him, belonged to his age and his creed. He was less statesman than soldier. He leaned to the most direct and boldest policy, and one of his last acts was to petition Richelieu for men and munitions for repressing that standing menace to the colony, the Iroquois.[3] His dauntless courage

---

[1] Le Jeune, *Relation*, 1636, 56 (Quebec, 1858).

[2] Vimont, *Relation*, 1643, 3 (Quebec, 1858). A supposed discovery, in 1865, of the burial-place of Champlain, produced a sharp controversy at Quebec. Champlain made a will, leaving 4,000 livres, with other property, to the Jesuits. The will was successfully contested before the Parliament of Paris, and was annulled on the ground of informality.

[3] *Lettre de Champlain au Ministre*, 15 *Aout*, 1635.

was matched by an unwearied patience, proved by life-long vexations, and not wholly subdued even by the saintly follies of his wife. He is charged with credulity, from which few of his age were free, and which in all ages has been the foible of earnest and generous natures, too ardent to criticise, and too honorable to doubt the honor of others. Perhaps the heretic might have liked him more if the Jesuit had liked him less. The adventurous explorer of Lake Huron, the bold invader of the Iroquois, befits but indifferently the monastic sobrieties of the fort of Quebec, and his sombre environment of priests. Yet Champlain was no formalist, nor was his an empty zeal. A soldier from his youth, in an age of unbridled license, his life had answered to his maxims; and when a generation had passed after his visit to the Hurons, their elders remembered with astonishment the continence of the great French war-chief.

His books mark the man, — all for his theme and his purpose, nothing for himself. Crude in style, full of the superficial errors of carelessness and haste, rarely diffuse, often brief to a fault, they bear on every page the palpable impress of truth.

With the life of the faithful soldier closes the opening period of New France. Heroes of another stamp succeed; and it remains to tell the story of their devoted lives, their faults, follies, and virtues.

END OF VOL. II.

INDEX.

INDEX.

ABENAKIS tribe, the, ii. 116.
Acadia, De Monts petitions for permission to colonize, ii. 65; derivation of name, ii. 65; occupation of, ii. 68-80; Poutrincourt and Lescarbot head expedition to, ii. 82; Poutrincourt determines to make it a new France, ii. 99; ruin of, ii. 136-147; French still keep a hold on, ii. 147; advantages of establishing fortified posts in, ii. 148; Sir William Alexander's attempts to colonize, ii. 262.
Adelantado of Florida, the, see *Menendez de Avilés, Pedro.*
Adirondack Mountains, the, ii. 30, 170.
Agniés tribe, the, ii. 30.
Alabama, i. 15.
Alava, d', i. 153.
Alexander VI., Pope, proclaims all America the exclusive property of Spain, i. 19, 26; Francis I. ignores bull of, ii. 22; his action repudiated by Pope Paul V., ii. 213.
Alexander, Sir William, attempts to colonize Acadia, ii. 262; builds fort on Cape Breton, ii. 271.
Algiers, beleaguered by Charles V., i. 23.

Algonquin tribe, the, ii. 30, 64; ii. 162; Champlain joins them against the Iroquois, ii. 162-178; broad use of the name, ii. 201.
Allen's River, ii. 93.
Allumettes, Isle des, ii. 201.
Allumettes, Lac des, ii. 202.
Alphonse, Jean, ii. 47, 76.
Alva, Duke of, Catherine de Medicis influenced by, i. 101.
Amboise, Peace of, i. 49.
America, discovery of, i. 9, 19; a region of wonder and mystery to the Spaniard, i. 9, 35.
American civilization, springs of, i. ix.
Anastasia Island, i. 132, 141.
Andastes tribe, the, ii. 225.
Anderson, i. 91.
Ann, Cape, ii. 77.
Annapolis Harbor, discovered by De Monts, ii. 71.
Annapolis River, the, see *Équille River* and *Dauphin River.*
Anquetil, ii. 37.
Antarctic France, i. 27; Spain and Portugal make good their claim to, i. 32.
Anticosti, Island of, ii. 21, 23, 52.
Antonio, Don, offers Gourgues command of fleet against Philip II., i. 178.

INDEX.

Appalache, mysterious mountains of, i. 78.
Appalache, village of, i. 12.
Appalachicola, i. 12.
Aquaviva, Claude, ii. 112, 144.
Arambec, ii. 38.
Archer's Creek, i. 41.
Arciniega, Sancho de, commissioned to join Menendez, i. 105.
Argall, Capt. Samuel, arrives at Jamestown, ii. 130; abducts Pocahontas, ii. 130; sails to expel the French from coast of Maine, ii. 131; attacks and defeats La Saussaye, ii. 132; interview with La Saussaye, ii. 133; saves his prisoners from the wrath of Sir Thomas Dale, ii. 137; commands a new expedition, ii. 138; demolishes Port Royal, ii. 139; interview with Biencourt, ii. 141; returns to Virginia, ii. 142; becomes Deputy-Governor of Virginia, ii. 146; knighted by King James, ii. 147.
Arkansas River, the, i. 15.
Arlac, Sergeant, i. 65; remains to fight battles of chief Outina, i. 66; victory over warriors of King Potanou, i. 67; fidelity to Laudonnière, i. 72; disarmed by mutineers, i. 73; attacked by the Indians, i. 87; embarks against the Spanish, i. 116.
Armouchiquois Indians, the, ii. 77; Chief Membertou's hatred for, ii. 96.
Aspinwall, Col. Thomas, ii. 5.
Asticou, Chief, ii. 127, 128.
Astina, Chief, i. 83.
Asturias, knights of, i. 104.
Athore, son of Chief Satouriona, i. 65.
Aubert, of Dieppe, ii. 13.

Aubigné, d', i. 5.
Aubry, Nicolas, ii. 70, 72.
Audubon, J. J., i. 59.
Audusta, Chief, i. 42.
Avezac, M. d', ii. 37.
Ayllon, Vasquez de, voyages and discoveries of, i. 11, 39.

BACCALAOS, ii. 10.
Bacchus, the Island of, ii. 24.
Bahama Channel, the, i. 108, 162.
Bahama Islands, the, i. 10.
Bailleul, ii. 132.
Balsam Lake, ii. 229.
Balthazar, Christophe, ii. 112.
Bancroft, George, i. 7, 160.
Barcia (Cardenas y Cano), i. 5, 11, 13, 19, 70, 99, 100, 105, 109, 112, 113, 119, 122, 123, 128, 132, 147, 151, 158, 160, 162, 165, 172, 179; ii. 20.
Barré, Nicolas, in command of the Coligny colonists, i. 44.
Bartrams, the, i. 59.
Basanier, i. 40, 47, 50, 53, 94, 114, 160, 165, 168.
Basques, the, ii. 9; brisk trade with the Indians, ii. 151; conflict with Pontgravé, ii. 152; make peace with Pontgravé, ii. 152; plot to place Quebec in the hands of, ii. 156.
Bauldre, François de, ii. 57.
Baumgartens, ii. 10.
Bayard, Le Chevalier, death of, ii. 19.
Bazares, Guido de las, sails to explore Florida coasts, i. 18.
Beauchamp, Rev. W. M., ii. 231.
Beaufort, Duchesse de, ii. 108.
Beaufort River, the, i. 40.
Beaufort, South Carolina, i. 41.
Beaumont, at St. Croix, ii. 74.
Beauport (Gloucester, Mass.), ii. 77.

INDEX. 287

Beaupré, Vicomte de, ii. 42.
Belknap, ii. 43, 147.
Belle Isle, Straits of, ii. 12.
Belleforest, derivation of the name of Canada, ii. 23; reality of Verrazzano's voyage, ii. 50.
Belœil, cliffs of, ii. 166.
Benin, negroes of, i. 160.
Bergeron, ii. 10, 13.
Berjon, Jean, ii. 74.
Berthelot, M., ii. 25, 27.
Berthier, ii. 154.
Beteta, i. 18.
Beverly, ii. 147.
Beza, Theodore, i. 49.
Biard, Pierre, the Jesuit, ii. 4, 10; named to join Poutrincourt's Acadian expedition, ii. 100; left behind by Poutrincourt, ii. 101, 110; sails for Acadia, ii. 111; friction with Poutrincourt, ii. 114; difficulty with the Micmac language, ii. 118; studies among the Indians, ii. 119; controversy with Biencourt, ii. 122, 123; a truce, ii. 123; relieved by La Saussaye, ii. 125; at Mount Desert, ii. 127; attacked by the English, ii. 132; experiences of captives under Captain Argall, ii. 136; accompanies Captain Argall on another expedition, ii. 138; destruction of Port Royal, ii. 139; accused by Poutrincourt of treachery, ii. 139, 140; returns home, ii. 146.
Biddle, ii. 20.
Biedma, i. 16, 17.
Biencourt, Vice-Admiral, son of Poutrincourt, ii. 103, 104; gains audience of Marie de Medicis, ii. 105, 110; returns to Acadia, ii. 112; left in charge at Port Royal, ii. 115; takes young Pontgravé prisoner, ii. 115; meeting with the Armouchiquois Indians, ii. 116; dislike for the Indians, ii. 117; discord and misery, ii. 119; succor from France, ii. 121; controversy with the Jesuits, ii. 122; a truce, ii. 123; among the Indians, ii. 139; interview with Captain Argall, ii. 141; partially rebuilds Port Royal, ii. 147; advantages of establishing fortified posts in Acadia, ii. 148.
Bimini, Island of, fountain of eternal youth said to be upon, i. 10, 11.
Biscay, knights of, i. 104.
"Black drink," the, Indian belief in the properties of, i. 167.
Black, Hon. Henry, i. xiii.
Blanc, Cap, ii. 78.
Block Island, ii. 17.
Bois-Lecomte, expedition to the New World, i. 27.
Borgia, General, i. 179.
Borgne, Isle du, ii. 201.
Boston Harbor, ii. 77.
Bouchette, ii. 153.
Boulay, ii. 74.
Bourbon, Charles de, see *Soissons, Comte de*.
Bourbon, Henri de, see *Condé, Prince de*.
Bourdelais, François, i. 168.
Bourdet, Captain, i. 70.
Brant Point, ii. 78.
Brantôme, i. 5; ii. 20, 37.
Brazil, i. 26, 28, 29.
Brébeuf, Jean de, the Jesuit, ii. 4, 173, 238; attempts to convert the Hurons, ii. 253, 270, 276, 280.
Brest, Governor of, feud with Villegagnon, i. 25.
"Breton," the, i. 83.
Breton, Cape, name of, ii. 10; ii. 271.

Breton, Christophe le, escape from butchery of Menendez, i. 145, 147.
Bretons, the, ii. 9.
Brevoort, J. Carson, ii. 50.
Briet, Padre Felipe, i. 137.
Brinton, i. 80.
Brion-Chabot, Philippe de, conceives the purpose of planting colony in America, ii. 20.
Brissac, the Maréchal de, ii. 195.
Broad River, i. 39.
Brown, John Carter, ii. 5.
Brulé, Étienne, ii. 221, 226, 228; adventures of, ii. 234-237; murdered by the Hurons, ii. 237.
Bry, De, i. 28, 35, 50, 147, 167.
Brymner, ii. 273.
Buckingham, Duke of, ii. 261.
Burke, i. 91.
Byng Inlet, ii. 223.

CABOT, Sebastian, discoveries of, i. 19, ii. 9.
Caen, Émery de, trade of New France conferred by the Duc de Montmorency on, ii. 251; "heresy" of, ii. 254; hatred of the Jesuits, ii. 254; success in the fur-trade, ii. 255; privileges annulled by Richelieu, ii. 258; reclaims Quebec from the English, ii. 274, 276.
Caen, William de, trade of New France conferred by the Duc de Montmorency on, ii. 251; success in the fur-trade, ii. 255; privileges annulled by Richelieu, ii. 258.
Cahiagué, the Huron metropolis, ii. 227, 241, 242, 243.
Calibogue Sound, i. 43.
Callières, Point, ii. 188.
Caloosa, River, the, i. 79.
Calos, King of, i. 79.

Calumet, the, Rapids of, ii. 210.
Calvin, John, Huguenots gather around, i. 21; pronounced by Villegagnon a "frightful heretic," i. 30, 31; Villegagnon's hot controversy with, i. 32; his heresy infecting France, ii. 22.
Calvinism, Rochelle the centre and citadel of, ii. 83.
Calvinistic churches, fast gaining strength, i. 23.
Canada, i. 19; country embraced by the name of, ii. 23; derivation of the name, ii. 23.
Canaveral, Cape, i. 79, 133, 149.
Cancello, efforts to convert the natives, i. 17; murdered, i. 18.
Canseau, ii. 97.
Cap Rouge, the River of, Cartier lands at mouth of, ii. 42; Roberval casts anchor before, ii. 47.
Carantouans, the, ii. 228.
Carayon, Auguste, ii. 112, 123, 138, 144, 253.
Carhagouha, ii. 225, 241.
Caribou, the, Rapids of, ii. 221.
Carillon, Rapids of, ii. 196.
Carli, Fernando, ii. 49.
Carmaron, ii. 225.
Caro, Annibal, ii. 50.
Caroline, Fort, i. 56, 60; discontent in, i. 68; famine and desperation at, i. 89; defenceless condition of, i. 117; attacked by the Spanish, i. 119-125; the massacre, i. 126-128; the fugitives, i. 128-130; repaired, i. 162. See also *San Mateo, Fort*.
Cartier, Jacques, efforts to plant colony in Spanish Florida, i. 19, ii. 10; most eminent in St. Malo, ii. 21; sails for Newfoundland, ii. 21; voyage a mere reconnoissance, ii. 21; receives second commission from Chabot, ii. 22;

INDEX. 289

sets out on second expedition, ii.
22; reaches the St. Lawrence
River, ii. 23; meeting with the
Indians, ii. 24; visit to Chief
Donnacona, ii. 25, 26; resolves
to go to Hochelaga, ii. 26;
warned by the Indians to desist,
ii. 27; sets out for Hochelaga,
ii. 28; reception by the natives,
ii. 31-33; farewell to Hochelaga, ii. 33; reaches Quebec, ii.
33; expedition afflicted with
scurvy, ii. 34; fort of, ii. 34;
waning friendship of the Indians, i. 34; takes Donnacona
and his chiefs forcibly on
board ship, ii. 36; sails for
France, ii. 36; appointed Captain-General of a new expedition, ii. 38; again sets sail for
the New World, ii. 41; again
reaches Quebec, ii. 41; sails up
the St. Lawrence River, ii. 42;
lands at mouth of the River of
Cap Rouge, ii. 42; explores
rapids above Hochelaga, ii. 42;
abandons New France before
Roberval's arrival, ii. 43; ordered to return but escapes, ii.
43; later life of, ii. 44; ii. 176.
Casco Bay, ii. 76.
Cathay, kingdom of, Verrazzano
despatched by Francis I. to find
westward passage to, ii. 14.
Cazenove, Lieutenant, i. 171.
Chabot, ii. 21; gives Cartier a
second commission, ii. 22; in
disgrace, ii. 37.
Chaleurs, the, Gulf of, Cartier
enters, ii. 21.
Challeux, i. 4, 112, 113; escape
from the massacre of Fort Caroline, i. 124, 125, 127, 129, 133,
145, 146.
Chalmers, ii. 43.

Chambly, Basin of, ii. 166.
Chambly River, the, ii. 166.
Champdoré, ii. 72, 80.
Champlain, Madame de, among
the Indians at Quebec, ii. 249;
later history of, ii. 250.
Champlain, Samuel de, i. 5; foremost in forest chivalry, i. 181;
the Father of New France, ii.
3; writings of, ii. 3; other
authorities concerning, ii. 4;
map of Quebec, ii. 25; finds
remains of Cartier's fort, ii. 34;
sterling merits of, ii. 59; visits
the West Indies and Mexico, ii.
59-61; his journal, ii. 60; erratic character of some of his
exploits, ii. 61; accepts post in
De Chastes' expedition to New
France, ii. 64; expedition sets
sail, ii. 64; explores the St.
Lawrence River, ii. 64; tries to
pass rapids of St. Louis, ii. 64;
return to France, ii. 65; important charts made by, ii. 71;
discovers St. Croix, ii. 71;
Mount Desert visited and named
by, ii. 76; on the coast of New
England, ii. 76-78; trouble with
the Indians, ii. 78; undertakes
a voyage of discovery with Poutrincourt, ii. 87; failure, ii. 88;
return to Port Royal, ii. 89;
"L'Ordre de Bon-Temps," ii. 91;
life at Port Royal, ii. 92, 93;
evil tidings, ii. 94; Port Royal
must be abandoned, ii. 95; sails
for France, ii. 97; radical defect in scheme of settlement, ii.
98; kindly relations with the
Indians, ii. 98; embarks on a
new enterprise to the New
World, ii. 149; views of colonization, ii. 150; lays the
foundations of Quebec, ii. 155;

conspiracy revealed to, ii. 156; winter sufferings at Quebec, ii. 160; return of Pontgravé, ii. 161; hopes of finding a way to China, ii. 161; joins the Hurons and Algonquins against the Iroquois, ii. 162-178; victory over the Iroquois, ii. 175; disposition of the prisoners, ii. 176; return to Quebec, ii. 177; returns to France, ii. 179; relates his adventures to the King at Fontainebleau, ii. 179; violent illness of, ii. 179; again sets sail for the New World, ii. 180; advantages of alliance with the Montagnais and the Hurons, ii. 180; on the St. Lawrence, ii. 180; war with the Iroquois, ii. 181-185; returns to France, ii. 186; encounters icebergs, ii. 187; returns to Tadoussac, ii. 187; lays the foundations for Montreal, ii. 188; trading with the Hurons, ii. 188, 189; taken down the rapids of St. Louis, ii. 189; in France again, ii. 190; gains the protection of the Comte de Soissons, ii. 190; De Soissons confers vice-regal powers in New France upon, ii. 191; the life of New France alone in, ii. 192; his two great objects, ii. 192; efforts to establish a trading company, ii. 192; deceived by Vignau, ii. 195; hastens to follow up Vignau's reported discoveries, ii. 195; difficulties of the journey, ii. 196-202; amazement of the natives, ii. 202; Chief Tessouat gives a feast in honor of, ii. 203, 204; asks for canoes and men to visit the Nipissings, ii. 205; Tessouat refuses, ii. 206; Vignau's falsehoods disclosed, ii. 207-209; return to Montreal, ii. 210; clemency to Vignau, ii. 211; religious zeal of, ii. 212; takes four of the Récollet Friars to New France, to convert the Indians, ii. 215; on the track of Le Caron, ii. 221; at Lake Nipissing, ii. 222; discovery of Lake Huron, ii. 223; regarded by the Hurons as their champion, ii. 225; meeting with Le Caron, ii. 225; the first mass, ii. 226; sets out on tour of observation, ii. 227; on Lake Ontario, ii. 229; attack on the Iroquois, ii. 232; wounded, ii. 233; loses prestige with the Indians, ii. 234; forced to winter with the Hurons, ii. 234; lost in the forest, ii. 239; made umpire of Indian quarrels, ii. 243; returns to Quebec, ii. 244; forced to rebuild at Quebec, ii. 245; his difficulties at Quebec, ii. 247; his efforts in behalf of the trading company, ii. 248, 249; brings Madame de Champlain to Quebec, ii. 249; a new monopoly, ii. 251; arrival of Jesuits, ii. 253; the Company of New France, ii. 258-260; refuses to surrender Quebec to Kirke, ii. 264; forced to capitulate, ii. 267; his character that of the Middle Age rather than of the seventeenth century, ii. 276; resumes command at Quebec, ii. 277; death of, ii. 281; severity of his loss to the colony, ii. 281; estimate of, ii. 281, 282.

Charavay, ii. 249.

Charente River, the, i. 39.

Charles I. of England, aids the rebels in France, ii. 261; restores New France to the French

INDEX. 291

Crown, ii. 272; letter to Sir Isaac Wake concerning restoration of New France to the French Crown, ii. 272.
Charles V., beleaguers Algiers, i. 23; ii. 37.
Charles VIII., ii. 13.
Charles IX., i. 41; helpless amid storm of factions, i. 49, 56, 101; petition for redress against Spain, to, i. 147; demands redress from Spain for massacres in Florida, i. 153; claims discovery of Florida prior to Columbus, i. 153; ii. 10; demands that Menendez be punished for massacres in Florida, i. 155, 156; refused redress, and submits, i. 157; fast subsiding into the deathly embrace of Spain, i. 157.
Charlesbourg-Royal, ii. 43.
Charlesfort, i. 41.
Charles River, the, ii. 77.
Charlevoix, Pierre François Xavier de, i. 5, 101, 128, 158, 162, 168, 171; ii. 25, 34, 55, 56, 110, 154, 173, 205, 259, 267, 271.
Charnock, i. 104.
Chastes, Aymar de, ii. 61, 62; fidelity to the King, ii. 62; reason and patriotism his watchword, ii. 62; receives patent for expedition to New France, ii. 63; death of, ii. 65.
Chatham Harbor, ii. 87.
Chatillon, ii. 50.
Chaton, Estienne, ii. 53.
Chats, Falls of the, ii. 198.
Chaudière, the, cataracts of, ii. 197.
Chaudière, Lake of the, ii. 198.
Chauveton, i. 147.
Chauvin, Captain, plans for fur-trading, ii. 57; sets out on enterprise, ii. 58; death of, ii. 63.

Chauvin, Pierre, left in charge at Quebec, ii. 179.
Chefdhôtel, despatched to bring convicts back from Sable Island; ii. 56; robs the convicts, but is forced to disgorge, ii. 56.
Chenonceau River, the, i. 41.
Chesapeake Bay, i. 103; Menendez urges immediate Spanish occupation of, i. 149.
Chevalier, ii. 94.
"Cheveux Relevés," the, ii. 242.
Chicora, i. 39.
China, hopes of Champlain to find a way to, ii. 161.
Choisy, l'Abbé de, ii. 108.
Cibola, wonderful land of, i. 38.
Clark, Gen. John S., ii. 231.
Cod, Cape, ii. 78.
Cohasset, shores of, ii. 78.
Cointac, i. 29, 30.
Colden, ii. 30.
Coligny, Fort, i. 28.
Coligny, Gaspar de, effort to build up a Calvinist France in America, i. 3; admiral of France, i. 22; a tower of trust, i. 23, 30; representative and leader of Protestantism of France, i. 34; plans second Huguenot colony to the New World, i. 34; the Puritans compared to colonists of, i. 35; again strong at Court, i. 49; requires Laudonnière to resign his command, i. 94; Philip II. demands his punishment for planting French colony in Florida, i. 154; waning power of, i. 157.
Colombo, Don Francisco, ii. 60.
Columbus, discoveries of, i. 9, 19.
Company of New France, the, formed by Richelieu, ii. 258; territory conferred on, ii. 258; powers granted to, ii. 258; re-

292   INDEX.

quirements of, ii. 259; the King heaps favors upon, ii. 260; gives succor to Quebec, ii. 261.
Condé, of the civil wars, ii. 191.
Condé, Prince de, i. 22; aspires to the Crown, i. 34; varying popularity of, i. 49; assumes protectorship of New France, ii. 191; history of, ii. 191, 192; imprisonment of, ii. 249; the Duc de Montmorency purchases the lieutenancy of New France from, ii. 249.
Condé, the great, victor at Rocroy, ii. 191.
Cordner, Rev. John, ii. 5.
Coronado, i. 15.
Cortés, Hernando, conquers Mexico, i. 11.
Cosette, Captain, i. 114.
Costa, Mr. de, ii. 50.
Coton, Father, confessor to Henry IV., ii. 99; urges the King to attach some Jesuits to Pontrincourt's expedition to Acadia, ii. 100.
Coudonaguy, the god, ii. 27.
Couexis, King, i. 43.
Council of the Indies, the, ii. 40.
Cousin, said by the French to be the discoverer of America, ii. 8.
Crow Indians, the, ii. 168, 169.
Crown Point, ii. 172.
Cuba, i. 10, 11.
Cumberland Head, ii. 170.
Cunat, Charles, ii. 39.

DACOTAH, the, remoter bands of, ii. 204.
Dale, Sir Thomas, Governor of Virginia, ii. 131; commissions Captain Argall to expel the French from the coast of Maine, ii. 131; wrath against Captain Argall's prisoners, ii. 137.

Daniel, Captain, exploit of, ii. 271.
"Dauphine," the, ii. 15.
Davila, i. 97.
Dawson, Doctor, ii. 30, 65.
Debré, Pierre, i. 165, 168.
De Chastes, Commander de, see *Chastes, Aymar de.*
De Choisy, the Abbé, see *Choisy, l'Abbé de.*
Deffiat, Maréchal, ii. 258.
Delaborde, i. 35, 49.
De Monts, Sieur, see *Guast, Pierre du.*
Denis of Honfleur, explores the Gulf of St. Lawrence, ii. 13.
Desdames, ii. 264.
Desimoni, Signor, ii. 50.
De Soto, Hernando, see *Soto, Hernando de.*
Des Prairies, ii. 183.
Deux Rivières, the, ii. 221.
Diamond, Cape, ii. 155.
Dionondadies, the, ii. 242.
Dolbeau, Jean, ii. 215; experiences among the Indians, ii. 216.
Dolphins, the, River of, i. 50, 113.
Donnacona, Chief, ii. 25; Cartier's visit to, ii. 25, 26; forcibly taken on board Cartier's ship, ii. 36; baptized, ii. 39; death of, ii. 39.
Dry Mountain, ii. 126.
Du Creux, ii. 279.
Du Jardin, ii. 111.
Du Parc, in command at Quebec, ii. 187, 210.
Du Plessis, Pacifique, ii. 215.
Dupont, war-ships of, i. 39.
Du Quesne, ii. 111.
Durantal (Darontal), Chief, ii. 234, 240; goes to Quebec with Champlain, ii. 244.
Dutch, the, find their way to the St. Lawrence River, ii. 94.
Du Thet, Gilbert, arrived in Acadia, ii. 122; returns to France, ii.

INDEX. 293

123; again sails for Acadia, ii. 125; death of, ii. 132.
Duval, plot to kill Champlain and deliver Quebec to the Basques and Spaniards, ii. 157; arrested and executed, ii. 157, 158.

EDELANO, island of, i. 79.
Eden, ii. 8, 10.
Eliot, Charles, ii. 79.
Eliot, Charles W., ii. 79.
Elizabeth, Queen, i. 47.
England, Florida claimed by, i. 19; relinquishes Quebec, ii. 276.
English colonization, compared with French colonization, ii. 217.
Entragues, Henriette d', see *Verneuil, Marquise de.*
Équille River, the, ii. 80; explored by Lescarbot, ii. 89.
Eries, the, ii. 225.
Espiritu Santo, Bay of, i. 14, 17.
Esquimaux, the, ii. 216.
Estancelin, ii. 8, 10, 13.
Etechemins, the, ii. 77.
Etechemins, la Rivière des, ii. 71.
Eternal youth, fountain of, i. 10.
Europe, Spain the incubus of, i. 20.

FAIRBAIRN, i. 91.
Faribault, G. B., ii. 5, 11, 25, 34, 35, 156.
Farrar, Capt. Constance, ii. 272.
Fayal, ii. 144.
Fenner, town of, ii. 231.
Féret, M., ii. 61.
Fernald, Mr., ii. 128.
Fernandina, i. 39.
Ferrière, La Roche, sent as emissary to distant tribes, i. 78.
Fiche, Isle de, ii. 12.
Fichet, Isle, ii. 12.
Fisher, ii. 25.

Fishot Island, ii. 12.
Five Confederate Nations, the, ii. 162.
Fleury, Capt. Charles, ii. 125, 127, 133, 146.
Florida, new documentary evidence connected with French occupancy of, i. vii; political and religious enmities, i. 3; Huguenot occupation of, i. 3; authorities for, i. 3; Ponce de Leon explores and names, i. 11; Ponce de Leon attempts to plant colony in, i. 11; coast outline becomes better known to Spaniards, i. 11; expedition of Narvaez to, i. 12; De Soto plans to conquer, i. 13; Cabeza de Vaca makes false statements concerning, i. 13; plan for colonization of, i. 18; territory embraced by name of, i. 19; rival claims to, i. 19; second Huguenot expedition to, i. 33; Laudonnière's expedition to, i. 48; coveted by Sir John Hawkins for England, i. 92; arrival of the Spaniards in, i. 95; Menendez commissioned to conquer, i. 100; Menendez takes formal possession of, i. 113; French and Spanish claims concerning discovery of, i. 153; Gourgues lands in, i. 164; abandoned by the Jesuits in disgust, i. 179.
Folsom, Charles, i. xiii.
Fontanedo, i. 11.
Forquevaulx, Sieur de, i. 154; demands redress for France from Spain for massacres in Florida, i. 155, 156.
Forster, ii. 10, 43.
Fort George Island, i. 163.
Foucher, ii. 263.
Fougeray, ii. 74.

INDEX.

Fourneaux, overpowers Laudonnière during illness, i. 72; compels Laudonnière to sign commission for West India cruise, i. 73; fortunes of the expedition, i. 75; captured by La Caille, i. 75; court-martialled and shot, i. 76, 77.

Française, la Baye, ii. 70.

France, Florida claimed by, i. 19; Spanish jealousy of, i. 19; vitality of, i. 21; corruption and intrigue run riot in, i. 22; Huguenot influence in colonizing the New World, i. 27; gliding towards religious wars, i. 33; trembling between the Catholics and the Huguenots, i. 101; indignation over the Spanish massacres in Florida, i. 145; the true pioneer of the Great West, i. 181; peculiar part assumed on borders of the New World, ii. 7; claims discovery of America, ii. 7, 8; vitality wasted in Italian wars, ii. 13; defeat in Italy, ii. 19; loss of Milan, ii. 19; death of Bayard, ii. 19; invasion of Provence, ii. 19; captivity of Francis I., ii. 19; heresy of Calvin infecting, ii. 22; Spain jealously guards America from the encroachments of, ii. 39–41; plunged into fratricidal war, ii. 51; advent of Henry IV., ii. 58; policy to mingle in Indian politics, ii. 163; the champion of Christianity, ii. 276.

"France in the New World," story of, i. ix.

France-Roy, ii. 47.

Francis I., of Angoulême, owner passes to, ii. 13; despatches Verrazzano to find westward passage to Cathay, ii. 14; captivity on the field of Pavia, ii. 19; treacherous escape from captivity, ii. 20; ignores bull of Alexander VI., ii. 22; sinking to his ignominious grave, ii. 37.

Francis II., i. 25.

Francis, Saint, of Assisi, characteristics of, ii. 213, 214.

Franciscans, the, i. 104, ii. 214; relax their ancient rigor, ii. 214.

Franklin Inlet, ii. 223.

French, the, new documentary evidence connected with occupancy of Florida, i. vii; their dominion a memory of the past, i. xii.

French Cape, i. 36.

French colonization, compared with English colonization, ii. 217.

French Protestantism, in America, crushed by Menendez, i. 180.

Frenchman's Bay, ii. 126.

Frontenac, Count, ii. 25.

Fundy, Bay of, explored by De Monts, ii. 70, 135.

Fur-trade, infancy of, ii. 52, 53.

GAFFAREL, i. 153, 157; ii. 8, 11.

Gaillard, M., i. 160, 162, 165.

Gaillon, Michel, ii. 48.

Galicia, knights of, i. 104.

Gambie, Pierre, i. 79.

Ganabara, i. 26, 28; falls a prey to the Portuguese, i. 32.

Garay, Juan de, voyages of, i. 11.

Garcilaso, de la Vega, i. 10, 13, 14, 17, 18, 19.

Garneau, ii. 154.

Garonne River, the, i. 39.

Gas (Guast), Mont du, ii. 155.

Gaspé, Cartier plants a cross at, ii. 21, 151.

Gastaldi, map of, i. 149.

Genesee River, the, ii. 225.

Genesee, the, valley of, ii. 171.

INDEX. 295

Geneva, Huguenots find refuge at, i. 21; sends large deputation to the New World, i. 27.
Genre, plans to kill Laudonnière, i. 69, 70.
George, Lake, ii. 171.
Georgia, State of, i. 15.
Georgian Bay, ii. 223.
Germany, the heresy of Luther convulsing, ii. 22.
Gilbert, abortive attempt to settle near mouth of the Kennebec River, ii. 115.
Gironde River, the, i. 39.
Gloucester Harbor, ii. 77, 87.
Goat Island, ii. 80.
Godfrey, i. 102.
Gomara, i. 10, 13; ii. 8, 11.
Gorges, ii. 147.
Gosselin, M., ii. 44, 52, 54, 56.
Gouldsborough Hills, ii. 126.
Gourgue, Captain, i. 5.
Gourgues, Dominique de, hatred of the Spaniards, i. 158; early life of, i. 159; resolves on vengeance, i. 159; his band of adventurers, i. 160; the voyage, i. 161; his plan divulged, i. 161; warmly welcomed by the Indians, i. 163; lands in Florida, i. 164; joins forces with Chief Satouriona against the Spaniards, i. 165; attack on the Spaniards, i. 171; victory over the Spaniards, i. 172; successfully attacks Fort San Mateo, i. 173; execution of Spanish prisoners, i. 175; his mission fulfilled, i. 176; return to France, i. 177; coldly received by the King, i. 178; invited by Queen Elizabeth to enter her service, i. 178; accepts command of fleet against Philip II., i. 178; sudden death, i. 178; tribute to, i. 178.

Gourgues, Vicomte A. de, i. 5, 7, 158, 160.
"Grace of God," the, ii. 113.
Granada, Spain's final triumph over infidels of, i. 9.
Grand Bank, the, ii. 151.
Grandchemin, i. 126.
Grande Isle, ii. 170.
Granville, ii. 154.
Gravier, Gabriel, ii. 57, 125.
Great Head, ii. 126.
Great Lakes, the, ii. 180.
Green Mountain, ii. 126.
Green Mountains, the, ii. 170.
Grotaut, i. 78.
Grotius, i. 179.
Guast, Pierre du, petitions for leave to colonize Acadia, ii. 65; plans for the expedition, ii. 66; pledges to Rome, ii. 67; expedition sets sail, ii. 68; Catholic and Calvinist, ii. 68; sights Cap la Hève, ii. 69; awaits arrival of Pontgravé, ii. 69; proceeds to St. Mary's Bay, ii. 69; the lost priest, ii. 70; discovers Annapolis Harbor, ii. 71; explores the Bay of Fundy, ii. 71; visits and names the St. John River, ii. 71; St. Croix chosen as site for new colony, ii. 71; Poutrincourt sails for France, ii. 74; winter miseries, ii. 75; weary of St. Croix, ii. 76; establishes himself at Port Royal, ii. 80; returns to France, ii. 80; in Paris, ii. 81; patent rescinded, ii. 94; transfers his claims to lands in Acadia to Madame de Guercheville, ii. 121; passion for discovery, ii. 149; views of colonization, ii. 151; sends Pontgravé and Champlain to the New World, ii. 151; failure to gain renewal of his monopoly,

ii. 179; acts without it, ii. 179; moving toward financial ruin, ii. 186.
Guast, Rivière du, ii. 77.
Guercheville, Marquise de, rare qualities of, ii. 106; relations of Henry IV. with, ii. 106-109; becomes the patroness of the Jesuits, ii. 110; assists Biard and Masse to sail for Acadia, ii. 111; sends succor to the Jesuits in Acadia, ii. 121; sweeping grant of territory in the New World given to, ii. 121, 122; prepares to take possession, ii. 124; pious designs crushed in the bud, ii. 146.
Guérin, i. 25, 48, 158; ii. 8, 56.
Guise, Duc de (François of Lorraine), i. 22, 26; varying popularity of, i. 49.

Hackit, Thomas, i. 38.
Hakluyt, Richard, i. 4, 11, 13, 17, 38, 47, 50, 53, 65, 70, 77, 80, 91, 117; ii. 10, 11, 15, 21, 38, 41, 43, 44, 52, 53.
Hamlin, E. L., ii. 128.
Hampton Beach, ii. 77.
Hampton Roads, ii. 136.
Harrisse, Henry, ii. 8, 38, 50.
Havana, i. 148.
Havre, i. 35.
Hawes, Nathaniel, ii. 131.
Hawkins, Sir John, i. 77; comes to relief of Laudonnière's company, i. 89; description of, i. 90, 91; covets Florida for England, i. 92, 113; ii. 154.
Hayti, i. 108.
Hazard, ii. 38.
Hébert, Louis, ii. 246.
Helyot, ii. 214, 215.
Henrietta Maria, Queen, important bearing of her dowry upon New France, ii. 272.
Henry II., i. 25, 27.
Henry IV., of France, characteristics of, ii. 58; patron of Champlain, ii. 59; insists that Poutrincourt attach Jesuits to his expedition to Acadia, ii. 100; murder of, ii. 104, 105; hope of Europe died with, ii. 105; relations with Marquise de Guercheville, ii. 107; attracted by Charlotte de Montmorency, ii. 191.
Henry VIII., of England, ii. 20.
Herrera y Tordesillas, Antonio de, i. 10, 11, 19; ii. 8, 10, 50.
Hilton Head, i. 39, 41.
Hispaniola, Gourgues lands at, i. 160.
"Hochelaga, River of," ii. 23, 25.
Hochelaga, town of, ii. 26; Cartier sets out for, ii. 28; Indians of, ii. 29; plan showing defences of, ii. 30; dwellings of, ii. 30; vanished, ii. 64.
Holmes, ii. 131.
Hornot, ii. 9.
Hospital of the Gray Nuns, the, ii. 188.
Hostaqua, Chief, i. 62; promises aid in subjecting Indians to rule of the French, i. 78.
Houël, ii. 212.
Hudson, Henry, voyage of, ii. 195.
Hudson River, the, ii. 172, 225.
Hudson's Bay, ii. 153, 180.
Huet, Paul, ii. 246.
Huguenots, the, occupation of Florida, i. 3; authorities for, i. 3; fugitives from torture and death, i. 21; gather about Calvin, i. 21; influence in colonizing the New World, i. 27; second colony sails for the New World, i. 33;

a political as well as a religious party, i. 34; experiences of the second expedition to the New World, i. 35-47; double tie of sympathy between the English Puritans and, i. 92; regarded Spain as natural enemy, i. 152; demand redress for massacres in Florida, i. 153; droop under Marie de Medicis, ii. 105; revolt against the King, ii. 261.

Hundred Associates, the, ii. 258-260; on the verge of bankruptcy, ii. 274. See also *Company of New France.*

Hungry Bay, ii. 229.

Huron Indians, the, i. 60; ii. 162; Champlain joins them against the Iroquois, ii. 162-178; advantages to Champlain from alliance with, ii. 180; Champlain's trading with, ii. 188, 189; tribal relations, ii. 223; population of, ii. 224; regard Champlain as their champion, ii. 225; Brébeuf attempts to convert, ii. 253.

Huron, Lake, discovery of, ii. 223.

Huron-Iroquois family of tribes, the, ii. 29.

Hyannis, ii. 87.

INDIA, passage to, ii. 21.

Indians, the, attack and kill Ponce de Leon, i. 11; treatment received from De Soto, i. 14; friendly reception to Coligny's colonists, i. 36; familiarity with the colonists, i. 42; religious festival of, i. 42; friendly reception to Laudonnière, i. 50; make offerings to pillar erected by Ribaut, i. 51; hatred between the tribes, i. 57; customs of, i. 57, 58; villages of, i. 58; social distinctions among, i. 58; French and Spanish treatment compared, i. 162; belief in properties of the "black drink," i. 167; meeting with Cartier, ii. 24; of Hochelaga, ii. 29; kind treatment received from Champlain, Lescarbot, and Poutrincourt, ii. 98; Biencourt's dislike for, ii. 117; power of dreams among, ii. 172; armor used by, ii. 175; custom of scalping among, ii. 176; cannibalism among, ii. 185; worship of the Manitou, ii. 197; better treated by the French than by the English, ii. 277.

Indies, the, Champlain's desire to find a route to, ii. 192.

Iroquois Indians, the, ii. 30, 162; Champlain joins the Hurons and the Algonquins against, ii. 162-178; Champlain's victory over, ii. 175; war with Champlain and the Montagnais, ii. 181-185; attacked by Champlain and the Hurons, ii. 232; attack Quebec, ii. 251; a constant menace to Quebec, ii. 281.

Iroquois, Rivière des, ii. 166.

Isle aux Coudres, the, ii. 23, 24.

Isle de Roberval, ii. 12.

Isles, Cap aux, ii. 77.

Isles of Demons, the, legends concerning, ii. 11; Roberval at, ii. 44; story of Marguerite on, ii. 44-46.

Isles of Shoals, the, ii. 77.

Italian wars, vitality of France wasted in, ii. 13.

JAMAY, Denis, ii. 215, 245.

James I. of England, ii. 133; grant made to the London Company, ii. 138.

James River, the, ii. 120, 129.
Jamestown, Capt. Samuel Argall arrives at, ii. 130, 137.
Jean, François, i. 120.
Jeannin, President, ii. 195.
Jérémie, ii. 195.
Jesuits, the, power over Spain, i. 96; abandon Florida in disgust, i. 179; strong at court, ii. 99; insist on taking part in Poutrincourt's Acadian expedition, ii. 100; Poutrincourt fears them in his colony, ii. 101; Spanish in origin and policy, ii. 101; the Marquise de Guercheville becomes the patroness of, ii. 110; supported by Marie de Medicis and the Marquise de Verneuil, ii. 110; sail for Acadia, ii. 112; arrive at Port Royal, ii. 113; vast extent of the influence of, ii. 113, 114; seize Poutrincourt for debt, ii. 124; the Récollets apply for the assistance of, ii. 252; increasing strength of, ii. 253; Émery de Caen's hatred of, ii. 254.
"Jesus," the, i. 89.
Joachims, the, rapids of, ii. 221.
"Jonas," the, ii. 83, 125.
Jordan River, the, i. 11, 39.

KAMOURASKA, ii. 154.
Kennebec River, the, explored by Champlain, ii. 76.
Kingston, ii. 238.
Kirke, David, ii. 262, 268; receives the honor of knighthood, ii. 273.
Kirke, Gervase, ii. 262; demands the surrender of Quebec, ii. 264; defeats Roquemont, ii. 265; return to England, ii. 272.
Kirke, Henry, ii. 262.

Kirke, Lewis, ii. 262; lands at Quebec, ii. 267.
Kirke, Thomas, ii. 262, 268; resigns Quebec, ii. 276.
Kohl, i. 149.

LABRADOR, legends concerning, ii. 11; Cartier coasts the shores of, ii. 22; derivation of name, ii. 37.
La Cadie, see *Acadia*.
La Caille, François de, i. 63; asks Laudonnière to allow the company to turn buccaneers, i. 71; fidelity to Laudonnière, i. 72; plot to kill, i. 72; captures the mutineers, i. 75; embarks against the Spanish, i. 116; interview with Menendez, i. 141.
La Chenaie, ii. 154.
La Chère, i. 44; killed and eaten by his companions, i. 46.
Laet, De, i. 5, 10, 11, 19; ii. 9, 10, 13, 38, 50, 55, 112.
Lafitau, ii. 30, 169, 173, 175.
La Flèche, Father, attempts to Christianize New France, ii. 102, 103.
La Grange, Captain, council of war, i. 115, 116; drowned, i. 133.
La Hève, Cap, De Monts sights, ii. 69.
Lairet River, the, ii. 34.
Lalemant, Charles, ii. 4, 176, 201, 205, 224, 242, 253, 255.
La Mota, de, i. 180.
La Motte, ii. 74, 132, 133, 146.
La Noue, Father Anne de, ii. 253, 254, 276.
La Popelinière, i. 5, 25; ii. 11.
La Potherie, ii. 25, 154.
La Roche, Marquis de, plans to colonize New France, ii. 53; titles and privileges conferred, ii. 53, 54; expedition sets out, ii. 54; lands convicts on Sable

INDEX.   299

Island, ii. 54 ; return to France, ii. 56; thrown into prison, ii. 56; death of, ii. 57.

La Roque, Jean François de, efforts to plant a colony in Spanish Florida, i. 19; a new champion of New France, ii. 37 ; honors conferred upon, ii. 37 ; powers of, ii. 38; detained by unexpected delays, ii. 43 ; discovers Cartier's ships returning to France, ii. 43; mixed complexion of company of, ii. 44; stern punishment of his niece Marguerite, ii. 44–46; arrives at Cap Rouge, ii. 47 ; houses built, ii. 47; famine and discontent, ii. 47, 48; severity of rule of, ii. 48; ordered back to France by the King, ii. 48 ; death of, ii. 49.

La Roquette, encourages discontent felt towards Laudonnière, i. 69.

La Routte, ii. 165, 166.

La Saussaye, sails for Acadia, ii. 125 ; arrives at Port Royal, ii. 125 ; sails to Mt. Desert, ii. 126 ; discontent among his sailors, ii. 127; attacked and defeated by Captain Argall, ii. 132; interview with Captain Argall, ii. 133 ; turned adrift in an open boat, ii. 134 ; reaches St. Malo, ii. 135; return home, ii. 146.

Laudonnière, René de, i. 4, 40, 47 ; origin, i. 48 ; commands expedition to Florida, i. 48; description of, i. 48; first sight of Florida, i. 50; friendly relations with the Indians, i. 50–54 ; selects site for the new colony, i. 54 ; builds a fort, i. 55 ; makes treaty with Chief Satouriona, i. 57 ; breaks his faith with Chief Satouriona, i. 64 ; determines to make friends with Chief Outina, i. 64 ; returns two prisoners to Chief Outina, i. 65 ; discontent among the followers of, i. 68 ; La Roquette and Genre plan to destroy, i. 69, 70 ; charges sent to France against, i. 70 ; disastrous exchange of soldiers for Captain Bourdet's sailors, i. 70 ; asked to allow his company to turn buccaneers, i. 72; fidelity of Ottigny, Vasseur, Arlac, and La Caille to, i. 72; overpowered by Fourneaux during illness, i. 72 ; compelled to sign commission for West India cruise, i. 73 ; entire command reorganized after departure of the mutineers, i. 74; capture of the mutineers, i. 75 ; court-martial of the mutineers, i. 76, 77; threatened starvation, i. 81 ; hostility of the Indians, i. 81 ; Outina attacked and captured, i. 84 ; ransom promised for release of Outina, i. 85 ; treacherous attack of the Indians, i. 87; famine and desperation, i. 89; relieved by Sir John Hawkins, i. 90–92; arrival of Ribaut, i. 93 ; required to resign his command, i. 94 ; determines to return to France to clear his name, i. 95 ; council of war, i. 115; defenceless condition of Fort Caroline, i. 117 ; escape from the massacre of Fort Caroline, i. 124.

Laudonnière, Vale of, the, i. 55.

Laverdière, Abbé, ii. 79.

La Vigne, i. 118, 123.

Le Beau, ii. 154.

Le Borgne, Chief, ii. 203.

300   INDEX.

Le Caron, Joseph, ii. 215; noteworthy mission among the Indians, ii. 216-219; discovery of Lake Huron, ii. 223; meeting with Champlain, ii. 225; the first mass, ii. 226; returns to Quebec, ii. 244.
Le Clerc, ii. 4, 19, 49, 213, 214, 215, 216, 219, 224, 230, 248, 253.
Ledyard, L. W., ii. 231.
Le Jeune, Paul, the Jesuit, ii. 4, 169, 201, 224, 238, 271, 276, 277, 278, 279, 281.
Le Moyne, Antoine, i. 4, 50, 55, 56, 64, 72, 74, 77, 80, 81, 112, 114, 115, 124, 126, 129, 145, 146, 167.
Léry, Jean de, i. 28, 30, 31; attempt at settlement on Sable Island, ii. 13.
Lescarbot, Marc, i. 5, 25, 128, 147, 159, 160; ii. 4, 9, 10, 13, 21, 23, 35, 38, 48, 50, 52, 53, 54, 55; sketch of, ii. 81; joins Poutrincourt in expedition to Acadia, ii. 82; first sight of the New World, ii. 84; arrives at Port Royal, ii. 85; left in charge of Port Royal, ii. 87; explores the river Équille, ii. 89; life at Port Royal, ii. 92, 93; evil tidings, ii. 94; Port Royal must be abandoned, ii. 95; sorrow at leaving Port Royal, ii. 97; sails for France, ii. 97; radical defect in scheme of settlement, ii. 98; kindly relations with the Indians, ii. 98, 100, 101, 102, 105, 111, 112, 115, 123, 140, 142, 147, 154, 158, 176.
Levi, Point, ii. 154.
Lévis, Henri de, see *Ventadour, Duc de*.
Liancourt M. de, ii. 108.
Libourne River, the, i. 40.

Limoilou, seigniorial mansion of, description of, ii. 44.
Liverpool Harbor, ii. 69.
Loire River, the, i. 39.
Lok, Michael, map of, i. 149; ii. 8.
London Company, the, grant made by James I. to, ii. 138.
Long Island, ii. 17, 170.
Long Saut, the, rapids of, ii. 196.
Lorraine, Cardinal of, i. 22, 30, 49.
Los Martires, i. 148.
Louis, the sagamore, ii. 123.
Louis XIII., gives sweeping grant of territory in the New World to Madame de Guercheville, ii. 121; Champlain recounts his adventures to, ii. 179; assassination of, ii. 186; power increased by Richelieu, ii. 257.
Lowell, Charles Russell, i. 7.
Loyola, Ignatius de, the mysterious followers of, ii. 253; sole masters of the field in Canada, ii. 278.
Luther, Martin, "heresies" of, i. 31; convulsing Germany, ii. 22.
Luz, St. Jean de, ii. 8.

Madeira, ii. 15.
Magin, Antoine, ii. 10.
Maine, seaboard of, ii. 18.
Maiollo, Visconte, di, ii. 49.
Major, Mr., ii. 50.
Mal Bay, ii. 268.
Mallard, Captain, rescues fugitives from Fort Caroline, i. 129.
Malo, M., ii. 154.
Malta, Knights of, i. 23.
Manitou, the, Indian worship of, ii. 197.
Manitoualins, the spirit-haunted, ii. 223.
Marais, ii. 161, 165, 166, 167.
Marets, Burgaud des, ii. 46.

INDEX. 301

Marguerite, story of her experiences on the Isles of Demons, ii. 44-46.
Marguerite de Valois, ii. 47.
Marot, psalms of, i. 34.
Marquette, Jacques, second discovery of the Mississippi, i. 15.
Marshall, O. H., ii. 201, 231.
Marshfield, shores of, ii. 78.
Martin, ii. 154.
Martines, map of, i. 149.
Martyr, Peter, i. 10, 11; ii. 8, 10.
Massachusetts Bay, ii. 77.
Massachusetts Indians, the, ii. 77.
Masse, Enemond, ii. 110; sails for Acadia, ii. 112; ill-success among the Indians, ii. 119; relieved by La Saussaye, ii. 125; turned adrift in an open boat, ii. 134; reaches St. Malo, ii. 135, 253.
Matanzas Inlet, i. 36, 133.
Matchedash, Bay of, ii. 223, 227.
Mattawan, the, ii. 221.
Mavila, Indian town of, i. 17.
May, River of, i. 38, 48, 49, 50, 54, 163.
Mayarqua, village of, i. 65.
"Mayflower," the, ii. 125.
Mayport, village of, i. 50, 163.
Mayrra, Chief of the Thimagoas, i. 61.
Medicis, Catherine de, struggle to hold balance of power, i. 22, 40, 41; helpless amid storm of factions, i. 49; leanings toward Spain, i. 101; influenced by the Duke of Alva, i. 101; defends rights of the French in Florida, i. 154.
Medicis, Marie de, becomes regent of France, ii. 105; characteristics of, ii. 105; supports the Jesuits, ii. 110.
Membertou, Chief, ii. 86, 92, 94; grief at parting with the colonists, ii. 96; characteristics of, ii. 96; war with the Armouchiquois, ii. 96; welcomes Poutrincourt, ii. 102; converted to Christianity, ii. 102; religious enthusiasm of, ii. 103; remarkable character of, ii. 118; death of, ii. 118.
Mendoza Grajales, Francisco Lopez de, i. 6; account of Menendez' expedition, i. 106, 107, 108, 109, 112, 113, 114, 118, 120, 128, 131, 132, 134, 139.
Menendez, Bartholomew, i. 131.
Menendez de Avilés, Pedro, i. 6; boyhood of, i. 98; early career of, i. 98, 99; petition to Philip II., i. 99; commissioned to conquer Florida, i. 100; powers granted to, i. 100, 103; plans of, i. 100, 103; force strengthened, i. 102; a new crusade, i. 102; formation of his force, i. 104; Sancho de Arciniega commissioned to join, i. 105; sailing of the expedition, i. 105; assailed by a terrible storm, i. 106; haste to reach Florida, i. 108; first sight of Florida, i. 109; first sight of Ribaut's ships, i. 110; interview with the French, i. 111; the French flee before, i. 112; founds St. Augustine, i. 113; takes formal possession of Florida, i. 113; a storm saves his ships from the French attack, i. 118, 119; attack on Fort Caroline, i. 119-125; the massacre, i. 126-128; return to St. Augustine, i. 131; tidings of the French, i. 132; interview with the French, i. 135; promises of protection, i. 137; treachery of, i. 138; massacre of the French, i. 139; interview with Ribaut,

i. 142; further treachery and murder, i. 143, 144; exaggerated reports to Philip II., i. 148; Charles IX. demands his punishment for massacres in Florida, i. 155, 156; high in favor in Spain, i. 179; re-establishes his power in Florida, i. 179; given command of the Spanish Armada, i. 179; sudden death of, i. 180; crushed French Protestantism in America, i. 180; Canadian fur trade, ii. 52.

Mercator, Gérard, map of, ii. 23.
Mercœur, Duc de, ii. 56, 59.
"Mer Douce," the, ii. 223.
Méry, ii. 147.
Mexico, Cortés' conquest of, i. 11; Champlain visits, ii. 60.
Mexico, Gulf of, i. 19.
Meyrick, ii. 174.
Mezeray, i. 160.
Miamis, the, cannibalism among, ii. 185.
Michel, Captain, ii. 262; bitterness against the Catholics, ii. 269; death of, ii. 271.
Micmac Indians, the, ii. 77.
Milan, France loses, ii. 19.
Mississippi River, the, i. 13; discovered by De Soto, i. 15; second discovery of, by Marquette, i. 15.
Mississippi, State of, i. 15.
Mitchell, Henry, ii. 79.
Mohawk Indians, the, ii. 30, 172.
Mohawk River, the, ii. 171.
Mohawk, the, valley of, ii. 171.
Mohier, Brother Gervais, experience with the Indians, ii. 246.
Mollua, Chief of the Thimagoas, i. 62.
Moluccas, the, i. 148.
Monomoy Point, ii. 87.
Monroe, Fortress, ii. 136.

Montagnais Indians, the, ii. 153, 177; advantages to Champlain of alliance with, ii. 180; war with the Iroquois, ii. 181-185.
Montcalm, ii. 25.
Monteil, ii. 8.
Montgomery, ii. 25.
Montluc, Blaise de, i. 160.
Montmorency, Charlotte de, ii. 191.
Montmorency, Duc de, i. 22; purchases the lieutenancy of New France from Condé, ii. 249; suppresses the company of St. Malo and Rouen, and confers the trade of New France to William and Émery de Caen, ii. 251; sells his viceroyalty to the Duc de Ventadour, ii. 252; holds ancient charge of Admiral of France, ii. 258; sells it to Richelieu, ii. 258.
Montpensier, Duc de, i. 159.
Montreal, ii. 28; Champlain lays the foundations for, ii. 188; importance as a trading-station, ii. 246.
Montreal, Mountain of, ii. 29.
Moorish wars, the, i. 9.
Motte, Isle à la, ii. 170.
Mount Desert, Island of, visited and named by Champlain, ii. 76; La Saussaye arrives at, ii. 126.
Mount Desert Sound, ii. 128.
Munster, map of, i. 149.
Murphy, Henry C., ii. 50.
Muskrat Lake, ii. 201.

Nantasket Beach, ii. 78.
Nantes, Jean de, ii. 48.
Narvaez, Pamphilo de, expedition to Florida, i. 12; death of, i. 12.
Nassau River, the, i. 169.
Natel, Antoine, ii. 156.
Nation of Tobacco, the, ii. 242.

INDEX.   303

Nausett Harbor, ii. 78.
Navarre, i. 22, 49.
Navarrete, ii. 11.
Neutral Nation, the, ii. 224.
New England, unfaithful to the principle of freedom, ii. 256; compared with New France, i. x; ii. 256.
Newfoundland, i. 103, 148, 149; visited by Bretons and Normans, ii. 10; importance of the fisheries of, ii. 11; Verrazzano reaches, ii. 18; Cartier sails for, ii. 21; trade steadily plied at, ii. 51.
New France, compared with New England, i. x; ii. 256; tragical opening of the story of, i. 3; Champlain the father of, ii. 3; division of, ii. 23; La Roche plans to colonize, ii. 53; De Chastes' expedition to, ii. 64; Poutrincourt's attempts to Christianize, ii. 102; the Jesuits in, ii. 114; the Comte de Soissons granted vice-regal powers in, ii. 190; the Prince de Condé assumes protectorship of, ii. 191; in Champlain alone the life of, ii. 192; poor prospects of, ii. 193; inseparable blending of spiritual and temporal interests in, ii. 212; Richelieu remedies the affairs of, ii. 258; to be forever free from taint of heresy, ii. 259; Kirke wrests power from the French in, ii. 265; restored to French Crown by Charles I., ii. 272; explanation of Charles I.'s willingness to make restoration to the French Crown of, ii. 272.
New Mexico, i. 19.
Newport, ii. 17.
Newport, Captain, ships of, ii. 129.

Newport Mountain, ii. 126.
Newport News, ii. 136.
New Spain, i. 12.
New York, Dutch trading-houses of, ii. 121.
Niagara, Falls of, ii. 65.
Nibachis, Chief, ii. 202.
Nichols Pond, ii. 231.
Nipissing Indians, the, ii. 205; village of, ii. 222; promise to guide Champlain to the northern sea, ii. 242.
Nipissing, Lake, Champlain at, ii. 222.
Noel, Jacques, ii. 53.
Noirot, Father, ii. 253.
Norembega, ii. 38, 76.
Normans, the, ii. 9.
North Carolina, coast sighted by Verrazzano, ii. 15.
"Northern Paraguay," the, strangled in its birth, ii. 148.
Nottawassaga Bay, ii. 223.

OATHCAQUA, Chief, i. 80.
O'Callaghan, Dr. E. B., ii. 5, 12, 143.
Ogilby, ii. 10.
Old Point Comfort, ii. 136.
Olotoraca, Chief, i. 167, 169, 171.
Onatheaqua, King, i. 62.
Oneida, Lake, ii. 229, 231.
Onondaga Indians, the, ii. 230, 231.
Onondaga, Lake, ii. 231.
Onondaga, the, valley of, ii. 171.
Ontario, Lake, Champlain on, ii. 229.
"Ordre de Bon-Temps, l'," ii. 91.
Orillia, town of, ii. 227.
Orleans, Channel of, ii. 64.
Orleans, the Island of, ii. 24, 154.
Ortelius, second map of, ii. 23; division of New France, ii. 23.
Orville, Sieur d', ii. 73, 74.

INDEX

Otis, ii. 79.
Otouacha, Huron town of, ii. 224.
Ottawa Indians, the, ii. 205.
Ottawa River, the, ii. 162, 218, 221.
Ottigny, Lieutenant, i. 52, 53, 59, 60; the Thimagoas offer to point out gold and silver to, i. 61; fidelity to Laudonnière, i. 72; disarmed by mutineers, i. 73; joins Chief Outina against King Potanou, on promise of being shown gold mines, i. 80; victory over King Potanou, i. 81; attacked by the Indians, i. 87; council of war, i. 115; embarks against the Spanish, i. 116; murdered by the Spanish, i. 147.
Ouadé, King, i. 43.
Outina, Chief, i. 57; lord of all the Thimagoas, i. 62; Laudonnière determines to make friends with, i. 64; Laudonnière returns two prisoners to, i. 65; Vasseur promises to join against King Potanou, i. 66; victory over warriors of King Potanou, i. 67; asks further aid of the French against King Potanou, promising to show gold mines, i. 80; victory over King Potanou, i. 81; refuses assistance to the colonists, i. 83; attacked and captured by the colonists, i. 84; ransom promised for release of, i. 85.
Overman, Captain, ii. 201.

PALATKA, i. 59.
Palfrey, John G., ii. 256.
Palms, River of, i. 19.
Panuco River, the, Spanish settlement on, i. 17.
Parkhurst, Anthonie, ii. 11.

Parmentier, Jean, ii. 10, 13.
Parry Sound, ii. 223.
Passamaquoddy, Bay of, ii. 65, 71.
Passamaquoddy Indians, the, ii. 71.
Patiño, i. 113.
Paul V., Pope, i. 179; repudiates action of Pope Alexander VI. in proclaiming all America the exclusive property of Spain, ii. 213.
Pavia, field of, ii. 19.
"Pearl," the, i. 127.
Pemetigoet River, the, ii. 76.
Penetanguishine, Harbor of, ii. 223.
Penobscot River, the, ii. 76.
Perez, Fernando, i. 122.
Peru, conquest of, i. 13.
Petuneux, the, ii. 242.
Philip II., i. 6, 21, 97; commissions Menendez to conquer Florida, i. 100; approval of Menendez' slaughters in Florida, i. 147, 151; resents expeditions of Ribaut and Laudonnière to Florida, i. 153; demands that Coligny be punished for planting a French colony in Florida, i. 154; refuses to give redress for Menendez' massacres in Florida, i. 155, 156; Gourgnes takes command of fleet against, i. 178.
Pierria, Albert de, left in command of the colonists by Ribaut, i. 41; extreme severity of, i. 44; murdered by his men, i. 44.
Pinkerton, ii. 52.
Pinzon, ii. 8.
Pizarro, Francisco, conquest of Peru, with De Soto, i. 13.
Place Royale, see *Montreal*.
Plymouth, ii. 148.
Plymouth Company, the, grant made by James I. to, ii. 138.
Plymouth Harbor, ii. 78.

INDEX. 305

Pocahontas, abducted by Capt. Samuel Argall, ii. 130; married to Rolfe, ii. 130.
Point Allerton, ii. 78.
Pointe à Puiseaux, ii. 155.
Pointe aux Rochers, la, ii. 151.
Pointe de Tous les Diables, la, ii. 151.
Pommeraye, Charles de la, ii. 22, 28.
Ponce de Leon, Bay of, i. 148.
Ponce de Leon, Juan, sets out to find fountain of eternal youth, i. 10; bargain with the King, i. 11; explores and names Florida, i. 11; attempt to plant colony in Florida, i. 11; death of, i. 11; new light thrown on discoveries of, i. 11.
Pons, Antoinette de, see *Guercheville, Marquise de.*
Pontbriand, Claude de, ii. 22, 28.
Pontgravé, plans for fur-trading, ii. 57; sets out on enterprise, ii. 58; takes part in De Chastes' expedition to New France, ii. 63, 64; overtakes De Monts, ii. 69; left in command at Port Royal by De Monts, ii. 80; life at Port Royal, ii. 85; sails for France, ii. 87; commands ship sent by De Monts to trade with the Indians, ii. 151; conflict with the Basques, ii. 151, 152; makes peace with the Basques, ii. 152; sails for France, ii. 158; return to Tadoussac, ii. 161; remains in charge at Quebec, ii. 161; returns to France, ii. 179.
Pontgravé (the younger) causes Poutrincourt trouble with the Indians, ii. 114; taken prisoner by Biencourt, ii. 115.
Poore, B. P., ii. 4.
Popham, abortive attempt to settle near the mouth of the Kennebec River, ii. 115.
Porcupine Islands, ii. 126.
Port Fortuné, ii. 87; treacherous slaughter at, ii. 98.
Port la Hève, ii. 103.
Port Mallebarre, ii. 78.
Port Mouton, ii. 69.
Porto Rico, harbor of, i. 107.
Port Royal, ii. 71, 74; De Monts establishes himself at, ii. 80; Lescarbot arrives at, ii. 85; life at, ii. 85; description of, ii. 90; must be abandoned, ii. 95; radical defect in scheme of settlement, ii. 98; no attempt to enforce religious exclusion, ii. 98; Poutrincourt arrives at, ii. 102; conversion of the natives to Christianity, ii. 102; the Jesuits arrive at, ii. 113; friction between spiritual and temporal powers, ii. 114; misery at, ii. 119; endless strife over, ii. 122; La Saussaye arrives at, ii. 125; demolished by Captain Argall, ii. 139; partially rebuilt by Biencourt, ii. 147; restitution to France, ii. 273.
Port Royal, South Carolina, i. 39, 40, 103.
Port Royal Basin, ii. 85.
Port St. Louis, ii. 78.
Portsmouth Harbor, ii. 77.
Portugal, i. 26; makes good its claim to "Antarctic France," i. 32.
Portugal, King of, sole acknowledged partner with Spain in ownership of the New World, ii. 40.
Portuguese, the, Ganabara falls a prey to, i. 32.
Postel, ii. 9.

VOL. II. — 20

Potanou, King, i. 57, 62; Vasseur joins Chief Outina against, i. 66; victory over, i. 67; Ottigny joins Chief Outina against, i. 80; victory over, i. 81.

Poutrincourt, Baron de, ii. 66; asks to remain on Annapolis Harbor, ii. 71; sails for France, ii. 74; resolves to go in person to Acadia, ii. 81; joined by Lescarbot, ii. 82; first sight of the New World, ii. 84; arrives at Port Royal, ii. 85; continues with Champlain on a voyage of discovery, ii. 87; failure, ii. 88; return to Port Royal, ii. 89; "l'Ordre de Bon-Temps," ii. 91; life at Port Royal, ii. 92, 93; evil tidings, ii. 94; Port Royal must be abandoned, ii. 95; sails for France, ii. 97; radical defect in scheme of settlement, ii. 98; kindly relations with the Indians, ii. 98; determines to make Acadia a new France, ii. 99; influence acting against his schemes, ii. 99; the King insists that Jesuits be added to the Acadian expedition, ii. 100; a good Catholic, ii. 100; fears the Jesuits in his colony, ii. 101; sets sail for Port Royal, ii. 101; mutiny on board ship, ii. 102; attempts to Christianize New France, ii. 102; narrow escape from drowning, ii. 104; friction with Biard, ii. 114; sails for France, ii. 115; accepts aid from Madame de Guercheville, ii. 121; seized by the Jesuits for debt, ii. 124; accuses Biard of treachery, ii. 139, 140; visit to Port Royal, ii. 147; death at Méry, ii. 147.

Prescott, i. 97.

Prescott Gate, ii. 155.

Prévost, Robert, i. 128, 147, 160, 162, 168.

Protestantism, Coligny the representative and leader in France, i. 34.

Prout's Neck, ii. 77.

Provence, invasion of, ii. 19.

Purchas, i. 13, 19, 91; ii. 10, 43, 52, 55, 57, 84, 131, 140, 141, 142, 147, 158.

Puritans, the, landing of, i. 35; compared with Coligny's colonists, i. 35; double tie of sympathy between the Huguenots and, i. 92; regarded Spain as natural enemy, i. 152; of New England, ii. 256.

QUEBEC, i. 19; language of, ii. 24; early name of, ii. 25; Champlain's map of, ii. 25; the Indians of, ii. 30; Cartier at, ii. 33, 41; origin of name, ii. 154; Champlain lays the foundation of, ii. 155; plot to put Basques and Spaniards in possession of, ii. 156; winter sufferings at, ii. 160; Pontgravé remains in charge at, ii. 161; Chauvin of Dieppe in charge at, ii. 179; Champlain bids farewell to, ii. 186; Du Parc in command at, ii. 187; signs of growth faint and few at, ii. 245; half trading factory, half mission, ii. 247; bad state of affairs at, ii. 250; attracted by the Iroquois, ii. 251; rival traders at, ii. 251; population of, ii. 255; the Company of New France give succor to, ii. 261; the English at, ii. 263, 264; suffering at, ii. 265; on the verge of extinction, ii. 266; restitution to France, ii.

INDEX. 307

273; reclaimed from the English, ii. 274; Champlain resumes command at, ii. 277; becomes a mission, ii. 279; propagandism at, ii. 279; policy and religion at, ii. 280.
Quentin, Father, sails for Acadia, ii. 125, 138.
Quirpon Island, ii. 12.

RABELAIS, ii. 46.
Ramé, ii. 44, 53, 54.
Ramusio, map of, i. 13; ii. 10, 11, 13, 15, 19, 21, 30, 38, 48.
Rand, ii. 65.
Ranke, i. 159.
Rathery, ii. 46.
Ravaillac, murders Henry IV., ii. 104, 105; execution of, ii. 177.
Razilly, Claude de, ii. 271.
Récollet Friars, ii. 213; authorized by Pope Paul V., to convert the Indians, ii. 213; four of their number sail for New France with Champlain, ii. 215; choose a site for their convent, ii. 215; assignment of labors, ii. 215; build a stone house for defence, ii. 245; missions established by, ii. 252; apply for the assistance of the Jesuits, ii. 252; unable to return to their missions, ii. 278.
Red River, i. 12.
Reform, the, i. 22, 23.
Religious wars, the, France gliding toward, i. 33.
Ribauld, i. 3.
Ribaut, Jacques, i. 127, 128, 130.
Ribaut, Capt. Jean, i. 3; commands second Huguenot expedition to the New World, i. 35; experiences in Florida, 35-41; friendly reception by the Indians, i. 36; delightful first impressions of Florida, i. 37;

journal of, i. 38; embarks for France, i. 41; Indians make offerings to the pillar erected by, i. 51; arrival in Florida to relieve Laudonnière, i. 93; arrival of the Spaniards in Florida, i. 95, 110; flees before the Spanish ships, i. 112; council of war, i. 115; bold plan of, i. 115; letter from Coligny, i. 115; characteristics of, i. 116; misfortunes of, i. 133; interview with Menendez, i. 142; treachery and murder, i. 143, 144, 146, 147.
Richelieu, supreme in France, ii. 257; strengthens the royal power, ii. 257; annuls the privileges of the Caens, ii. 258; forms the company of New France, ii. 258; at Rochelle, ii. 261.
Richelieu River, the, ii. 166, 180.
Rideau, the, ii. 197.
Rio Janeiro, harbor of, i. 26.
Rip Raps, the, ii. 136.
Robert, Master, i. 125.
Roberval, Sieur de, see *Roque, Jean François de la.*
Robin, associated with Poutrincourt in his Acadian scheme, ii. 99.
Rochelle, the centre and citadel of Calvinism, ii. 83; Richelieu at, ii. 261.
Rocher Capitaine, the, ii. 221.
Rohan, Catherine de, Duchesse de Deux-Ponts, ii. 106.
Rolfe, marries Pocahontas, ii. 130.
Rome, i. 30.
Roquemont, ii. 261; defeated by Kirke, ii. 265.
Rossignol, ii. 69.
Rougemont, Philippe, death of, ii. 35.

INDEX.

Royal, Mont, ii. 33.
Ruscelli, map of, i. 149, 153.
Russell, A. J., ii. 201.
Rut, John, ii. 10.
Rye Beach, ii. 77.

SABLE, Cape, ii. 69, 135.
Sable Island, Baron de Léry's attempt at settlement on, ii. 13; La Roche lands convicts on, ii. 54; left to their fate, ii. 55; Chefdhôtel despatched to bring them home, ii. 56.
Saco Bay, ii. 77.
Sagard, Gabriel, ii. 4, 68, 173, 175, 185; ii. 201, 213, 216, 219, 223, 224, 237, 245, 248, 264, 266.
Saguenay River, the, ii. 24, 57, 152.
St. Ann's, ii. 196.
St. Augustine, i. 50; founding of, i. 113; Menendez returns in triumph to, i. 132.
St. Augustine, Fort, i. 147.
St. Bartholomew, carnage of, i. 101.
St. Charles River, the, ii. 25, 155.
Saint Cler, i. 118.
St. Croix, chosen for site of new colony, ii. 71; fort built, ii. 72; winter miseries, ii. 75; De Monts weary of, ii. 76.
St. Croix, Island of, ii. 138; settlement on, ii. 140.
St. Croix River, the, ii. 25; boundary line between Maine and New Brunswick, ii. 72.
St. Eleana, i. 104.
St. Helen, Island of, ii. 195.
St. Helena, i. 39.
St. Jean, ii. 154.
St. John, ii. 25.
St. John, the Bay of, ii. 10; Roberval enters, ii. 43.
St. John, Islets of, ii. 166.

St. John's Bluff, i. 52, 55, 121.
St. John's River, the, i. 38, 50, 51, 54, 59, 65, 110; visited and named by De Monts, ii. 71, 166.
St. Just, barony of, in Champagne, owned by Poutrincourt, ii. 101.
St. Lawrence, Bay of, ii. 23.
St. Lawrence, Gulf of, i. 103; explored by Denis of Honfleur, ii. 13.
St. Lawrence River, the, i. 148, 149; Cartier reaches, ii. 23, 42; Roberval sails up, ii. 47; Champlain explores, ii. 64, 154; the English on, ii. 271.
St. Louis, castle of, ii. 245.
St. Louis, Lake of, ii. 189.
St. Louis, Rapids of, Champlain tries to pass, ii. 64, 189.
St. Louis River, the, ii. 166.
St. Malo, town of, ii. 20, 44; sends out fleet for Canadian fur-trade, ii. 53, 135.
St. Martin, mines of, i. 149.
St. Mary's Bay, i. 103; De Monts enters, ii. 69, 72.
St. Mary's River, the, i. 39, 163.
St. Peter, Lake of, ii. 64, 165.
St. Quentin, victory of, i. 98.
St. Roche, ii. 154.
St. Roque, ii. 25.
St. Sauveur, La Saussaye arrives at, ii. 126; destruction of, ii. 134.
Sainte Marie, council of war, i. 115.
Salazar, i. 137.
San Agustin, i. 113.
San Mateo, Fort, i. 150; repaired, i. 162; Gourgues' attack on, i. 173; rebuilt by Menendez, i. 179.
"San Pelayo," the, flag-ship of Menendez, i. 104, 107, 108, 110, 112, 113, 114.
Sautander, Dr. Pedro de, i. 18.
Santilla River, the, i. 163.

Sarrope, Island of, i. 80.
Satouriona, Chief, i. 51; makes treaty with Laudonnière, i. 57; Vasseur makes false report to, i. 63; expedition against the Thimagoas, i. 63; hatred toward Laudonnière's company, i. 81; warm welcome to Gourgues, i. 163; cruel treatment from the Spaniards, i. 164; joins with Gourgues against the Spaniards, i. 165; attack on the Spaniards, i. 171; victory over the Spaniards, i. 172.
Saut au Récollet, ii. 254.
Sant St. Louis, ii. 188, 210, 235.
Savalet, ii. 97.
Savannah River, the, i. 43.
Schooner Head, ii. 126.
Scituate, shores of, ii. 78.
Seine River, the, i. 39.
Seloy, Chief, i. 113, 119, 132.
Seneca Indians, the, ii. 231.
Severn River, the, ii. 227.
Seville, Cardinal of, ii. 40.
Sewell's Point, ii. 136.
Shea, John Gilmary, i. xiii.
Sibley, John Langdon, i. 7.
Simcoe, Lake, ii. 227, 229.
Sismondi, ii. 37, 192.
Sister Creek, i. 170.
Skull Creek, i. 40.
Slafter, Edmund F., ii. 79.
Smith, Buckingham, i. 7, 12, 19, 104, 180; ii. 41, 50, 147.
Smith, Capt. John, ii. 130.
Snake Indians, the, ii. 168.
Soames's Sound, ii. 128.
Society of Jesus, the, ii. 100, 113, 122.
Soissons, Comte de, granted vice-regal powers in New France, ii. 190; confers them upon Champlain, ii. 191; death of, ii. 191.

Solís, Dr. de las Meras, i. 6; account of Menendez' expedition, i. 132, 134, 135, 137, 138, 139.
"Solomon," the, i. 90.
Sorel, town of, ii. 166.
Sorel River, the, ii. 166.
Soto, Hernando de, conquest of Peru with Pizarro, i. 13; plans to conquer Florida, i. 13; treatment of Indians by, i. 14; discovers the Mississippi, i. 15; death and burial of, i. 16; his fate an insufficient warning to adventurers, i. 17.
Sourin, ii. 74.
South Seas, the, i. 104.
Spain, final triumph over infidels of Granada, i. 9; exalted ideas of America, i. 9; Florida claimed by, i. 19; Papal bull gives Florida to, i. 19, 26; jealousy of France, i. 19; the incubus of Europe, i. 20; makes good its claim to "Antarctic France," i. 32; watching to crush the hope of humanity, i. 33; sends expedition to Florida, i. 95; subject to the monk, the inquisitor, and the Jesuit, i. 96; the citadel of darkness, i. 97; Catherine de Medicis turns toward, i. 101; ascendancy of the policy of, i. 101; regarded by English Puritans and French Huguenots as their natural enemy, i. 152; Charles IX. demands redress for massacres in Florida, i. 153; refuses redress, i. 156; Charles IX. fast subsiding into the deathly embrace of, i. 157; jealously guards America from encroachments of the French, ii. 39–41.
Spanish Armada, the, Menendez given command of, i. 179.

310 INDEX.

Spanish Florida, efforts to plant a colony in ancient, i. 19.
Sparks, Jared, i. 169; ii. 5.
Stadaconé, language of, ii. 24.
Stith, ii. 147.
Stow, i. 91.
Straits of Belle Isle, ii. 21, 22, 44.
Stuart, Mary, of Scotland, espousals with Francis II., i. 25.
Sturgeon Lake, ii. 229.
Suffolk, Lord, ii. 154.
Sully, ii. 65; loses his power under Marie de Medicis, ii. 105.
Susane, ii. 174.
Susquehanna River, the, ii. 236.
Suza, Convention of, restores New France to the French Crown, ii. 274.
"Swallow," the, i. 90.
Swan, Major, Indian belief in properties of the "black drink," i. 167.

TADOUSSAC, efforts to establish fur-trade at, ii. 57, 63, 64, 69, 151; centre of the Canadian fur-trade, ii. 152; fur-traders at, ii. 186; importance as a trading-station, ii. 246.
Tadoussac, Bay of, ii. 149.
Talbot Inlet, i. 169.
Tampa Bay, i. 12, 14.
Tequenonquihaye, Huron town of, ii. 225.
Ternaux, i. 4, 50.
Ternaux-Compans, i. 4, 11, 12, 14, 18, 50, 53, 106, 125, 127, 128, 160; ii. 35.
Tessouat, Chief, location of village of, ii. 202; remarkable graveyard of, ii. 203; gives a feast in honor of Champlain, ii. 203, 204; refuses to give Champlain canoes and men to visit the Nipissings, ii. 286.

Têtu, reveals conspiracy to Champlain, ii. 156.
Thevet, André, i. 16, 29; ii. 12, 23, 24, 40, 46, 48, 49, 52.
Thimagoa Indians, the, i. 54, 57, 59; offer to point out gold and silver to Ottigny, i. 61; Vasseur makes alliance with, i. 62; Satouriona's expedition against, i. 63.
Thomas, Champlain's interpreter, ii. 206.
Thou, De, i. 5.
Three Rivers, importance as a trading-station, ii. 246.
Thunder Bay, ii. 223.
Ticonderoga, Fort, ii. 171.
"Tiger," the, i. 90.
Touaguainchain, Huron town of, ii. 225.
Tourmente, Cape, ii. 24.
Trenchant, i. 73, 75.
Trent River, the, ii. 229.
"Trinity," the, flag-ship of Ribaut, i. 110, 112.
Trinity, Bay of the, ii. 153.
Turnel, ii. 143, 144, 145.
Two Mountains, Lake of, ii. 196.

ULPIUS, Euphrosynus, globe of, ii. 49.

VACA, Alvar Nuñez Cabeça de, i. 12; false reports concerning Florida, i. 13.
Vasseur, makes alliance with the Thimagoas, i. 61, 62; makes false report to Chief Satouriona, i. 63; takes prisoners back to Chief Outina, i. 65; promises to join Chief Outina against King Potanou, i. 66; fidelity to Laudonnière, i. 72.
Ventadour, Duc de, purchases the

INDEX. 311

viceroyalty of New France from the Duc de Montmorency, ii. 252.
Vera Cruz, i. 148.
Verdier, i. 93.
Verneuil, Marquise de, supports the Jesuits, ii. 110.
Verrazzano, Hieronimo da, ii. 49.
Verrazzano, John, voyage of, i. 19; early history of, ii. 14; despatched by Francis I. to find westward passage to Cathay, ii. 14; doubts concerning reality of the voyage, ii. 14; the voyage begun, ii. 15; sights the coast of North Carolina, ii. 15; meeting with the Indians, ii. 15; coasts the shores of Virginia or Maryland, ii. 17; enters the Bay of New York, ii. 17; Long Island, Block Island, and Newport, ii. 17; repelled along the New England coast, ii. 18; coasts the seaboard of Maine and reaches Newfoundland, ii. 18; writes earliest description of the shores of the United States, ii. 19; joyfully received in France, ii. 19; misfortunes of France prevent planting a colony in America, ii. 19; few remaining traces of fortunes of, ii. 19; hanged as a pirate, ii. 20; supposed shipwreck of, ii. 27; theories concerning voyage of, ii. 49, 50.
Verreau, Abbé, ii. 50.
Vicente, i. 113.
Viel, Nicolas, ii. 253.
Viger, Jacques, ii. 5, 61.
Vignau, Nicolas de, volunteers to winter among the Indians, ii. 194; return to Paris, ii. 194; remarkable report brought by, ii. 194, 195; his falsehoods disclosed, ii. 207, 209; allowed to go unpunished, ii. 211.
Villafañe, Angel de, failure to reach Florida, i. 18.
Villaroel, Gonzalo de, i. 175.
Villegagnon, Nicolas Durand de, i. 23; exploits of, i. 24, 25; characteristics of, i. 24; expedition to the New World, i. 26; severity of, i. 27; welcome to new colonists, i. 28; wrangles with the colonists, i. 30; pronounces Calvin a "frightful heretic," i. 30; religious bigotry, i. 31; returns to France, i. 32; hot controversy with Calvin, i. 32.
Vimont, ii. 201, 281.
Vincelot, ii. 154.
Virginia, English colony of, ii. 121.
Vitet, ii. 8.

Wake, Sir Isaac, letter from Charles I. explaining restoration of New France to the French Crown, ii. 272.
Wampum, description of, ii. 243.
Weir, Lake, i. 80.
Wells Beach, ii. 77.
West Indies, Champlain visits, ii. 59–61.
White Mountains, the, ii. 76.
Willes, ii. 8, 10.
William Henry, Fort, ii. 172.
Williams, Roger, ii. 176.
Wilmington, South Carolina, site of, ii. 15.
Wolfe, ii. 25.
Wytfleit, map of, i. 5; ii. 10, 11, 19, 38, 50.

Yonville, council of war, i. 115.
York Beach, ii. 77.

Zacatecas, mines of, i. 149.

CPSIA information can be obtained
at www.ICGtesting.com
Printed in the USA
LVHW032234310321
683129LV00008B/447